**Consulting in
Child Custody**

Consulting in Child Custody

An Introduction to the Ugliest Litigation
for Mental-Health Professionals

Melvin G. Goldzband, M.D.
University of California,
San Diego

LexingtonBooks
D.C. Heath and Company
Lexington, Massachusetts
Toronto

Library of Congress Cataloging in Publication Data

Goldzband, Melvin G.
  Consulting in child custody.

  Includes index.
  1. Custody of children-United States.
  2. Forensic psychiatry-United States. I. Title.
KF547.G668   346.7301'7   81-48024
ISBN 0-669-05246-9   347.30617   AACR2

Published simultaneously in Canada

Printed in the United States of America

International Standard Book Number: 0-669-05246-9

Library of Congress Catalog Card Number: 81-48024

*To my colleagues in the American
Academy of Psychiatry and the Law,
who helped me become more sensitive
to the ramifications of what I do*

Contents

Preface

Any judge or trial lawyer, any forensic psychiatrist or other mental-health specialist will affirm that child custody is, indeed, the ugliest of all litigations. The cases are sufficiently distressing to discourage most psychiatrists, psychologists, and other behavioral scientists and counselors from participating. Even most lawyers and judges face them with distaste. Such resistance to helping often leads to mishandling and poor decisions, creating further problems for both the torn children and their torn parents.

My goal in writing this book is to provide a guide for participation in custody cases for the large number of specialists who, despite the need, persist in avoiding most legal cases, especially child-custody cases. Horror stories abound, some real and some apocryphal, and avoidance reactions are generally based on fear. I hope this book will alleviate some of the fears of those mental-health experts who avoid the legal arena like the plague. Those specialists need to know about the law—how lawyers think and plan their cases, and especially how lawyers, courts, and litigants all need the help of expert witnesses. Child-custody suits are increasing, and the need for more expert-witness participation is obvious. This book should help defuse the apprehension felt by most behavioral scientists and other clinicians who are called into court, willingly or no. They can never forget that they will occasionally have to go to court regardless of their attitudes toward it. Obviously, I also hope that those specialists who already participate in the evaluative processes in child custody find this book helpful as well.

This book is the second-generation offspring of a symposium on child-custody litigation I organized and chaired in San Diego in 1976. That program was sponsored by the San Diego Psychiatric Society and the San Diego County Bar Association, with the special cooperation of the Superior Court of California, San Diego County, and the Department of Psychiatry at the University of California, San Diego. Communication with the many psychiatrists and attorneys who participated in that and subsequent meetings demonstrated clearly that child custody was a neglected and shunned area for both lawyers and the mental-health specialists the courts needed to help them with these difficult cases. The book that was eventually produced was a practice guide for lawyers: *Custody Cases and Expert Witnesses: A Manual for Attorneys* (New York: Law & Business, Inc., Harcourt Brace Jovanovich, 1980).

A dilemma then arose: a guide was now available for the lawyers, but none was available for the expert witnesses on whom they increasingly must call. Thus the present book, which complements the book for lawyers but has a totally different format, was designed for a vastly different readership with different needs.

This book is also complementary to another recently published work. In 1980, following a long gestation period, a review was published by the Committee on the Family of the Group for the Advancement of Psychiatry (GAP), *Divorce, Child Custody and the Family* (New York: Law & Business, Inc., Harcourt Brace Jovanovich, 1981). It is not at all like this book. According to its introduction, "It is designed to convey an overall view of the family emotional processes which encompass every member of the family before, during, and after divorce, and which, if understood, can contribute to better decisions about child custody. . . ." The GAP book provides a psychosociohistoric context within which a number of factors affecting the problems of child-custody disposition are outlined. Unlike this book, it is in no way intended as a manual of procedure. However, it is highly recommended as an outstanding review of the social and theoretical background of numerous elements affecting family life and its dissolution.

Consulting in Child Custody is, frankly, a "how-to" book. As such, it sets out to establish and maintain a practical outlook, although experience has dictated that individuals who have had little, if any, forensic experience also have little, if any, forensic or legal background. Behavioral scientists play in the law's ball park when they serve as consultants to lawyers and to courts. Therefore, they must know the rules of the game and the parameters. They also must learn what is expected of them in terms of the actual job to be done, and how the results of that job may best be communicated to the agencies that can best use the findings. I have tried to incorporate this necessary background in this book so that the practical aspects will be seen to have realistic bases.

I am a psychiatrist, and my experience is, of course, based on my own professional participation. The courts, however, call on members of various disciplines and professions to help them. Psychiatrists, psychologists, social workers, agency workers with various backgrounds, physicians and counselors of all types, members of the clergy, and a variety of other professionals become involved in the ugliest litigation. I hope that all my colleagues working in the custody arena, regardless of their backgrounds, will find the direction, guidance, and counsel we all need to function adequately in that arena. The principles, cautions, and rules apply equally to all expert witnesses who are needed to help—and plenty are needed.

During the original child-custody symposium in 1976, a distinguished San Diego family-law specialist, John Lightner, commented that participation as an expert witness in litigations should not be a frightening situation. Rather, he felt, it could and should be a stimulating one. I have found that this is true, and that such participation can be gratifying as well, especially if both the attorneys and the courts succeed in learning what I am there to teach them. The most gratifying aspect is not the ego satisfaction of being heard in these cases but, rather, the feeling that my ideas and findings may have a positive effect on the beleaguered families and their children, the principals in these dreadful cases that become more dreadful the more we stay away from them.

Another family-law specialist, a lawyer from Chicago, Michael Minton, has recently addressed numerous groups and published several articles on the economic value of a wife and homemaker. As a good divorce lawyer, he hopes this issue will be addressed in the difficult financial settlements that also plague divorce actions. Such material is fascinating in itself; more pertinently, however, it highlights the value that cannot be measured by any economic yardstick—the value to a developing, dependent child of a parent of *either* sex who can meet the fundamental needs of that child. Mr. Minton and his fellow attorneys have the ability to work out the mathematics on their own. They need us, however, to determine the more important emotional economics. My sincere hope is that this book will make it easier for all of us in the mental-health or helping professions to fulfill that need.

Acknowledgments

After I wrote my previous book, I recommended that other potential authors keep their books within themselves. The process of giving birth to a book can be long and painful. But like many people who hear advice from psychiatrists, I did not take it!

My patient family has developed more patience and tolerance, increasingly remarkable virtues. To say that I am grateful to them is an understatement. John Donne was right: no man is an island. He must have the support, love, and encouragement of his loved ones in order to fulfill his creative urges with any degree of real emotional satisfaction. I am, indeed, a lucky man.

I am also lucky in my friends, who include many leading forensic psychiatrists and legal scholars. The participation of such distinguished lawyers and psychiatrists in the mock trial presented as part II of this book speaks for itself; but there is a long list of other, equally distinguished providers of support and critical encouragement. Henry H. Foster, Jr., professor emeritus at New York University Law School and past chairman of the Family Law Section of the American Bar Association should lead it. He spent considerable time poring over several early versions of this manuscript, providing invaluable corrections and suggestions. Such eminent forensic psychiatrists as Drs. Jonas R. Rappeport, consultant to the Supreme Bench of Baltimore, founding president of the American Academy of Psychiatry and the Law, and chairman of its Ethics Committee; Park Elliott Dietz and Dennis Koson of the Department of Psychiatry at Harvard Medical School; Richard Rada, assistant chairman of the Department of Psychiatry of the University of New Mexico; and James L. Cavanaugh, Jr., of the Isaac Ray Center at the Rush Medical College, should all be mentioned specifically here, as should a host of other good friends and colleagues. These were not rubber-stamp artists; they each focused on specific issues and demanded clarification or emphasis where needed. I am honored that the present book suits them. They are a demanding panel.

Like all my colleagues, I miss two brilliant contributors to the area of the mental-health sciences and the law. Professor Browning Hoffman of the University of Virginia and Professor Jonas Robitscher of Emory University both passed away recently at tragically youthful ages and in the midst of increasingly significant labors. Both were very encouraging to me, especially in this effort. They are irreplaceable in our hearts and in our science.

I have been fortunate to maintain a constant relationship with my typist for many years. Marguerite L. Mueller typed and her husband, Richard, proofread. I have piled a lot on them over the years, but they have stuck with me. I am fortunate not only in my family, but in my extended family as well.

**Part I
Problems in Child Custody**

1

The Law and Other Roots of Child-Custody Problems

Statistics seem to indicate that the social fabric of the United States is unraveling. For example, the terms *household* and *family* can no longer be routinely accepted as synonymous. The Bureau of the Census has reported that nearly half of the nation's 71.1 million households are occupied by one or two persons. In 1970, 10.9 million Americans lived by themselves; by 1975 this figure had risen to 13.9 million. Similarly, the number of two-person households (a large proportion of these are households with one parent of either sex and a child) rose from 18.3 million in 1970 to 21.08 million in 1975.[1] By 1977 two-person households accounted for 38 percent of all American families.[2] By 1979, 19 percent of families with children at home were maintained by one parent. During the 1970s the percentage of one-parent households maintained by divorced women climbed from 29 percent to 38 percent. The proportion headed by never-married women rose from 7 percent to 15 percent.[3] The Census Bureau's Marriage and Family Branch, which prepared these figures, interprets them to mean that the American family is becoming increasingly fragmented and isolated. They also predict a trend toward an increase in those figures, so that two-person or single-person households will become proportionately even more significant. Forty-nine percent of the one-person households are occupied by individuals under 35. The number of men under 25 living alone tripled between 1970 and 1977, and the number of women under 25 living alone doubled. Obviously, declining birthrates and increased numbers of divorces and separations have led to a reduction in the number of Americans who live together over long periods of time. Many contemporary sociologists feel that the increased incidence of young couples living together more or less casually has not yet had a definite effect on these statistics because such couples seldom stay together for long periods of time. In fact, that lack of mutual long-term commitment has been interpreted as both cause and effects of the social unraveling.

Marriage and divorce rates have increased since 1960, but the increase in divorce rates has been dramatic, whereas the increase in marriage rates has more closely paralleled general population growth. In 1970 the divorce rate was less than 400 per 100,000. By 1978 the divorce rate had climbed to 520 per 100,000.

The situation in Canada is very much the same. By no means can the divorce explosion be interpreted as a strictly American phenomenon. In the entire nation of Canada in 1922, there were 543 divorces. In 1977 that number had risen to 55,370, indicating a remarkable rise in the divorce rate per 100,000 from 6.1 to 237.7. The divorce rate in western Canada far exceeds that in eastern Canada, more closely approximating the figures for the United States.[4]

The breaking up of marriages, if not yet endemic, certainly appears to have reached epidemic proportions. Like most epidemics, it respects no political boundaries and few social ones.

Divorce

Most nonlawyers—and this obviously includes the bulk of mental-health professionals—have very little knowledge of the legal aspects of divorce beyond vague generalities, even when they have gone through the process themselves. Surprises usually abound for lay persons who begin to deal with the law as an institution. Behavioral scientists and mental-health counselors who deal with the difficulties and the products of divorce should also have some knowledge of its legal aspects.

The basic issue—and, surprisingly, the one often least understood by lay persons—is that divorce is a legal rather than a personal action. As such it is subject to statutes, laws that may be quite different from state to state. It is defined in legal terms, in ways that sometimes appear strange to nonlawyers and are certainly unfamiliar to mental-health workers whose definitions originate from different sources. One example is taken from the case of *People* v. *John,* 44 N.Y.S. 2d 806 (1943).[5] In that case the court wrote, "Divorce is the legal separation of husband and wife, effected, for cause, by judgment of a proper court." That is a basic and, by and large, complete definition. Other definitions only serve to provide depth and commentary. A Utah decision, *Morrison* v. *Federico,* 120 Utah 75 (1951), states that a divorce action, ". . . is primarily a controversy between husband and wife as to who is at fault in causing their domestic difficulties, and is an attempt to disrupt the family unit. . . ."

Regardless of what dictionaries or encyclopedias may say, the definitons provided by courts are the definitions used in the law. Moral value judgments are often part and parcel of these definitions because, regardless of how behavioral scientists may feel about it, the courts reflect the values of the societies they serve. They interpret the laws that are written by the legislatures; these are known as *statutes.* They also hand down decisions that, by precedence, come to be known as *case law* (as differentiated from statutes). The shadings of the definitions and the applications of the laws often differ from court to court, certainly from state to state but also within the same state and even within the same jurisdiction. Judges, of course, differ from one another.

A good example of moral value judgment may be found in the definition provided in the aforementioned case, *Morrison* v. *Federico*. It expresses the concept that fault is to be found in every divorce and that the marriage would continue were not one of the partners so fault-ridden that the other partner could no longer live with him or her. This is the classic background of most of the earlier divorce laws in most states in this country. Although created by a contract between husband and wife, marriage is a legal relationship of a particular nature, with certain mutual rights and obligations determined not only by private agreements but by the state law as well. Thus, in a very definite sense, the state has an interest in every marriage. If they are legally married by means of registration with the state, the parties cannot terminate that relationship by themselves, any more than any legally defined business partnership or corporation can break apart without legal action and recognition by that state or, through reciprocity, by another state. Before the development in recent years of what has come to be known as *no-fault divorce,* the state would allow the marriage contract to be broken only for what the state determined to be proper grounds. The most common grounds were adultery, desertion, and cruelty. When grounds were needed, divorce was a very difficult process, often involving messy trials in which the reputations of both parties were raked over the coals.

Divorce was deliberately made difficult because of the state's interest in maintaining the sanctity of the institution of marriage. Marriage, of course, is also a religious rite. In England, the country of origin of most U.S. laws, both marriage and divorce were originally under the jurisdiction of the ecclesiastical courts, which followed canon law. Not until 1857 did Parliament give secular, judicial courts power to grant complete dissolution of marriage. Because ecclesiastical courts were never established in the United States, that aspect of the English Common Law never crossed the Atlantic. Instead, the Constitution granted to the states the power to legislate and act on marriage and divorce. Nonetheless, religious influences over the concepts of marriage and its sanctity have always been strong in this country. The expressions of public morality as defined by U.S. courts have often been colored by the religious standards of the Judeo-Christian tradition, even if they have not been spelled out in that fashion. As stated in *Solomon* v. *Solomon,* 13 Ohio Dec. 517 (1903), "Divorce is the legal dissolution of the marriage status, and while the law favors marriage, it disfavors divorce. . . ." Even in this current era of somewhat easier divorce, the law still tends to favor marriage over divorce, as seen by such criteria as tax provisions (except for federal income taxes), insurance rates, and so forth.

The law, as an institution similar to most organized religion, has generally served as a brake against rapid social change. Social changes are not generally reflected in law until some years have passed; by then, societal values may well have swung back to earlier positions as a result of numerous factors. Social volatility cannot practically be reflected in the law. Certainly, regarding divorce, the population in general may *seem* to favor it over marriage, as the statistics indicate. That, however, is only a superficial judgment based on the numbers and not on the feelings of people who, for instance, may repeatedly enter into relationships in hopes of finding the "right one."

Despite the tendency of the law to favor marriage and disfavor divorce, lawyers, like everyone else, know that a wellspring of feeling exists throughout the country to liberalize the statutes affecting the dissolution of marriages. Ellen Goodman, the Pulitzer Prize-winning syndicated columnist, wrote a commemorative article that began:

> September 4 is a 10th anniversary of sorts, but don't send presents. It's the anniversary of a divorce law. On this day in 1969, Ronald Reagan signed the nation's first no-fault divorce law.
>
> By now every state in the Union—except Illinois, Pennsylvania and South Dakota—has some kind of a no-fault option in their range of divorce laws. [Since then, Pennsylvania has adopted no-fault provisions.] But the controversy continues about whether no-fault is at fault for the rising divorce rate, or for lowering the economic status of divorced women and their children.
>
> In some places, there are as many people blaming no-fault as formerly blamed each other. . . .[6]

Lawyers also know that there are more divorces, in states without liberalized laws as well as in the liberalized ones. And lawyers must prepare themselves for even higher divorce rates. According to an article in *The Wall Street Journal,*

> . . . the courts are still playing a hopeless game of catch-up with the 91% jump taken by the divorce rate between 1970 and 1978. More than half the civil suits now filed are divorce cases, and, because the number of judges has risen only slightly, couples who disagree on the terms of their divorces sometimes are forced to wait as long as two years for their day in court. . . . Most lawyers agree with Beverly Hills attorney Harry Fain who calls family law, "the most hated and actually ostracized branch of law."[7]

Easier Divorce

Easier divorce does not necessarily mean easy divorce. Breaking up a household generally creates a considerable emotional, legal, and financial wrench. However, breaking a relationship can sometimes be easier than keeping it, regardless of the severity of the divorce laws. A continuing marriage is often a testimonial to the capacity of each partner to sacrifice his or her own immediate ego satisfactions for the sake of maintaining the relationship, which is seen as more important than the individual needs of either partner. "Do it now," was the battle cry of the 1960s. The idea that if something feels good, nothing should stand in the way of doing it, delivered a blow to the contrasting idea of maintaining a relationship that must be worked at if it is to survive.

Some scholarly viewers of the current scene have stated flatly that marriage is a thing of the past, that it is no longer a viable institution in this culture. They cite the statistics given earlier to back their notions. However, the death of marriage as an institution, like Mark Twain's, may be prematurely reported. This is a remarkable period of transition in American life. Perhaps we shall have more answers after another fifty or hundred years. Meanwhile, we are faced with a current state of flux. All mental-health counselors have much work to do in dealing with the manifold anxieties arising in the population because of the breaking up of relationships and the failure of alternative provisions for the emotional needs that result from people's increasing isolation. In recent years, many offshoots of psychiatry and psychology have developed in response to the absolute as well as the relative increase in symptoms of anxiety. New approaches to therapy have attempted to deal with anxiety symptoms in a number of new and sometimes bizarre ways. The presence of these therapies only attests to the number of people who need relief.

Easier Divorce and Hostility

Divorce is becoming not only easier but more mechanical as well. One type, known as *actuarial,* is carried out by the divorcing partners themselves, without lawyers. The couple fill out and file their own forms. Divorce by actuarial means is a growing phenomenon, obviously related to all the sociologic factors and legal trends mentioned earlier. Marriages may now occur without the kinds of underlying commitments previously held sacred. There may even be a contractual basis that allows for adherence to predetermined actuarial conditions if the marriage breaks up. A decrease in actual litigation between partners will result. The trend toward actuarial divorce originated in those states that incorporated as part of their revised divorce statutes a mechanism by which the property held by the divorcing couple is divided equally between the parties. That property gained by the couple following their marriage, even if only one spouse ostensibly earned it, is known in those states as *community property.* The concept is based on the idea that both spouses contributed equally to the marriage; therefore, they should share in the distribution of the assets from it. Although there are some technical legal differences, those states that have statutes defined as equitable distribution can be considered for the purposes of this exposition as community-property states. In community-property states, actuarial divorce is not at all difficult. Attorneys' warnings of the pitfalls of do-it-yourself divorce may result in legislation to eliminate those pitfalls, rather than in forcing couples seeking divorce again to beat paths to attorneys' offices. This is, of course, a genuine economic problem for attorneys—one that may get worse. The burgeoning number of attorneys also may create economic problems for them, and those problems may affect the way they practice in, for example, cases of divorce with possible custody problems.

Again, a reminder must be given that *easier* divorce does not necessarily mean *easy* divorce. Community property or equitable distribution might make it easier in the end to determine property division and such appurtenances as alimony, support for children, and so forth; but it cannot be expected to work smoothly in every case. Even in community-property states, court battles are fought over such matters as the determination of whether assets are really community property or whether they represent separate property that should be considered as probably owned by one partner prior to the wedding. Even with those types of battles, however, the marriage dissolution process is far easier on both the individuals and their families than in those situations in which grounds for divorce had to be listed, often embarrassingly, and accompanied by mutual finger pointing.

Thus, if divorcing parents are going through their own processes, filling out the legal forms themselves and agreeing without any mediating lawyers about property division, alimony, and so forth, at the same time that the number of lawyers is growing rapidly, it stands to reason that the practice of family law and the economics of that practice must be adversely affected. Lawyers who can see and evaluate nationwide trends in this direction predict that in such cases the children might well be the only focus of disagreement between the dissolving partners. Lawyers see this from the viewpoint of the threat to their economic existence, but this trend may represent a threat from another point of view as well.

People who divorce each other are generally very angry with each other. This obvious phenomenon is overlooked by many individuals, who may idealize the divorce process, naively expecting the contesting partners to behave civilly toward each other. Although there are some "friendly divorces," these represent the exception. Most divorces are notoriously unfriendly. It is realistic to anticipate extraordinary hostility between divorcing partners, even if this is covered by a veneer of civility. If the divorce procedures between two mutually hostile people are carried out in a sterile, actuarial, figure-out-the-numbers manner, then one must wonder what happens to the hostility. Complaining to friends or family about the miseries caused by one's spouse may not be an effective or efficient way to discharge that hostility. Divorce lawyers are as familiar as therapists or marriage counselors with the need many divorcing couples demonstrate to fight with each other. Often, peripheral issues are selected as points of contention by one or the other party. The contending parties simply cannot deal more effectively with the wellspring of hostility they feel toward each other, and they must act it out by finding "red herrings."

Custody Suits and Attorneys

If community-property settlements and actuarial, lawyerless divorce represent trends, what can the contesting antagonists fight about? The answer is obvious. Even without these trends, all of us have seen horrible cases in which children are used as pawns in attempts to "get at" opposing marital partners. If trends toward actuarial divorce are borne out, we can expect to see even more of this. More children of these breaking marriages will need even more care and guidance, and their dispositions will become a matter of even greater determinative importance. Child custody will become a specialty in itself, perhaps replacing much of the practice currently devoted to the more routine aspects of divorce litigation.

Any lawyer who says that he or she does not have to deal with the emotional needs of clients during wrenching times of separation or divorce is being very unrealistic. Although psychotherapy is not a function of the attorney-client relationship, support and encouragement and, above all, approachability and accessibility are definite and appropriate functions mandated by the needs of the clients. Lawyers must develop sensitivity to those needs and must learn to provide for them without falling into the traps of overinvolvement or its opposite, withdrawal and coldness. As advocates, attorneys may have difficulty seeing themselves in a role such as that described here, but an advocate can certainly demonstrate understanding and provide emotional support. Often their friends, colleagues, and teammates in the mental-health professions can help them do this more effectively.

The Best-Interests Standard

The lawyers and their mental-health-expert consultants must understand the needs of the children of breaking marriages. If the lawyers cannot do so on their own, then the mental-health consultants must provide the needed understanding for them. The phrase, "the best interests of the child," is paid lip service throughout the United States and in Canada, but it may not really be adhered to if the custody decision has to be made in court.[8] The advocacy positions generally assumed by attorneys in divorce actions and in custody suits sometimes prevent the attorneys from seeing that the best in-

terests of the children might not be served by the litigations they are direct-
ing. Attorneys often identify with the causes of their clients; this, too,
blinds them against recognizing the depth of some of the problems involved
in these cases. Besides, the best-interests standard itself has created a
number of doubts among observers of the child-custody scene.

Painter v. Bannister, 258 Iowa 39 (1966), may have focused increased
attention on the problem of judges arbitrarily imposing decisions emanating
from their own viewpoints and prejudices instead of from real indications
or even common sense. In this notorious case, the issue centered on whether
the child in question should be returned to his father instead of being reared
by his maternal grandparents. The mother had been killed in an automobile
accident in California, where she had lived with her husband, and the father
had sent his son to the mother's Iowa parents while he pulled himself
together following the loss of his wife. The relationship between the boy
and his grandparents deepened, and the latter were loath to release him to
his father, whom they described as a person whose California standards and
life-style were unsuitable for meeting the boy's needs. A child-development
specialist, a school colleague of the grandfather, testified in the Iowa court
that this was indeed the case; and the court awarded custody to the grandparents.[9] Psychiatrists often criticize the judges in that case. It should be
remembered, however, that expert testimony was given, which led the
judges to make a decision they considered to be based on the best interests
of the child, even though that decision led to a result we might well reject.
Expert witnesses have much to learn from Painter v. Bannister. They, too,
can be victims of their own prejudices.

Even before that famous Iowa case, much dissatisfaction existed among
lawyers and judges, who were overwhelmed by the responsibilities of making decisions about the disposition of children whose parents fought over
them. Nothing has replaced the best-interests standard, however, and it is
unlikely that anything will—or, for that matter, that anything should, if the
standards are truly imposed on the basis claimed. For example, the Uniform
Marriage and Divorce Act uses that standard,[10] and the American Bar
Association has endorsed that act, although there was controversy over the
custody sections once they were promulgated.[11] The provisions regarding
custody are especially notable for their elimination of marital fault or
misconduct of either partner toward the other as factors to be *routinely* considered in decisions of custody. The provision directs the court to consider
"all the relevant factors" in the case but prohibits consideration of the
"conduct of a proposed custody that does not affect his relationship to the
child. . . ."

The main objections voiced by the American Bar Association to the
Uniform Marriage and Divorce Act centered on their impression that
criteria were lacking as to when there had been a complete breakdown of the

marriage. Ultimately, following considerable activity by the Family Law Section, criteria were developed. However, there is still controversy over the idea of whether any external agency has any capacity to establish such criteria. One or both marital partners ought to be able to agree on their own criteria, but this is not the way courts operate. All litigation comes to trial simply because the standards and ideas of the contestants do not meet, and because no mutuality of understanding, much less agreement, is possible between them.

The Tender-Years Standard

The best-interests standard is a relatively recent concept in the law, and although it is widely used there are a number of factors that often tend to mitigate against its actual force. Perhaps the main stumbling block is the retention of the so-called tender-years standard, in common use throughout most states since the turn of the century. Although Henry Foster, professor emeritus of the Law School at New York University and past chairman of the Family Law Section of the American Bar Association, dates this back to *Helms* v. *Franciscus* in Maryland in 1830, many courts throughout the nineteenth century considered children chattel and automatically turned them over to their fathers in the then relatively rare instances of divorce. According to Foster,

> The Maryland Court, after stating that the father is the sole and legal guardian of all his infant children, and that generally, no court can take them from him and give them to his wife, went on to say by way of dicta, "yet even a court of common law will not go so far as to hold nature in contempt, and snatch helpless, puling infancy from the bosom of an affectionate mother, and place it into the coarse hands of the father. The mother is the softest nurse of infancy, and with her it will be left in opposition to the general right of the father. . . ."[12]

Foster comments further that

> There. . . is uncertainty as to just what are "tender years." Generally, it is agreed that preschool age children so qualify, but there is a conflict in the cases as to older children. It may be that there is a maternal preference for daughters to an older age than that for sons. There also is some evidence that there is a recent trend to reduce the operative years for the tender years doctrine.
>
> A recent check of the American jurisdictions indicates that the tender years doctrine has lost ground so that in 1978 it is either rejected or relegated to the role of "tie breaker" in most states. The doctrine itself remains "gospel," but may be subordinated to the assumed best interests of the children in some fourteen states. In at least twelve states there is a prefer-

ence for a "fit" mother, other factors being equal. And in twenty-two
states the tender years doctrine is rejected by statutes or court decision. It
has a doubtful status in three states. . . .

One of the amazing things about the tender years doctrine is that it has
often persisted even in the face of "equalization" statutes or state Equal
Rights Amendments (ERA). . . . In the seventeen states presently having
ERA provisions, the tender years doctrine is alive and well in eight states,
and has been supposedly discarded in nine states. Although considering the
wording of ERA provisions, and the intent and purpose back of them, it is
difficult to see how the tender years doctrine could have survived in a state
having ERA, courts wanting to do so have found ways around the law. One
way is to stress the best interests of the child and then to assume that ordinarily the child's welfare will be best served by being with the
mother. . . . As has been noted, sexual stereotyping of the loving, tender,
and self-sacrificing mother makes any other choice as to custody a more
detrimental alternative. Uncritical sentimentality towards mothers in
general came to be as unsupportable as the feudalistic premises that the
father-husband was lord and master by natural right. . . .[13]

The Bases of Custody Decisions

Foster, of course, warns that regardless of the texts of the statutes, decisions
are made by people who themselves are often prisoners of their own needs,
of which they may or may not be aware. Lip service to the best-interests
standard is practiced nearly everywhere, but the effectiveness of the doctrine may often be compromised. Behavioral scientists who serve as consultants in custody cases must learn that, although they see that the best interests of a child might be served by a decision in one direction, a judicial
decision may be based on a different interpretation of the child's best interests. It is the decision of the court that counts, not that of any expert
witness. Many expert witnesses are unaware that they do not make decisions
but, rather, only attempt to explain matters so that the courts' decisions can
be based on something substantial.

In a recent symposium, Dr. Albert Solnit of Yale University Medical
School warned that clinical experts must be very careful not to overstep the
legitimate limits of their roles. Solnit defined the role of the consultant to
the courts in these cases quite narrowly. He stated that they must resist the
temptation to become "caught up in the fray" or to volunteer opinions on
how the case should be settled, even when invited to do so by a lawyer or a
judge. According to Solnit, "We're in the position of being able to answer
questions about the nature of the relationship between parent and child or
about the child's state of development, not to apply the law. We mustn't be
afraid to say, 'I don't know'."[14]

Most forensically trained and experienced witnesses in the mental-
health professions would second Solnit's encouragement of their saying, "I

don't know," when that is, indeed, the case. Most, however, would probably provide the court with their requested opinions regarding the disposition of the child based on their view of the child's best interests. Even with the expression of that opinion, however, the clinical expert remains only a consultant. As in any consulting situation, no matter how well the consultant's conclusions are presented or buttressed with data, they may be accepted or rejected by the person who request them.

Some expert witnesses express the opinion that they will no longer appear in the legal arena unless their opinions are accepted and put into action. They do not see that their presence, regardless of outcome, serves a valuable purpose, whereas staying away does not help anyone at all. Besides, as Foster again points out,

> At least 90-95% of custody issues are resolved out of court; it is the exceptional (pathological?) case that gets into litigation. When the custody case is litigated, the court is compelled to determine the issue on the basis of the evidence presented and within the framework of traditional values. The "best interests" of the child may be the paramount consideration but it is not the only one. . . .[15]

Much more often than not, custody issues are resolved without any input from behavioral scientists, whether the cases reach the courtroom or not.

Discussions of dissolving families and social fabrics, as well as of trends in the law regarding marriage, divorce, and standards by which custody of children is awarded, tend to stress the automatic assumption that custody cases only involve disputes between spouses or splitting parents. That assumption represents very restrictive thinking, however. The subject of custody also appears in many other types of proceedings, including adoption, guardianship, placement, and juvenile-court actions.

In many cases the opponents are not the parents. Perhaps one or both parents may proceed against a legal or governmental agency, as in a recent California case in which deaf parents successfully fought to regain custody of their child, taken from them originally by a perhaps overzealous probation department.[16] Even political considerations can enter the child-custody arena, as in Chicago recently, when the 12-year-old son of a Ukrainian family became the subject of a custody battle. Although his parents were unhappy in the United States, the boy did not want to return to the Ukraine with his family. No charges of parental inadequacy or neglect were ever made, but a judge ruled that the county should assume temporary custody of the boy because his parents wanted to take him back with them to the Ukraine. Like statutes in most states, Illinois law holds that evidence must be brought forth to demonstrate that the child's "welfare or safety or the protection of the public cannot be adequately safeguarded without removal. . . ." None was provided, but the renewed cold war climate appeared to override that issue.[17]

Apolitical but nonetheless competing relatives or nonrelatives may also involve themselves in guardianship or similar cases. A particularly complex custody issue centers about the question of who gets custody of the surviving minor child if the custodial parent dies. Despite considerable urging by bar associations and media campaigns, many Americans have not prepared wills, and many of those who have done so have not incorporated any instructions for the disposition of their surviving minor children.

In many intact families, the parents have arranged for guardians for the minor children in case of their death. Those guardians may be relatives or trusted friends who have agreed to assume this responsibility. However, a child of divorce whose custodial parent dies may face the likelihood of being sent to the noncustodial parent, even if that parent was previously ruled unfit. Even if a guardian had been named by the deceased custodial parent, the noncustodial, surviving natural parent may contest that aspect of the will. Many courts are likely to recognize the rights of the natural parents over named guardians. This is a facet of the so-called *reversion doctrine,* which in many jurisdictions is applied in the event of death of the custodial parent, especially where the authorities disagree over the disposition of the children. In some cases, courts have named different persons as guardians of the person of the minor and of the minor's property, respectively.[18]

Obviously, it is the attorney's responsibility to plan for such contingencies and their sometimes dreadful complications. However, the mental-health expert evaluating the contesting custodial parents might well ask about plans regarding such issues. Not only can he or she render a service by making the parents even more aware of their overall planning responsibilities, but the expert also can gain insight into their respective planning capacities.

Many other types of custody litigations are also common, but they all have in common the threads that children are involved and that decisions are made in a legal arena, albeit by judges instead of by juries, except in Texas. Even these other types of cases are increasing, however, along with those stimulated directly by the increased divorce rate, because the familial instabilities resulting from family breakups lead to mushrooming ramifications. A cause-and-effect relationship exists between the decline in stable families as we once knew them and the increasing variety of parent substitutes. The more variables, the more conflicts.

Child Advocates and Expert Witnesses

Professor Foster wrote "A Bill of Rights for Children" in anticipation of this tendency.[19] In it he urges the use of a third attorney in the courtroom, one who serves solely as a legal advocate for the child or children in question, ensuring that their legal rights are upheld. This practice has been adopted in a few courts in some jurisdictions and has also been advocated by Goldstein, Freud, and Solnit.[20] This practice is too new to evaluate critically, but to paraphrase Clemenceau's famous dictum about war and generals, "Child-custody litigation is too important to be left to the lawyers." Most attorneys would probably agree, although they might well legitimately add, "or to the mental-health experts"! Certainly, most indicate their approval of the concept of child advocacy, but they feel very anxious about having to make decisions about the future welfare of children without help from experts in the field. Attorneys who have served as child advocates or, as they are called, guardians *ad litem,* have often complained that they felt a need for special help throughout the cases in order to alert them to situations, cues, and clues that indicate problem potentials for their minor clients. They do not feel that same need in representing the contesting adults, although the same cues and clues may certainly be expressed and overlooked.

Certainly, lawyers must develop more knowledge of the needs of their adult and/or child clients, and of their adult clients' children. However, they cannot realistically expect to see themselves as expert or authoritative child advocates in the sense of the mental-health experts who also use the term. (See the further discussion of child advocacy in chapter 5.) Those "third lawyers" will have to turn increasingly to expert professional sources for consultation. This certainly represents no new thinking in the way the law is practiced. Expert testimony has been used in the courtrooms of many countries since the fourth century A.D. In this country a number of states have included stringent criteria for expert evaluation of the needs of the children in custody cases in order to determine what would serve the children's best interests. In California the codes prescribe that

> Before the court makes any order awarding custody to a person or persons other than a parent, without the consent of the parents, it must make a finding that an award of custody to a parent would be detrimental to a child, and the award to a nonparent is required to serve the best interests of the child. . . .In a proceeding for dissolution of a marriage, the probation officer or domestic relations investigator when so directed by the court, must conduct a custody investigation and file a written confidential report thereupon. . . .[21]

The family Law Department of the Los Angeles Superior Court, for example, provides the services of a panel of court-appointed psychiatrists who are available to consult in matters of custody, visitation, dissolution, abandonment, adoption, and paternity. A fee schedule is set up as a part of that service. The orders for psychiatric evaluation may be obtained either by a written notice of motion to the opposing party with declarations of why the procedure is needed, by oral stipulation in open court that consultation is needed, or by submission of a jointly signed stipulation to the court without need for hearing. In these cases all parties are available for evaluation by the examining psychiatrist.[22]

Not all courts have family-law sections or divisions, and not all courts have access to a pool of mental-health professionals who may be specifically well trained to evaluate the situations surrounding contests over children. Not every community has such individuals; yet the courts and their officers must take sometimes unfamiliar factors into consideration in child-custody cases. Who, then, determines what is really in the best interests of the child—and how?

Such advanced proposals as the Uniform Marriage and Divorce Act or the California Family Law Act impose remarkable burdens on the individuals who must implement these laws.[23] Likewise, many jurists and attorneys resent the intrusion into their judgmental domain by the mental-health professionals, who, in rendering clinical opinions, actually create forces that often tend to carry the judicial decisions along with them. In criminal cases over the years, some psychiatrists and psychologists have pleaded that they did not want to usurp the powers of judges and juries and that they did not want the mantle of judgmental responsibility laid on them. It can be argued that the testimony of experts regarding the best interests of the children may carry more weight than the testimony of experts discussing legal insanity and criminal responsibility. In contrast, however, judges who see the mental-health sciences as confused and confusing may consciously or unconsciously reject the data or findings of mental-health professionals. They say that they can consider on their own all the factors that the law requires to be considered, and that common sense and a review of the evidence are adequate for decision making for children.

Although this type of thinking may make mental-health experts bristle, it must always be remembered that the judges, not the expert witnesses, are triers of fact, and that often those triers of facts have lost respect for the mental-health professions by witnessing interminable battles of the experts in their courtrooms. One of the goals of this book is to reduce the incidence of such courtroom battles, in which experts with apparently equal competence and credentials testify in mutual opposition, to the frustration of the listeners and the likely detriment of the children.

Obviously, most legal experts should not be expected to be experts in matters of family psychodynamics, mental illness, or child development, any more than behavioral scientists can be expected to speak authoritatively on matters of law. However, unfair expectations are placed on jurists by the laws and by the communities those laws represent. Lawyers have little enough help in that area. Often there is little meeting ground between psychiatrist and attorney. Most law schools lack adequate courses in law and the behavioral sciences, and those courses offered may be taught by attorneys without any participation by behavioral scientists. Attorneys and judges are too often left to flounder; when cases arise in which mental-health or emotional factors are prime considerations, they need all the help they can get. Under the U.S. court system, the fact-finding function must proceed with the aid of whatever experts the courts or their officers can get to provide that help.

Notes

1. U.S. Bureau of the Census, *Statistical Abstracts of the United States: 1975,* 96th ed. (Washington, D.C.: U.S. Government Printing Office, 1975). See esp. table 96, p. 68.

2. U.S. Bureau of the Census, "Households and Families by Type," series P-20, no. 313 (Washington, D.C.: U.S. Government Printing Office, March 1977).

3. Associated Press, "Increase of 80% in One-Parent Homes Reported," *Los Angeles Times,* 17 August 1980, p. 1.

4. *Statistics Canada, Catalogue 84-205 Annual,* vol. II: *Marriage and Divorces* (1979).

5. By virtue of the fact that the case is *People* v. *John,* it is seen that the issue at hand is a state offense rather than a civil one. If it were the latter, the case would be labeled *So-and-So* v. *John,* or *Some Institution* v. *John.* The *People* are really the *government of the state* in which the crime took place; a crime is considered to be an offense against the *people* of the state. The numbers following the name of the case are known to lawyers as a citation, a reference to the book in which the court's judgment can be found. In this case the reference is to the second series of decisions handed down by the New York State Supreme Court, vol. 44, p. 806. The decision was written in 1943.

6. Ellen Goodman, "Critics Are Quick to Find Fault with No-Fault Divorce Laws," Syndicated Column, *Los Angeles Times,* 4 September 1979, p. II, p. 7. ©1979, The Boston Globe Newspaper Company/Washington Post Writers Group, reprinted with permission.

7. Kathryn Christensen, "Disputes over Money and Children Swamp U.S. Divorce Courts," *The Wall Street Journal,* 28 January 1980, p. 1. Reprinted by permission of *The Wall Street Journal,* ©Dow Jones & Company, Inc., 1980. All rights reserved.

8. J. Goldstein, A. Freud, and A.J. Solnit, *Beyond the Best Interests of the Child* (New York: Free Press, 1973).

9. H. Painter, *Mark, I Love You* (New York: Simon and Schuster, 1967).

10. The Uniform Marriage and Divorce Act is not a statute per se. Rather, it is an attempt by leading legal scholars to formulate a model that might well be adopted by all fifty states. Obviously, it has not been.

11. M. Wheeler, *No-Fault Divorce* (Boston: Beacon Press, 1974), esp. chap. 5, pp. 72-97.

12. H.H. Foster and D.J. Freed, "Life with Father: 1978," *Family Law Quarterly* 11 (Winter 1978):321. Reprinted with permission of Sanford N. Katz, Editor-in-chief, *Family Law Quarterly*, and Henry H. Foster.

13. Ibid.

14. *Clinical Psychiatry News* (September 1981):14.

15. H.H. Foster, personal communication, quoted with permission.

16. J. Kendall, "Deaf Couple Wins Custody of Daughter," *Los Angeles Times*, 2 March 1978, pt. II, p. 1. See also Editorial, "Justice Returns a Child," *Los Angeles Times,* 3 March 1978, pt. II, p. 4.

17. J. Miller, "Government Goofed in Polovchak Case," *Chicago Sun-Times*, 29 August 1980, p. 43.

18. The reversion doctrine was overturned in a recent San Francisco case (reported by Philip Hager, *Los Angeles Times*, 21 October 1981, p. 3). There, the California Court of Appeals ruled that a 15-year-old boy with Downs' syndrome could remain with a family to which he had become very attached instead of with his biological family. The child had been institutionalized nearly all his life. The biological parents had objected to medical tests that might lead to consideration of corrective surgery for the boy's congenital heart condition. They reasoned that the child might then outlive them and be left without financial support. The appellate court confirmed the decision by the trial court that the boy had established such close ties to the second family that they had, in effect, become his psychological parents. The appellate court stated that he could remain with them over the objections of the natural parents. It remains to be seen whether similar decisions may be made in cases that do not involve life-preserving surgery or similarly dramatic events.

19. H.H. Foster, *A Bill of Rights for Children* (Springfield, Ill.: Charles C. Thomas, 1974).

20. Goldstein, Freud, and Solnit, *Beyond the Best Interests*.

21. *California Practice Review* 144:128-130 (1970).

22. Los Angeles County Bar Association, Family Law Section, *Family Law Symposium, 1975*, esp. K. Raiford, "Investigation in Custody Matters," and T.A. Curtis, "The Court-Appointed Psychiatrist."

23. Family Law Act, *California Civil Code* 4000-5174, enacted 1970.

2 The Lawyers versus the Experts

Lawyers may have a terrible time finding any mental-health expert in private practice who will work with them in child-custody cases. Going to court is a prospect most behavioral scientists dread.

When lawyers must consult with behavioral scientists and depend on their testimony, which is based on what lawyers see as alien and troublesome concepts, it is obvious why the gulf between the disciplines of law and the behavioral sciences has maintained itself for so long. That gulf remains despite the formalities of law, which insist that the two disciplines must work together toward common ends.

In his characteristically elegant manner, Dr. Jonas Robitscher, late professor of law and psychiatry at Emory University, clarified some of the basic conflicts. He said:

> Law is all logic and reason, or at least it sets out to be so. But for a legal system to function, it must be more than merely logical and reasonable. It must be definite. It must be based on precedent. It must rely on rules. And so, in the course of time all functioning legal systems become legalistic, and in the process some of the logic and reason gets left behind. . . . Psychiatry deals with the illogical and the unreasonable. Freud's central idea was that human actions have their sources both in the conscious, which may be governed by reason, and in the unconscious, which is not governed by reason, intellect or logic, and which in fact, is by definition *unreasonable*. In attempting to describe and deal with the illogical and unreasonable actions of humans, psychiatrists are somewhat contemptuous of precedent, and they often fail to please the court when asked to categorize and place information in neat cubbyholes in the fashion that lawyers approve. When these two disciplines meet, therefore, we may expect to find confusion, complexity and mutual dissatisfaction. . . .[1]

In his foreword to Dr. Robert Sadoff's standard text on forensic psychiatry, a distinguished Detroit professor of law, Ralph Slovenko, asks a pointed series of questions: "Is psychiatry too good for the law? Is law too good for psychiatry? Do they simply not go together, like some chemicals?"[2] Ralph Slovenko won the 1975 Guttmacher Award from the American Psychiatric Association for his distinguished efforts in the field of forensic psychiatry,[3] so one might anticipate that his answers to his own questions would all be emphatic "no"s. He and others are attempting to develop emulsifiers for the immiscible oil-water combination he describes as the usual result of attempts to combine the law and the mental-health sciences.

Psychiatrists and psychologists probably resent working in domestic-relations litigation even more than in criminal matters. As expert witnesses in criminal proceedings, they tend to resent the law more impersonally—as an institution. There they see what amounts to a sham, at least in their eyes, in which lip service may be paid to their expertise regarding the makeup, motivations, and controls of the individual on trial—if, in fact, that material is allowed to be presented at all. They also see a vast, compartmentalized system in which trial, sentencing, and punishment—or what is sometimes euphemistically called rehabilitation—have no meaningful interrelationship.[4]

In domestic-relations matters, however, the issues become more personal. The lawyers may appear to be more intense in their roles as advocates because the individuals they represent are so mutually and openly hostile. In child-custody cases, especially, it is more common than not for the consultant-evaluators to wind up with little if any respect for either contestant. Often, those parties have so much invested in their own personal and deeply narcissistic needs that the needs of the children are only peripherally acknowledged.

Many lawyers recognize this, too; and they may have hard times advocating for clients they may despise. Nonetheless, they must advocate. In contrast, the needed expert witnesses are likely to say, "A plague o' both your houses"—not only to the clients, but to the lawyers as well. Instead of avoiding all this ugliness, however, those needed experts who eschew forensic work should step back and look at the heated situation from an objective (and safe) distance. Then they would see that the very rage of the contestants, which so often drives expert witnesses away from participating in such litigation, is in fact expected, perhaps even healthy. More often than not, divorce is ugly and hateful. In fact, according to a social-science rather than a legal definition, it is a formalized, institutionalized expression of hostility, one that is usually accepted as such by all the lawyers, judges, and mental-health authorities working in the field.

Advocates and the Adversary System

Most expert witnesses in any field have problems coping with the adversary system, regardless of the type of case at hand. They often have the impression that the adversary system inhibits the development of the ideas and knowledge they need to present in court. Many feel that they can better function in a neutral zone, perhaps as *amici curiae*, ("friends of the court"). These are experts asked by the court itself to give opinions. They are paid by the court, and there is no question of undue financial or other influence from either side. In child-custody cases, especially, it is felt that this approach nips in the bud the kinds of preexisting hostility so often demonstrated in court by both the contestants and their attorneys.[5] However, most attorneys will not relinquish their classic advocate roles for such a procedure. Even though in many states there are mechanisms by which judges can appoint impartial experts in custody cases, many lawyers initially resist such appointments or else seek their own experts, who well may be less than impartial. The law spawns *advocates*, who champion their causes regardless of intrinsic rightness or wrongness. The law correctly insists that every issue raised by a contestant can be heard and defended, and many lawyers are suspicious of psychiatrists who insist that they can function best outside the adversary arena, unrelated to either side. But the expert witness must *educate* the contesting parties if he or she is to serve as a needed, impartial advocate for the child, as described in chapter 4.

The consultants are right, of course. They can function best outside the arena—but is that what lawyers want or, for that matter, need? If it is not what lawyers want, are *they* right? Judge David Bazelon has written:

> My experience has shown that in no case is it more difficult to elicit productive and reliable expert testimony than in cases that call on the knowledge and practice of psychiatry. . . . In my experience they try to limit testimony to conclusory statements couched in psychiatric terminology. Therefore, they take shelter in defensive resistance to questions about the facts that are or ought to be in their possession. Thus, they refuse to submit their opinions to the scrutiny that the adversary process demands. . . .[6]

Judge Bazelon is a noted critic of U.S. forensic psychiatrists because of problems that arose in criminal cases, not family-law cases. However, his remarks are appropriate here because of his contention that the adversary system provides the most reliable and meaningful form of meting out justice, and that all experts, including psychiatrists, must function within the system if truth is going to emerge from their testimony.

Judge Bazelon states that facts can be brought out only by stringent direct and cross-examination. However, nothing would prevent this kind of tough questioning by each attorney if behavioral scientists operated as *amici curiae*, either. Child-custody cases are handled by trial lawyers, individuals with particular commitments to do battle for their clients. Although in matters of child custody, evaluating experts should have access to all participants, advocacy may be too deeply entrenched in the basic identification processes of most attorneys to allow this without a struggle.

Solow and Adams have written recently:

> We do not believe that the adversary process is an indispensable or even desirable method for determining matters of child custody, as do Tuchler

and Bazelon. The heart of the custody matter is not who is guiltier or more deserving, but which parent can provide the more likely environment for nurturance and growth of the child. This is seldom the true focus of the adversary process as we have observed it.

We propose going several steps beyond the notion of the expert panel and beyond the widely advocated neutral stance of the psychiatrist as expert "friend of the court," in helping the judge to reach an equitable decision on behalf of the child. We suggest that the psychiatrist himself is more qualified to make such a complex evaluation and decision. . . .[7]

Their argument is not unique among psychiatrists or their colleagues in the mental-health professions. However, jurists can certainly debate whether the decision-making process ought to be in the hands of behavioral scientists. The system is simply not set up that way; like it or not, the courts will continue to call on expert witnesses to help them, *not* to decide for them. With more and better input by trained family specialists, the courts can reach more appropriate decisions. If both contesting parties and their attorneys agree to the type of effective, thorough evaluation described by Solow and Adams, or to the type of workup to be described later in this book, the desired effect—preventing a courtroom battle—is achieved. If, however, as often happens, the contestants refuse to sit down with each other and discuss their children realistically and objectively, or if other sources of hostility between the contestants are fueling the custody fight, then the courts and the adversary system will become necessary. At that point the legal trier of fact becomes of necessity the recipient of the expert's advice. In some cases, he may even take it!

Psychiatrists, psychologists, and social workers resent attorneys who ask them to participate in litigation proceedings for other reasons, too. The basic conflicts of the adversary system are only one springboard for their complaints. Philosophic differences aside, the mental-health professionals feel that the adversary system reduces their position to a debasing one of tactics, and that much pertinent material is often overlooked because of the real purpose for which the attorney is presenting "his" or "her" expert. Behavioral scientists often feel that attorneys are not genuinely interested in the real meat of what they have to say unless it suits their contesting tactical purpose, and that feeling is often correct. This, of course, provides them with a remarkably self-justifying point of view regarding the law as an instituion. However, it also betrays a vast lack of understanding and appreciation of the requirements of the adversary system and its demands on all parties.

Financial Arrangements

Money has also been a classic problem for all expert witnesses in private practice when they become involved in medicolegal procedures. Often experts are loath to demand their justifiable fees in advance or even at the times of their work. Although attorneys do this routinely, counselors in the helping professions who are inexperienced in forensic work do not usually do likewise. In my own practice, when I become involved in a private medicolegal evaluation (as distinct from a court-appointed one), I clarify at the outset with the attorney and his or her client that my fees are to be paid at the times of the evaluations, and that the total bill will depend on the number of sessions needed. If I have developed a close, ongoing relationship with an attorney with whom I have often worked before, he or she may tell me that sufficient funds are set aside in a trust account for my workup and participation, and that I can send a bill for the entire procedure at its conclusion. In such cases I usually will do so, although such attorneys generally agree with me that it is appropriate to send me a letter explaining the payment procedure and noting that they understand my fee structure. If I have to go to court to testify, my fee for appearing there is usually paid in advance, at least to the extent of the initial half-day service. Although many lawyers may try to reassure the expert witness by saying, "Doctor, I don't think you'll be away from your office for more than an hour," experience dictates otherwise. Commitments to a smooth, ongoing patient schedule necessitate careful advance planning, and it is generally unwise to count on less than a half-day absence. That security makes for less tension in the courtroom session.

Many colleagues complain that they are unable to collect from either the litigants they have seen or the litigants' attorneys. They have usually erred by not setting forth the plan for fee payment *as the workup began* and not making sure that the responsible party understood and would follow through. The attorneys also err, however, by not bringing this matter up at the outset with the consultants they call. They should explain that it is preferable to arrange the fee schedule and payment schedule with the responsible party whom the consultant generally sees first. The expert should routinely advise the attorney of his or her fee schedule at that time so that no misunderstandings occur. Sometimes, of course, individuals fail to follow through with the payment for the workup as it progresses. In such cases I do not refuse to see the parties, but I explain to them that, even though I am seeing them that day, I shall not proceed with any communications to their attorneys or to the courts until the bill has been paid as previously agreed.

A fundamental error many attorneys make is failure to prepare their clients properly. Neither lawyers nor clients may appreciate the costs involved in a proper and complete psychiatric or psychological workup; and if the attorneys do not wish a proper and complete workup, they should have none at all. Attorneys must discuss these issues with their clients and stress the importance of the workup, even if the findings do not help their cause. When attorneys do not prepare their clients properly, resentments and problems may germinate. When lawyers prepare their clients, and when they communicate freely and openly with the consultants whose help they actively seek, the clients manifest no resentment about the appropriate and expected routine for payment. They know that litigation is expensive and that the psychiatric evaluation will increase that total expense to some extent. Similarly, the expert witness need have no hesitation about frankly announcing his or her fees if asked in the courtroom. Also, the consultant assumes an automatic obligation to attempt to contain the expenses by avoiding unnecessary aspects of the investigation. Determination of these limits is a manifestation of professional judgment.

For the most part, since custody trials are nonjury proceedings, questions about fees are rare. This is in contrast to trials in which a cross-examiner will want to embarrass the witness before impressionable juries. In any case, the witness need not be embarrassed when asked to discuss his or her fees.

When litigants simply cannot afford private consulting fees, attorneys should avail themselves of the services of court-appointed experts. In most jurisdictions a panel of qualified psychiatrists or psychologists serves the court for fees considerably lower than private scale, just as court-appointed lawyers do. Often, probation departments or other court-affiliated agencies have contracted mental-health experts available at a low fee or no fee at all. Some states have established conciliation courts in which trained investigators and evaluators can work with contesting parents.

Ethical Considerations

Ethics may be as significant a problem as fees. Certain relationships exist between mental-health counselors and the people they evaluate that allow for the presentation of material about those people in court; other relationships may preclude such presentation. For example, a therapist who is already involved in a treatment relationship with one or more of those concerned in a custody suit will generally not want to involve him- or herself in the litigation, and may actually refuse to do so. Such involvement would violate previous agreements with the patients that the treatment relationships will be confidential and inviolate. The patient's involvement in a lawsuit in which his or her emotional status is in question waives privilege; but therapists have nevertheless fought to reserve the right to maintain their silence, even if their testimony might be favorable to the patient's cause.[8] The therapists have always lost, sometimes even suffering contempt-of-court citations, although things generally do not get so far out of hand.[9] Nontreating evaluators do not confront such thorny problems. The evaluator, the attorney, and all the subjects of the consultant's examinations know that the purpose of those examinations is one that encompasses the elaboration of findings in a courtroom; hence privilege and confidentiality are not considerations.

Although that sounds simple enough, gray areas sometimes develop that can become quite sticky ethically. For example, in my own practice I consider it of urgent importance to emphasize that the individual seen for evaluation is *not* my patient because I have assumed no clinical or therapeutic responsibility. I routinely explain this to the people I see at the outset of my workups. I may, however, find that therapy is sorely needed for an individual I have evaluated. My own usual practice is not to take that person into psychotherapy myself. Instead, I recommend therapy for the person and make appropriate referrals. At times this can be difficult. For example, an individual may refuse to see anyone other than me. In practically every instance, however, I am able to convince the potential patient that it would be a violation of medical ethics for me to take him or her on as a patient. It would be as if I were soliciting a patient: someone comes to see me for another reason, but I convince him that he needs treatment and promptly begin collecting fees for long-term treatment.

As another example, there may be no other therapist available to treat the individual. Many communities lack needed mental-health facilities. The evaluator in such a case will have to make a difficult decision, perhaps in favor of providing treatment for a needy person. However, doing so and then going into court during the time the treatment is continuing invites considerable problems in the relationship with the patient. Of course, those problems can also adversely affect both the patient's and the doctor's relationships with the attorney, thereby undermining the entire litigation.

I have served in the novel capacity of liaison psychiatrist on several occasions, each time with the obviously necessary approval of the contacting attorneys and their clients. In such cases I perform an evaluation of all significant parties and then discuss the case as I see it with the therapist already involved with one or all parties. The therapist checks my data and conclusions, and, via instruction, agrees or disagrees with all or part, sometimes adding further materials. My function as liaison preserves the relationship between therapist and patient(s) while allowing the court to get a fuller view of the necessary findings addressed to the issues in specific question.

The procedure has met with favor when used thus far. However, it requires much hard work by both liaison and treatment psychiatrist who must convince the adversary attorneys of the value of a sacrosanct therapy relationship for the long-term sake of their clients.

Communication with Attorneys

Behavioral scientists speak a different language than attorneys do, and both must strive to make themselves understood. Perhaps the most significant point—one that is often neglected—is that each must genuinely want to understand the language, viewpoints, and needs of the other. If either has the attitude that the other will simply have to adapt him- or herself entirely, there can be no productive relationship. This must go beyond burying the hatchet in the long-standing feud between the disciplines; it must extend to eager and open cooperation and anticipation. Otherwise, things will bog down in court, with the expert rambling far afield and the attorney's unfulfilled expectations going even further off the mark.[10]

Most mental-health experts are drawn into child-custody cases when they are called by a lawyer. The attorney must be pleased with the communicative powers of the expert he or she contacts and must develop a feeling that he or she and the consultant can work well together.

The expert becomes part of a team whether he works with only the referring attorney or, if possible, with both attorneys. As a team member, the expert must explain his reference points, procedures, findings, and conclusions simply and clearly. He must also expect the attorney(s) to explain the pertinent law and their views as clearly to him. Nothing substitutes for a series of face-to-face conferences. No expert witness in any kind of case should set foot in a courtroom without the opportunity for such conferences and the mutual clarification and understanding they provide.

As with questions about fees, no embarrassment ought to follow the expert's being asked in cross-examination if he has previously met with the lawyer who called him, and if he has previously discussed his testimony with the lawyer. The meeting would be not only appropriate, it is essential. A feeling of security in one's position as an expert witness can counter any apprehension about the demands of the adversary arena and the tactics of the adversaries.

Notes

1. J.B. Robitscher, *Pursuit of Agreement* (Philadelphia: Lippincott, 1966).

2. R.L. Sadoff, *Forensic Psychiatry* (Springfield, Ill.: Charles C. Thomas, 1975).

3. R. Slovenko, *Psychiatry and Law* (Boston: Little, Brown, 1973).

4. M.G. Goldzband, "Schizophrenia in the Adversary Arena," *Cal. Western Law Rev.* 12 (1976):247.

5. T.L. Trunnell, "Johnnie and Suzie, Don't Cry; Mommy and Daddy Aren't That Way," *Bull. Amer. Acad. Psychiat. & Law* 5 (1976):120.

6. D. Bazelon, "Psychiatrists and the Adversary Process," *Scientific American* 230 (1974):18. Reprinted with permission.

7. R.A. Solow and P.L. Adams, "Custody by Agreement: Child Psychiatrist as Child Advocate," *J. Psychiat. & Law* 5 (1977):77. © Federal Legal Publications, Inc., 157 Chambers St., New York, N.Y. 10007. Reprinted with permission.

8. Most forensically shy workers in the mental-health professions are shocked to find that the privilege of maintaining confidentiality is usually not their's but, rather, the patient's. By this is meant that the patient must grant the therapist permission to violate the confidentiality. Exceptions to this are rare and generally refer to situations concerned with public safety.

9. *In Re Lipschutz*, 8 *Cal. Rptr.* 829 (1970). A related case dealing with the waiver of privilege of a parent is *Matter of Edward D.*, 132 *Cal. Rptr.* 100 (1976).

10. M.G. Goldzband, *Custody Cases and Expert Witnesses* (New York: Law & Business, Inc., Harcourt Brace Jovanovich, 1980).

3 Who Listens? The Judges

Relationships between lawyers and mental-health experts have been described as problematic. Those between behavioral scientists and judges may be even more so. On the one hand, behavioral scientists may feel considerable rejection when they appear before judges who may deprecate the behavioral sciences, as many judges do. Even judges who respect contemporary psychiatric and psychological thought may disagree with the expert's conclusions, arousing feelings of rejection, hurt, and anger in the inexperienced expert witness. On the other hand, judges may have sat and listened to considerable testimony of remarkably poor quality by many experts. Testimony that is not backed by cogent reasons or understandable data often causes judges to despair, not only of the witness but often of the witness's profession.

The concept of child advocacy will be elaborated in later chapters. Within that concept is the dictum that child-advocating experts must try to resolve disputed custody cases before the cases end in court. All expert witnesses, however, must learn about court procedures and officers, even if they hope that, through their efforts, they will never have to see the inside of a courtroom or face a judge. If the behavioral-scientist consultant is unable to deal with the contesting parties effectively enough that they can resolve their conflict without resorting to trial, then that consultant must present his or her findings openly and completely before the judge. Therefore, the consultant must learn some things about judges.

Judges who sit as deciders in nonjury civil trials may have even greater need for clarification of the emotional factors in the cases before them than, for example, criminal-court judges who preside over situations in which juries make decisions. Lawyers have developed considerable faith in the jury system, and most attorneys would rather plead cases before juries than before judges. Like judges, juries are notoriously unpredictable, but in different ways. Attorneys place their confidence in that very unpredictability and in the dilution effect of twelve individual thought processes. In a judge-decided case, characteristic of family law, the expert witness may have to work even harder to explain him- or her-self clearly because there is no such dilution effect. Most judges are former trial lawyers who, for conscious or unconscious reasons of their own, have decided to abandon the fray. Judges' identification with the processes and tactics of the trial lawyer remains great, however; often one can see that identification transparently at work as judges intervene in the presentations of cases. Experienced lawyers know their judges well; after all, they have worked with, against, or before them for years. In judge-decided cases the expert witness must ask the experienced attorney about the judge hearing the case so that presentations can be planned for the best effect.

Judges have inherited the impossible task of dispensing the wisdom of Solomon in custody cases, and few have it. This is no slap at judges; no one seems to have such divinely inspired guidance these days. Judges have a nasty job to do, and they do it—often very well. The fact that it is done badly at other times is incontrovertible, but blame can not be placed broadly. Making the best of bad situations in which choices often represent the lesser of two evils is an unenviable task, and many judges have complained that presiding over a child-custody case is their most discomfiting duty.

The trier of facts in a case must be stimulated by the presentation of findings he or she sees as bearing weight. Expert witnesses must provide this through clear exposition of material that is sensible, logical, and easily assimilable. Judges may, indeed, have a greater *capacity* for understanding psychiatric material than do many jurors, but this does not automatically mean that they have a better understanding. College is far behind them for most judges, whose post-law-school education, furthermore, may have been sparse or nonexistent. Attorneys and the experts they call on must create the sparks needed to activate the thought processes of the judge who presides over a matter that is just a distasteful to him or her as to any other sensitive human being.

Who are the judges? How are they selected? The answers to these questions vary from one locale to another. In some jurisdictions, judges are elected; in others they are appointed. Does this make a difference in the capacities of the judges to be stimulated? Attorneys too often complain that one judge or another is "hopeless," and some decry all the judges in their jurisdiction as political hacks. Of course, attorneys who criticize so sweepingly leave themselves open to question. But even assuming that the generalizations are accurate, those attorneys must simply react by working harder. Inadequate judges must be seen as special challenges, and appearing before them must stimulate the attorneys to work more closely than ever with their expert witnesses to present material that not only is pertinent and moving, but also is presented in imaginative and stimulating ways. Audiovisual aids are often helpful, and expert witnesses especially skilled in such presentations sometimes use videotape interviews or observations. These are often effective but can backfire if material is too blatant or somehow offensive to the observers. Judges can be offended as easily as jurors. Articulate witnesses often develop their own techniques for clarifying issues relevant to custody cases, such as the stages of psychodynamic development of children, the various stresses children undergo and against which they must be protected by perceptive parents or other authorities, and so forth. Even the most somnolent or antagonistic judges can be roused to interest with a simple "chalk talk."

This does not mean that an attorney and his or her consultant should plan a presentation that talks down to a judge. Patronizing a judge can be lethal because the judge is as capable as anyone else is of recognizing a situation in which he or she is being put down. Instead, just as the specific cause-and-effect relationship between offense and *mens rea* must be clarified beyond misunderstanding in criminal cases, so the concepts relating to the comparative capacities of contesting parents must be elucidated in custody cases, along with the specific needs of the children. Such difficult issues as, for example, the oral, anal, and oedipal phases of psychosexual development must be explained in terms that are only understandable but also palatable. Judges are much like jurors in that they come from disparate backgrounds, with families of their own about which they have many conscious and unconscious feelings. Those factors are always at work within judges, just as they are within jurors and within behavioral scientists.

The judge generally is not a psychoanalytic patient, and if he were it would not be the attorney's couch on which he would be lying. Thus lawyers probably have little idea of the deep feelings of the judges with whom they are familiar, but they may have pretty good ideas about how these judges have operated. These ideas can provide consultants with some data on which to base presentation modes. Of course, those consultants also share the responsibility of trying to determine the judge's attitudes, even during the heat of their own direct and cross-examinations. They must try to get their messages across in the ways they see as most effective, gauging the responses of the judges according to numerous factors, including posture, facial expressions, interjections, and so forth. "Getting the message across" is, in fact, the expert witness's job. Too often, potentially expressive and astute professionals have been justifiably discouraged from serving the needs of courts because getting the message across is misinterpreted as undignified. If it is, then so is teaching in any capacity.

Who are the judges with respect to their interests? Are there judges with particular interests in family-law matters in the specific jurisdiction? If so, why are they particularly interested in family-law matters? Do they see their functions as, for example, preventing drastic increases in divorce rates, preventing children from being parted from their mothers at any cost, or fighting for the emerging rights of fathers who wish to assume custody of children? Some behavioral scientists are "trendy," quickly adopting ideas and methods that are new or controversial, simply for the sake of being in the vanguard. Some judges are like that, too. Is the judge divorced? If so, what are his relationships with his children? Are his religious feelings and practices anti-thetical to divorce or to the acceptance of psychiatric or psychologic opinion?

How busy are the courts? Judges in most jurisdictions are overworked, with calendars so crowded as to defy description, and certainly to prevent adequate hearing of all cases. If the judges hear general calendars, with criminal as well as civil trials, does this affect the way they see family matters generally, as well as the way they try family-law cases?

Is there a family-law division in the local courts? If so, what are the advantages of this? Do the judges there avail themselves of any continuing-education programs? Are they participants or enrollees in any of the seminars held by various schools and agencies all over the country? If so, does this mean that the judges can be expected to develop a level of sophistication and understanding that allows for increased use of mental-health professionals in their courts—and increased *listening* to them?

The expert witnesses must expect the attorneys to inform them about all these factors and about other, related quantities as well. For example, the local probation department or juvenile-protective agency may serve as an arm of the court and, as such, as a scouting and information-gathering mechanism for the judge. What kind of people work for that agency? Is the agency well funded so that it can attract topflight, experienced social workers with considerable background and training? Even if it has that kind of personnel, do the judges who use it do so only perfunctorily, or do they really dig into the reports prepared by the probation-department workers?

In my own experience, when I am involved in a case, the probation workers generally contact me and ask for input that often becomes crucial in the preparation of their reports. I routinely discuss this eventuality with the attorneys who call me, and I tell them that it is urgent to have a probation report. Sometimes lawyers are defensive about their clients or what they perceive as their clients' positions, but experience shows that they will have more reason to be defensive when the judge asks why a probation report was not prepared. Resistance to such a report by an attorney usually flashes a red light before a judge. An independent, unbiased outside agency can be very valuable to any decider of factors or dispositions. If judges are accustomed to probation reports and have confidence in the workers who prepare them, then input from an authority who points out specific issues and questions might be quoted more effectively in the probation report than on the witness stand.

A relatively recent development in family-law courts in many jurisdictions in the United States and Canada is the proliferation of *conciliation courts*. These arms of the trial courts represent a specialized outgrowth of the aforementioned probation or other juvenile-protective services. Conciliation courts developed originally for the purpose of trying to determine whether any factors existed within the quarreling couple's relationship that could be used in an attempt to preserve the marriage or, at least, to ease the divorce process. Subsequently the conciliation courts assumed the tasks of investigating the contesting parties in custody battles. Some judges routinely refer custody cases to the conciliation courts attached to their trial courts. Others may choose to ignore the existence of conciliation courts. In some jurisdictions, lawyers can refer their clients directly.

The conciliation courts themselves vary widely in the professionalism of their personnel and in their use by judges and by lawyers. Unfortunately, some judges use conciliation courts as bludgeons against the contesting couple rather than as true investigative or mediating agencies. Some judges, in fact, have expressed marked satisfaction with some of their conciliation-court personnel who demonstrate ability to hammer out their own, sometimes hasty decisions for the quarreling couple, who generally yield to the force of that hammer since it is wielded by an arm of the court. That type of externally imposed decision may save time and trouble for the judge, but it may create further problems for both the parents and their children. Fortunately, most conciliation courts, despite the pressures of numbers and of time, attempt to meet the real needs of the couple and the children by performing as adequate an investigation and evaluation as they can. Even then, however, lack of training on the part of some personnel may betray their good intentions and sincerity. Often, moral value judgments that do not really affect custodial capacity are noted in the reports, as is obvious identification with one or the other contestant. Even more significant in many cases is the absence of any evaluation in depth of the special needs of the children, which of course do not necessarily dovetail with the findings regarding their parents.

Despite these shortcomings, however, conciliation courts have established themselves rightfully as significant and valuable assisting bodies in family-law courts. Increasing professionalism and further training of personnel are goals most conciliation courts strive for, and numerous training programs and seminars are offered for their staffs throughout the country. In California the Civil Code affecting marital dissolution was amended as of 1 January 1981, when mediation became mandatory in all cases of disputed custody or visitation. Obviously, the California conciliation courts will play increasingly influential roles in these cases on the basis of the new law, which is being observed carefully by family-law specialists in other states as well. If an outside consultant is called into a case, the results of the evaluation by the conciliation court often have to be heeded carefully by that independent expert. Issues raised by those recommendations and conclusions will have to be addressed specifically, whether for confirmation or contradiction.

By and large, judges try to do as good jobs as they can, generally under trying circumstances. Practically all judges lack special training in the crucial areas of child development and evaluation of the parents' abilities, but they must sign the decisions in contested cases. Those decisions are the outgrowth of several factors. Many are based on what judges like to call "common sense," generally a blend of unconscious biases and prejudices based on the judges' own life experiences. Other decisions are the result of skillful persuasion by trial lawyers who have honed their capacities to present particular points of view to the status of a fine art.

Most decisions, however, are probably based on the preponderance of evidence—as they ought to be. It is here that attorneys and mental-health experts must work closely as a smoothly functioning team. The evidence presented can be historic, with witnesses or investigative agencies citing events that occurred some time ago. If these facts are damaging to the case presented by an advocate, then the advocate must determine with his or her expert whether changes have been made in the accused individual, or whether changes can be made that would allow for the continuance or resumption of custody or visitation.

One of the most significant things a behavioral scientist can present to any court—family, civil, or criminal—is his or her perception of how much an individual has changed or can change, and of what the court can expect from that individual. Some predictions are more difficult to make than others, but with appropriately intensive investigation of a person and a situation, a general range of adaptive behavior can be predicted. Judges need those predictions because they have to base their decisions on what they expect the future to hold.

Judges' decisions are also predicated on specific issues in the law affecting custody disposition. For example, the same amendment of the California Civil Code that called for mediation in contested custody cases also mandated consideration of joint custody in all cases of divorce in which there are children. The amended Family Law Act provides that, *where both parents agree to an award of joint custody*, a presumption exists that such an award is in the best interests of the child or children. If the court declines to award joint custody, it must state its reasons for refusing.

Joint custody has been defined by so many people in so many different ways that a single, specific definition cannot be given here. By and large, the concept entails the award of custody to both parents equally, providing that physical custody of the children somehow be shared in such a manner as to ensure frequent and continuing contact between the children and both parents. However, the court may award joint legal custody without specifying joint physical custody. This often forms the basis for the confusion in definitions. It is generally accepted that joint legal custody indicates that both parents share equally the right to make decisions regarding such matters as the care, control, education, health, and religion of the children.

Conflicting opinions cloud the determinations of whether shared decision-making is permitted with respect to the childrens' friends or social activities, clothing, sports or other activities, and so forth, unless actual physical custody is granted.

Joint custody is a creative approach to maintaining necessary relationships between children of divorce and both their parents—*if* the parents are capable of communicating with each other about the children without mutual acrimony. As Levy and Chambers, of the Conciliation Service of the Circuit Court of Cook County, Illinois, state:

> Two divorced parents who amicably can make joint decisions are better than two contradictory or fighting parents. . . . If, in reality, they can jointly work out planning for and with the children, all will profit. A separate custodial and visitation order does not prevent their co-parenting. They do not need a joint custody award in court. . . .[1]

Goodwill can overcome all kinds of legal problems, but goodwill is generally lacking in contested situations.

Sucessful joint-custody arrangements have, indeed, been worked out informally by parents who loathe each other and who fight terribly over other issues. Nonetheless, in those cases, they were able to relate quite well and effectively about their children. In such situations, though, the children ordinarily do not transfer from home to home, nor do the parents move in and out of the home in which the children are constants. Usually, the children live with one parent, who maintains good communication with the other. Ideally, the noncustodial parent has free access to the children, encouraged by both the custodial parent and the new spouses of both parents. (In the recently amended California Family Law Act, noncustodial parents were guaranteed access to records and information about their minor children from doctors, dentists, schools, and other agencies.) This type of joint custody is a metaphysical phenomenon rather than a geographic one. It is not the type of arrangement that can be expected to work well when the parents fight over the children. In such an instance, splitting the weeks and the addresses will probably not work well, either.

In contested cases, some judges may award joint custody in desperation when they simply cannot determine which parent is better. Judges also may make such awards because of the current popularity of this type of decision; for reasons of their own they may feel a need to be "with it." Faddish ideas often develop considerable force, and media exposure of those ideas creates a further impetus to act on them. In the case of joint-custody decisions in contested cases, this is unfortunate.

Even in contested cases, however, joint custody has adherents. One New York researcher, Judith Brown Greif, has written extensively about enforced joint custody, even in cases in which one or both parents do not wish such an arrangement.[2] She points out that parents often disagree about their children during their marriages; were they to remain married, they would have to find a way to rear their children despite those differences.[3] However, most behavioral scientists feel that in such cases the stresses imposed on the children by disparate parental ideas and by the constant friction between the parents lead to considerable anxiety on the part of the children. That type of anxiety might be dealt with best by separation of the parents. Elissa and Richard Benedek of the University of Michigan speak for the consensus when they point out:

> Without corroborative research that is far more extensive and convincing than that which is currently available, the arguments of the proponents of joint custody are not sufficiently persuasive to justify a legal presumption favoring joint custody or any predisposition to award joint custody in preference to traditional dispositions. Furthermore, it is difficult to envision a situation in which it would be appropriate to impose joint custody on a parent who fully understands this form of custodial disposition but, nonetheless, remains adamantly opposed to it. There is also insufficient evidence for concluding that joint custody must be categorically avoided. . . .[4]

In any instance, joint custody, like any other custody decision, must be determined on the basis of the individual indications for or against it. That basis is best formulated by means of a thorough examination of all concerned by a competent evaluator who is able to present his or her ideas and reasons clearly to a judge who has the responsibility of making the decision. That decision must be individualized in each case. This is what makes the job of a judge so unenviable.

In his recent excellent review for psychiatrists of the historical trends affecting child-custody cases, Dr. Andre Derdeyn of the University of Virginia spotlights the increasing load borne by judges:

> The major recent changes relating to the custody of children revolve about alterations in the relative advantages of parents with respect to custody. The weakening of the tender years presumption, the increasing concern about discrimination by sex, and the moderate decrease on emphasis on parental fault in awarding custody all herald a trend toward equalization of the struggle for custody between former spouses. An important effect of this equalization is that it requires judges to exercise ever-increasing freedom or discretion in each interparental custody decision. . . .[5]

Neither psychiatrists nor judges possess crystal balls; the future is always "iffy." However, in courts nationwide lawyers, judges, and behavioral scientists can and do work as effective teams, especially when those experts have been effectively trained to present their material understandably and in a manner not likely to alienate suspicious, cynical, bored, or jaundiced judges. If the expert can also train the attorney so that he or she understands the meaning of what the consultant is trying to express, then that meaning will be able to be brought out and developed clearly. The judge then will be properly stimulated and impressed with thinking that he can then incorporate into his own decision-making process.

Notes

1. B.A. Levy, and C.R. Chambers, "The Folly of Joint Custody," *Illinois Bar Journal* 69 (March 1981):412. See also *Family Advocate*, ABA Family Law Section 3 (Spring 1981):6.

2. J.B. Greif, "Fathers, Children and Joint Custody," *Am. J. Orthopsychiatry* 49 (1979):311.

3. J.B. Greif, "Joint Custody: A Sociological Study," *Trial Magazine* (May 1979):32.

4. E.P. Benedek and R.S. Benedek, "Joint Custody: Solution or Illusion?" *Am. J. Psychiatry* 136 (1979):1540. Copyright 1979, American Psychiatric Association. Reprinted with permission.

5. A.P. Derdeyn, "Child Custody Contests in Historical Perspective," *Am. J. Psychiatry* 133 (1976):1369. Copyright 1976, American Psychiatric Association. Reprinted with permission.

4

The Expert's Tasks and Goals

In child-custody cases the tasks and goals assumed by the expert are complex and sometimes even mutually incompatible. Unless—unfortunately—he has no ambivalence about being a "hired gun," the consultant must present him- or herself as the advocate for the contested children (see chapter 5 for further discussion of the concept of child advocacy). He or she must also serve as a teacher to the courts and the attorneys while avoiding the risk of being a boring or pontifical lecturer. The mental-health professional, though initially sought as an expert witness for the purpose of serving in litigation, may possibly provide a service for the contesting couple as well as for the children in question. This difficult but rewarding process might be seen more clearly if it is defined as a series of goals.

Establishing a Relationship with the Attorney

The initial goal is the creation of a working relationship with the referring attorney. In the usual situation, the attorney calls the potential expert and asks if the expert will help him or her in the case. More often than not the attorney is unaware of the expert's points of departure and his or her concept of his own role. Nothing can substitute for a face-to-face interview between advocate and expert. If the lawyer and the consultant are already well known to each other, the telephone request may be enough. Even then, however, it is necessary to repeat such admonitions to the familiar attorney as, for instance, the expert's need to serve as an independent evaluator.

The potential expert should set up an appointment with the attorney, who can then come to the office and discuss the issues in the case as he or she sees them. The lawyer will express his or her particular needs for expert evaluation and reporting and will help structure the necessary business arrangements for the workup. The expert must then tell the lawyer his or her own views about child-custody cases generally. It is hoped that these would center about the ideas that these cases are generally traumatic for the children as well as for the contesting adults, and that settlements are generally best made out of court before difficult adversarial battles need to be fought. Further, it is hoped that the expert will assume the stance of advocate for the contested children, explaining that stance to the referring attorney and pointing out that he or she will also explain that viewpoint to the contesting parents, both of whom need to be seen. As a child advocate, the expert must teach the attorney that he or she is to be an independent evaluator of all parties, who might well develop a recommendation the attorney and his client will dislike. The expert may need to remind the adversarial-minded attorney that the expert's credibility as an evaluator/witness is enhanced thereby.

The attorney's views must be heard and understood by the potential expert witness during that initial session. The fact that the attorney serves as an advocate for one contesting party should not diminish him or her in the expert's eyes. That is the attorney's job. It is even more important that the potential consultant understand the attorney's attitudes toward the value or effectiveness of the mental-health professions. Mental-health experts are often acutely sensitive to what they perceive as others' demeaning attitudes toward them and their work. At times this is realistic, but at other times this sensitivity may be merely defensive. The expert must make peace with his or her ability to work with attorneys who may not respect the mental-health professions, and with his or her own hostility toward lawyers and courts. Considerable missionary work is needed. The laborers in these relatively virgin fields will find much hostility—most of it expressed indirectly—among lawyers, jurists, and witnesses. Sometimes this hostility is direct, as, for example, if the referring attorney cannot get the opposing counsel to agree to the appointment of an expert as an independent evaluator for all parties. Here the opposing counsel may demean mental-health experts by saying, in effect, that neither he nor, in his opinion, the judge cares about any possible effect of the testimony of behavioral scientists, and that his side has no intention of using expert testimony. In reality he may fear that the expert's testimony will be damaging to his client's case. In other words, he may actually be overvaluing the effect of the expert testimony—hardly a demeaning reaction.

Sometimes it comes as quite a shock when the *referring* attorney belittles the expert in a sense by using the expert's testimony only tactically. Every expert witness must recognize at the outset that much more often than not his or her opinions—and only experts give *opinions*; other witnesses are restricted to *facts*—are going to be used for tactical purposes related to the adversary system. The effective expert will acknowledge that fact but will use the opinions and their bases as springboards to teach the courts the value of the expert evaluations and testimony. This is analogous to dealing with a patient's hostility in a psychotherapeutic setting. The opinions of hostile institutions cannot be changed by adopting the holier-than-thou position described in an earlier chapter. Mental-health professionals have an opportunity to work in the arena in which lawyers and judges function. Only if they do so under the current legal ground rules can the opinions of lawyers, judges, and (eventually) legislators be made more favorable toward the behavioral sciences and their practitioners.

Obviously, however, if the child-advocating consultant can get the litigants to see the wisdom of settling the issues without a court fight, then the expert will have won the battle on his or her own turf. This goal must be made clear at the outset to the attorney and, subsequently, to the litigants during the initial sessions with them.

Decisions whether or not the case will be accepted are predicated on these issues and a number of others, mainly centered about the consultant's and lawyer's abilities to work together in an atmosphere of mutual respect. The consultant must be willing to go the route if he or she accepts the case. This means a possible appearance in court, with sometimes stringent cross-examination by the attorney for the contestant not recommended by the expert. This also means recognizing the possible instabilities of the contesting parties on both sides, which may lead to even further entanglement, including, possibly, further litigation and appeal.

Dealing with Restrictions

The consultant must determine whether he or she will accept the case even if all principal parties are not made available for examinations. Perhaps the contesting attorney prevents this; perhaps he or she wants it but the client does not. Perhaps even the children are unavailable for examination.

Some mental-health professionals refuse to see *any* parties if they are not allowed to see *all* parties in a custody case. Solow and Adams describe their "suggested nonadversarial model within the legal process." They insist on seeing all parties and also insist on the contestants' signature to an agreement stating that the "parties hereto agree to abide by the evaluation and recommendations of the psychiatrist with respect to the custody of said children and with respect to any treatment which may be recommended. . . ."[1]

Most consultants do not go that far but nonetheless feel the need to see all the pertinent parties in a custody case.[2] Common sense dictates that necessity. It is impossible to get a bead on an individual's personality structure without actual contact with that individual, and the capacity to be a good parent is in great part based on the personality structure. Many lawyers agree with that concept, but some see it as a threat to their advocacy position. In fact, some say that in many cases an advocate should prevent a mental-health professional from evaluating the client because of the client's personality problems. Such lawyers feel that their primary loyalty is to their clients and that their clients' causes must be defended regardless of any possible deleterious effect on the children in question. The idea of creating a cloud of suspicion by preventing an examination by a consultant is dismissed by many attorneys who espouse that kind of protection of their clients. They believe it is easy to influence a possibly skeptical court that no purposes are served by such evaluations and that the records and testimonial evidence speak for themselves.

Other attorneys and most behavioral scientists argue that judges, regardless of their possible prejudices, become suspicious whenever a participant in a child-custody litigation is prevented from seeing a mental-health professional; the judges begin to wonder what there is to hide. That jaundiced view certainly cannot do the "protected" client any good. This becomes even more striking if an investigation is mounted by the probation department or a conciliation court, which has the power to see all parties. If a contending spouse will speak with a probation officer, then why not with a psychiatrist, psychologist, or social worker? If any consultant does not see him- or herself as an advocate for the child but, rather, as an advocate for one of the contesting parties—as still often happens, unfortunately—then it is certainly not unreasonable for an attorney to keep his or her client away from the "unfriendly" expert. Under the division of labor contemplated by the adversary system, the lawyer's function is to present evidence favorable to his or her client, not that which is unfavorable. Of course, if a consultant is appointed by a court as an evaluator of all parties, the objections of the attorneys or their clients fall by the wayside.

By and large, consultants who accept the invitation of an attorney to work on a custody matter should ask that attorney to discuss with the other lawyer the likelihood of his or her evaluating all participants. If that lawyer is agreeable, most experts will want to meet with him or her as well in order to discuss the role in which the consultant sees him- or herself. Perhaps he or she will meet with both attorneys together, perhaps separately. However, everyone involved in the case must be made aware that the expert, if he or she functions as a child advocate, will want to see everyone and arrive at his or her own opinion regardless of which attorney initially contacted him or her.

If the other lawyer is resistant to the idea as presented by the initial attorney, the consultant should call him or her to discuss the issue. If the opposing lawyer refuses to allow the expert to interview his or her client (and/or the children, if they are currently in the custody of his client), the consultant is faced with a dilemma. More often than not, he or she will probably take the case anyway, working with the attorney who made the contact; interviewing that attorney's client and the other witnesses standing by that client; and reviewing any pertinent records from schools, other doctors, and so forth.

The consultant's report under such conditions must be a restricted one, stating that it is restricted and why. In such a situation, most experts will attempt to determine if there are any factors operative within the examined contestant that would make that person an unsuitable parent. Most will look for any contraindications to custody being awarded to that parent, and the presence or absence of those contraindications will provide most of the bases for his or her limited conclusion. The consultant may also refer to charges made by the one spouse about the other contending spouse whom he or she was not allowed to see, or about the children whom he or she was not allowed to examine. Extreme caution must be used in these instances, and allegations must be spelled out specifically as such. Often, however, internal logical consistency in the allegations and their patterns may reflect personality factors, structures, and problems.

The expert must use care and discretion if he or she indicates the possible presence of personality disturbances in the unseen litigant on the basis of the examined litigant's allegations. The American Psychiatric Association, in its Tenets of Ethics, disallows diagnoses of unexamined individuals. Also, as will be discussed later, diagnoses per se ought not to be used in custody cases except in rare instances. The consultant should always be aware that if he or she is going to present a report indicating personality disturbances in the unseen litigant, he or she is especially likely to be called as a witness in the hearing. In such an instance cross-examination will be especially severe. The expert will have to detail his or her reasons for developing his or her theoretical conclusions, all the time facing the relentless probing of an advocate for the maligned client who wishes to destroy the expert's credibility.

The internal logical consistency of the allegations can also redound against the originally referring attorney's case. The emerging patterns can be those that indicate to the consultant that the "friendly" attorney's client may be sick, vengeful, or basing the fight on needs that serve no good purpose for the children. The consultant must always remember that he or she must be open and frank with the referring attorney, who will probably be quite grateful for that information. The expert may withhold information deleterious to a client; but this usually emerges somehow in the trial, causing great embarrassment for the expert, the referring attorney, and the client.

I have occasionally accepted cases in which my contacts were restricted. Each time, I did so in the hope that my ability to spell out the limited nature of my conclusions would warn the judge that one of the sides was fearful of laying its cards on the table. In some cases, this worked. The judge ordered examinations of the resistive parties and the withheld children, delaying the trial and, incidentally, making for very hostile and defensive interview subjects. That trouble, however, is more than compensated for by the chance to see, evaluate, and work with the recalcitrant parties in order to gain and transmit to the court a far more complete understanding of the issues. The best compensation, of course, is provided when, on the basis of the now-complete workup, the trial is aborted and decisions reached in conference.

Becoming the Second Expert

Occasionally a potential consultant will be approached after another expert has already seen the parties and performed an evaluation. Perhaps that evaluation has resulted in a recommendation against the referring attorney's client. This can sometimes be sticky, depending on one's knowledge and opinion of the first expert, who also may be in a different mental-health field than the second expert. The second opinion is a time-honored practice in all consultation, so the requested consultant need have no ethical conflicts about it. Likewise, all experts should be aware that, as with a patient, the person for whom they provide an opinion may or may not accept that opinion. Medical ethics teach that the doctor's responsibility is to provide the best opinion and advice possible. The patient has no obligation to accept it. Certainly a lawyer need not accept recommendations he sees as harmful to his or her client, even if the consultant feels strongly about them, spells them out, and makes sure that both lawyer and client understand them. Courts may not accept these recommendations, either.

It may even be more important that the second expert let the attorney and the client know that the results of this examination may be just as un-favorable as the one by his or her predecessor. If, however, certain issues are spelled out in the previous reports, and those issues are seen as specific bones of contention by the advocates, then the second expert must pay special attention to these and attempt to clarify these. The second expert needs to have access to all the first expert's sources as well as to the first expert's report. Obviously, the second expert discussed here is not just a "hired gun"—a person who simply makes a case for the hiring attorney.

A related example occurred recently when I was asked to evaluate the contesting father of a 16-year-old boy. The child was living with the father and wished to continue living with him. Most states would allow a 16-year-old boy to express his own choice in such cases, but all states reserve the right to reject that preference and to consider possible harmful situations. In this case the wife alleged that the husband was dangerous and prone to violent episodes because he suffered from temporal-lobe epilepsy. Her attorney had contacted a forensically inexperienced psychiatrist who, without seeing the father, had written a general, two-page letter about temporal-lobe epilepsy and possible violent behavior. Although the father was not specifically named in that paper as a person who fulfilled the prediction the psychiatrist saw as representative of the disease, the effect of the letter on the trier of fact would nonetheless be considerable.

As expected, I was unable to see the wife but was able to see both the boy and his father, as well as the results of a recent electroencephalogram and consultation with a competent neurologist who was treating the father. I had warned the referring attorney that I might find this man's interictal states and his seizure behavior characteristic of a person whose hostile impulses might get out of control, but the attorney accepted this proviso. I specifically described my report as limited and restricted only to the issue of the father's dangerousness. I made no recommendation as to the disposition of the boy; I commented only on his relationship with the father and on the father's stability and capacity to serve as a parent in his own right.

Establishing Relationships with the Litigants

Once a working relationship is finally established with the referring attorney, such a relationship must also be established with that attorney's client. Obviously the optimal situation derives from speaking with both contesting attorneys before the contesting parties themselves are seen, with the agreement that the expert will serve as an independent evaluator for all contesting parties. In such cases all contesting litigants relate to the expert more easily in their evaluative interviews.

More often than not, however, both attorneys will not be seen even though they may agree that all parties be seen by a single evaluator. Then the consultant must be sure to clarify his or her attitudes and goals, preferably in writing, to all parties. The party responsible for the fee must be told in no uncertain terms that he or she is paying for independent consultation from an expert whose point of departure is the best interest of the child, not that of either adult litigant. Both contesting parties must know the ground rules and the consultant's attitudes from the outset, including the roles the consultant plays in the child-custody setting. Those roles are: (1) data collector and independent evaluator from the standpoint of advocate for the child, and (2) recommender and possible effectuator of the recommendation. These issues must be clarified with the attorneys and with the contesting parties themselves before the workup begins. Often, the contestants will pay lip service to the expert's attitude. In reality, however, they may have no intention of agreeing with an adverse recommendation, even though they may agree that they do not want the horrors of a courtroom battle to affect their children as well as themselves.

Limits of the Consultant's Role: Ethical Problems and Ground Rules

The expert must have a very clear idea about the limits of his or her role. Whether hired by the court or by one attorney, does he or she stop after reporting to the lawyers or to the courts, or after sitting down with the parents (if, indeed, he or she does this) and letting them know of his or her findings and recommendations? The consultant must be aware that at this point all kinds of mutually conflicting attitudes and even ethical tenets may interfere with his function as he sees it. If he explains his findings and recommendations to the attorneys, this usually raises no problems except for expressions of argument and/or disdain from the disappointed advocate. That advocate, however, might well serve as an excellent counselor to his client by simply pointing out to that client that the odds do not favor his or her position. Experienced lawyers have learned over the years to let their clients down very gently. Many experts who serve as consultants in custody suits find that the lawyers can do this with their clients much better than can the evaluators themselves, who represent the foci of clients' resentment.

Whether court-appointed or individually hired, unless the examiner announces at the outset his intention and reasons for doing so, he puts himself in considerable ethical jeopardy if he decides to effectuate his recommendations by sitting down with the disappointed contestant and trying to get that litigant to see the wisdom of his conclusions. The expert should recognize that the contestant might not have agreed to enter into a relationship with the expert for the purposes of psychotherapy, and it can be argued successfully that such effectuating interviews constitute psychotherapy. The basic role and function of a mental-health professional in such a situation may be in question. Is he or she simply a skilled investigator and reporter whose point of departure is based on the contention that his or her recommendations are centered about the best interests of the child? Or is he or she an agent somewhat separate from the investigative aspects of the litigation process, who can act as a combined investigator and therapist for those people whom he or she is investigating?

Most child-advocating consultants discuss the issues and recommendations with the contesting parties after all the materials have been collected and interpreted. They really function as rather directive therapists, guiding the contesting parties into a frame of mind in which they might well accept the conclusions reached by the experts without having to go to court. This is, of course, a perfectly valid role for a consulting behavioral scientist, *as long as all the significant parties are told beforehand that they will be discussing the findings and recommendations with him or her prior to court and that they might well consider acting on them.* Certainly the method proposed by Solow and Adams, referred to earlier, in which the contestants agree in writing to abide by the professional decisions of the independent experts, spells out all the roles beforehand so that no surprises or false expectations are created.

As Levy expressed in his own paper:

> The efficacy of the consultant room setting rests . . . primarily on the effort which the family members are ready to put forth to solve their prob-

lems. . . . In depth exploration takes place in the course of a series of conferences held in the informal setting of the psychiatrist's consultation room
rather than in the adversarial setting of the court. . . . In this setting a kind
of freewheeling atmosphere prevails wherein appreciation of needs and
behavior neutralizes the impulse toward polarization of the family into two
warring sides. . . .[3]

Some mental-health professionals and a number of attorneys disagree.
They say that it is inappropriate for the expert to assume the position that
the court ought to assume, and that a consultant's conference that moves
parties to abandon litigation may well deprive those parties of rights and
possibilities of winning their cases. Aside from that, the experience of many
behavioral scientists who become involved in custody cases, even those
whose stances are staunchly those of child advocacy, is that many of the
contestants are simply unable to make the kind of effort Levy describes. If
they can do so, obviously this represents the ideal setting in which to resolve
the debated issues over the best interests of the contested children. Cases
such as these represent the type hoped for by the California legislature when
it passed the law referred to in the previous chapter mandating mediation of
all cases involving contested custody or visitation, "prior to or concurrent
with the setting of the matter for a hearing. . . ." This move obviously
represents a giant step forward in statutory attempts to remove custody
litigation from the adversary arena. It is hoped that other states will follow
this lead and will also set up the necessary machinery—for example, more
and better conciliation courts—to effect it.

However, if one of both contestants is unwilling to consider this approach or refuses to agree to the recommendations made by the expert, even
if there is prior agreement that he or she will do so, then there is nowhere to
turn but the courts. All mental-health experts and all legislatures, must be
prepared to accept that as a distinct possibility, if not a likelihood; and they
must be prepared to accept the propriety of the use of the courts.
Sometimes, like all the king's horses and all the king's men, behavioral
scientists cannot get people together again, even to the extent of communicating effectively. The question of those professionals acting as
mediators bears further scrutiny, however.

When is the consultant an investigator, and when is he or she a
therapist? In my own training I was taught that psychotherapy begins when
the patient phones me for an appointment or comes through the door. Each
communication from the patient is grist for the therapeutic mill, and some
mental-health professionals may have the capacity (or, in some cases, the
temerity) to start interpreting to the patient what the patient is *really* saying
even before the patient becomes familiar with the process and its ground
rules. The techniques of psychotherapy are not easily set aside, even in
situations in which the specialist functions "only" as an investigator or

diagnostician. He or she listens carefully and specifically spotlights areas of anxiety that may be either known to or unrecognized by the patient or the subject.

The consulting mental-health expert must focus on those areas, in an effort to open them more fully, so that the sources and meanings of the anxiety-producing material can be seen. This can be done in evaluative interviews as well as in therapy. If it is not done, there is no value in having a skilled behavioral scientist perform those interviews: any routine interviewer could get the superficial facts of the case. Many professional counselors might define such in-depth interviews as therapy, and certainly therapeutic techniques are used. Is there such a great gulf between the use of those techniques and postrecommendation counseling? Perhaps not, but the expert's role must be explained and understood by all parties. The goal is certainly a laudable one. Every child advocate should want to keep the children out of court and should try to get the contesting parents to agree to act together for the sake of the children.

Will the contesting parents do this? *Can* they? Most lawyers have seen recalcitrant clients who are so obsessed with the need to win custody of the children that discussion with them is like whistling into the wind unless the subject is strategy for satisfying the client's obsession. The behavioral scientist is in a unique position here. It is he or she who can perceive and perhaps make the parent perceive the underlying causes of that single-mindedness. For example, the contesting parent really may be clinging to the shreds of a lost marriage by fighting for the children. It may turn out that the children are less important than the relationship with the estranged, hated spouse, whose face or expression is seen in the faces or expressions of the children. Most attorneys would probably agree that it is appropriate for an examiner to try to deal with this unresolved ambivalence, but they might not agree that a child-custody workup is the appropriate place to deal with it. In any case, attorneys cannot resolve the unconscious conflicts of their clients even if they perceive them; and deciding judges usually only prolong them by arbitrary decisions.

Divorcing couples are often depressed as well as overtly angry. Psychotherapists often note that depression may color an individual's judgment. When that judgment affects only the patient, that is one problem. If that distorted judgment affects a fought-over child, however, that is another problem, one that any child-advocating consultant must confront. Evaluations of contesting parents must include not only factors specifically related to their children, but also factors related to the ways they feel. If they are depressed, how is the depression manifested? What are the specific responses to the loss represented by the breakup of the marriage that represented such a major investment for the partner? Is there grief and overt depression? Or is there disguised depression—for example, in the form of overcompensation through numerous impetuous sexual involvements that allow the depressed partner to reassure him- or herself of continued sexual acceptability? Are such sexual involvements—or, as another example, dependence on alcohol—the examples of behavior used by the opposing partner as the evidence that the contestant is not a fit parent for the contested children?

The actual treatment of the depression ought not to be the focus of the intervention by the expert evaluating the custody situation, but that expert ought to relate with the affected parent(s) in such a way that the depression can be recognized by the sufferer(s) and appropriate treatment instituted elsewhere. The behavioral scientist hired to evaluate the custody situation is definitely not working as a marriage counselor or, for that matter, specifically as a divorce counselor to the contesting parents. However, the evaluator must respond to the needs of the parties at least to the extent of making the parties aware of them. Participants' attitudes toward doing something about themselves also provide excellent clues to their capacities to be good parents and their motivations in that direction.

The evaluator also must attempt to determine the attitudes of each contestant toward a decision that might not be favorable to him or her. How will each individual respond to not being awarded custody of the children? How does that expected response correspond to previous responses to disappointments or rejections? How did those individuals eventually learn to adapt to those disappointments or rejections—or did they learn? A sensitive, perceptive evaluator can work toward some resolution of these conflicts within the historical analysis of the contestant's prior ways of operating.

Of course, it is obviously therapeutic rather than purely evaluative to attempt to draw parallels for the contestants in the hope that they can recognize the common threads in the various conflict-ridden situations in their lives. However, this is not really inappropriate in a custody evaluation. On the contrary, it is extremely valuable. Attempts to make life easier for any of the contestants do not conflict ethically or otherwise with the need to determine the best interests of the contested children. Such attempts may, in fact, enhance those best interests by strengthening the custodial or, for that matter, the noncustodial parent.

Wallerstein and Kelly, who have written extensively on divorce and custody problems, illuminate some of the specific issues and problems related to visitation and other facets of the relationships between children and their noncustodial parents. Visitation, like custody per se, is a subject that must be evaluated by the behavioral scientists who serve as expert witnesses. Even if it is not mentioned as a matter for specific investigation at the outset of the workup, it is necessary to determine each contestant's attitude toward visitation, how each parent would use visitation time, and how each would adapt to visitation by the other parent. Some evaluators, however, seem to overemphasize this. In some cases they have made decisions regarding custodial disposition on the basis of how the awarded parent will allow for visitation by the other. That, of course, is a distortion of the multifaceted approach to the custody-disposition problem. Visitation conflicts and problematic attitudes can be dealt with and should not be made the prime consideration upon which disposition is based. In a recent paper, Wallerstein and Kelly state succinctly:

> After a marital separation, both parents and children, without rehearsal or available role models, need to adapt their feelings and mutual needs in the relationship to the narrow confines of a visit. We have conceptualized this process as a funneling that requires complex, and sometimes exquisite, maneuvers from the several participants. . . . Unfortunately, the courts and the embattled partners and their attorneys have focused on imposing restrictions and strict conditions that further encumber a relationship that, even under the best circumstances, needs encouragement. [Wallerstein and Kelly could easily have added mental-health expert witnesses to this list because they, too, generally afford this crucial aspect a distant second place.] Divorcing families could benefit considerably from guidance during this difficult transition, which could help them create new or maintain close and affectionate bonds between the visiting parent and the child.[4]

Dr. Henry Friedman has discussed the effects of divorce on the father-child relationship. His work in treating fathers undergoing divorce has led him to the conclusion that the bonds between fathers and children can be strengthened even when those fathers are noncustodial parents.[5] Often, the fathers have been away during their marriages or preoccupied with the marital struggles that have led to the divorce. After the divorce they may be able to devote more time and effort to developing worthwhile, mutually beneficial relationships with their children. They may not resort to becoming "Disneyland fathers" who allow the visits to be guided by the facilities of the local amusement center.

Again, the expert-witness evaluators asked to participate by the attorneys or the courts are not the people who should serve as therapists for these fathers (or mothers) or work with them to the extent required to duplicate Friedman's results. However, it behooves the expert witness to try to be alert to these types of potential difficulties and to guide the participant contestants into appropriate treatment elsewhere. Such treatment does not necessarily need to be psychoanalysis. Newly organized groups of custodial and noncustodial parents have been formed throughout the United States. They may provide appropriate leverage toward more definite therapy, if necessary. In any case, the evaluating expert witness must be able to use the techniques of therapy, including the often derided empathic response to the suffering and conflict-ridden parent, to determine any needs for further support or therapy that will help both parents and children.

In the many situations in which unconscious psychodynamics rule the need for entering into custody litigation in the first place, it is best for the examining consultant to sit down with both attorneys and discuss the findings and recommendations with them. If there is to be any counseling or explanation to one or both contestants that their motives are unconsciously dictated and do not represent what is best for the child, that intervention ought to be performed only *after* the contestants' attorneys decide that it is best to do so. Often behavioral scientists are surprised to find that some attorneys also see themselves as child advocates and that they, too, want to see the custody determined without a court fight. Even in such favorable circumstances, however, the expert must state his goals and *modus operandi* at the outset. Again, the examining mental-health professionals are operating on turf that is not theirs, functioning within a framework of rules not of their making or choosing, for purposes generally different from those held by therapists. Those specialists correctly continue to insist, however, that their participation in a legal rather than a therapeutic setting must not result in their doing harm to any client or child. Failure to participate at all, of course, may invite such harm by default.

Most experienced divorce lawyers know that their clients are extremely anxious and fearful. Husbands may be just as frightened as wives; they, too, may have dependent needs that the breakup of the marriage leaves unmet. Most experienced lawyers have had to learn how to put their clients at ease and relieve some of the clients' more overt and disabling anxiety. It is often enough simply to be a strong figure on whom the client can depend. At times when nothing seems to assuage the client, however, an effective partnership between lawyer and behavioral scientist can be very helpful.

An even more effective partnership in that situation is that between the behavioral scientist and both lawyers if the opposing attorney recognizes that the anxiety of *either* client can disrupt the case. In such situations, the evaluator's interventions may be eagerly sought by even the most antagonistic lawyer. Even there, however, the expert must recognize, as the lawyer does, that the client is entitled to his or her day in court, even if mediation is statutorily mandatory. That entitlement must be balanced against the needs and best interests of the child. Those needs and best interests can be explained to all parties, but the consultant cannot expect the parties always to see them clearly or to accept them.

Often they cannot expect the lawyers to accept them, either. Professor Henry Foster has pointed out:

> If I am fighting for the custody of my son, I don't want a "helping agent" representing my interests. . . . I want my own counsel, not a distinterested neutral, to represent me. . . . There is and should be room for a "friend of the court" but not at the expense of depriving a party of individual representation and expert testimony. . . .[6]

If the consultant insists on trying to get the recalcitrant parent to work through his or her rage, to see the underlying or unconscious roots of the need to prolong the suit, and so forth, he may get involved in a situation he will later regret—unless these were the goals accepted at the outset. If such a case is eventually heard in court, the recalcitrant parent's attorney will be able to point out the expert's lack of credibility as an independent consultant, regardless of the expert's intentions.

Probably more cases are settled without court hearings following adequate independent evaluations than are continued in a courtroom. The settlement process is generally initiated by wise attorneys, who are often better able to deal with their clients. Mental-health experts must always remember that the vast majority of custody conflicts are decided without any consultation involvement at all. Experts are invited into the minority of these cases.

The Evaluation Process

After working relationships are established with the attorneys and their clients, and ground rules and points of departure explained, the business of evaluating begins. Some consultants advocate joint interviews with both contesting parents. Others, feeling that these may demonstrate no more than the well-known hostility between the parents, do not see the parents together. Styles of examination and evaluation differ among examiners. The important issue is to be able to defend one's method as a valid method—albeit not the only one—for collecting and evaluating data. Whether or not the contesting parents are seen jointly, obviously they must be seen individually, often over several sessions. Sometimes interviews are arranged in which one or both parents come with their children. This may permit the evaluators to see better into the relationships between each contesting parent and the children, as well as between the contestants. In any case, both children and parents must be seen individually.

The expertise of child psychiatrists is, of course, especially welcome in child-custody litigation. Unfortunately, though, that expertise is seldom seen there. If there is a spectrum of psychiatrists with respect to avoidance of the legal arena, child psychiatrsists generally would fall at the avoidance extreme. Perhaps this is due to the rigorous demands of their therapy schedules, which may need to be more flexible and unbroken for the sake of their young patients than the schedules of psychiatrists who treat adults. Perhaps it is due to the shortage of competent child therapists, which results in greater demands on their time than they can meet.

Many general psychiatrists, psychologists, and social workers disagree with the contention of some child psychiatrists that a child psychiatrist is the best resource person in these cases. Those specialists who disagree, as well as many attorneys, claim—incorrectly—that the parents generally need to be evaluated more than the children do. Admittedly, the court is interested in the relative capacities of the contesting adults to be good parents, under the assumption that the best interests of the children will be served by assigning them to the best parents. General psychiatrists, as well as competent clinical psychologists and psychiatric social workers, are certainly capable of evaluating parents; most also ought to be able to evaluate children, if not to the depths sometimes plumbed by child therapists. Many very young children can be quite open and articulate in the presence of a kind, nonthreatening adult. Play techniques are probably unnecessary in the evaluation of most children in custody cases. Most mental-health specialists have developed techniques for interviewing small children successfully, including the capacity to detect telltale signs of coaching.

Regardless of the controversy centering about whether the expert serves as some kind of therapist for the contesting adults, all parties must agree that his or her role with the children should be therapeutic, even in a purely evaluative setting. Children cannot avoid rage between the contesting parents; it is probably impossible for the parent with whom they live to avoid venting rage toward the contesting parent. Similarly, during visitation with the other parent, that parent's resentment toward the custodial parent is hard to hide.

Rage does not have to be verbalized in order to be perceived; children are particularly perceptive, sensitive creatures, whose antennae are finely turned to the nuances of their parents' moods. Most children will become frightened during protracted litigation and the accompanying investigation. The evaluator must use his or her skills not only to seek information from the child, but also to calm the child and ease the child's burdens. He or she must not only do this with the child directly but through the parents as well. Regardless of the controversy regarding counseling of the parents, all parties probably would agree that it is necessary to instruct the contesting parents about how to discuss the case with the children, and to try to make sure that the parents describe each other to the children as people who love the children but are having problems between themselves that do not affect that love.

Levy has recently reviewed the controversy over the practice of asking the children about their preferences regarding custody. When cases come to trial, judges often interview the children. In some cases children are placed on the witness stand instead of taken into the supposedly less threatening atmosphere of the judge's chamber. Although numerous writers have commented on the fact that the child's statements necessarily place him or her in a no-win, guilt-provoking situation, many examining experts nevertheless ask the children their preference. Levy encourages the evaluator to understand the underlying meaning of the child's stated preference. He states:

> Our task is to interpret the child's statement and to examine its relationship to the various factors affecting its development. Conscious and unconscious levels of meaning must be considered. . . . Adults, be they parents, mental health professionals or judges, owe it to children to listen carefully and fully to their statements. A commitment to listen does not bind one to be influenced accordingly. It will, however, commit one to a fuller exposition of the meaning of the children's statement in regard to their family relationship at that time. . . .[7]

Obviously, the children must be told by every listener that their preferences might not necessarily coincide with the way the case is decided, even though the listener thinks that the child's preferences are very important.

In my own practice, I have occasionally used a child psychiatrist with very young children in such a manner that the child psychiatrist is shielded from the courtroom arena. The child psychiatrist serves as a consultant to me, submitting a report to me similar to any other school, laboratory, or medical report. These reports form part of the basis of my conclusion, which will be presented and tested in the courtroom. The child psychiatrist is not then called into court.

Mention of other reports serves to remind the examining consultant of the need to obtain data not only from the parents and the children but from significant others as well. Examples include reports from schools or preschools, from doctors and pediatricians (always with the judicious use of a release-of-information form and with the attempt to reassure the doctors that their furnishing these data may help to keep them from having to go to court about the matter), from churches and ministers, and especially from county probation departments or other independent juvenile protective agencies. I have found reports by probation officers very helpful in illuminating specific issues to which my attention is directed. Sometimes those issues are legitimate; at other times they represent the biases of earnest but relatively unsophisticated probation officers. In all cases, however, they are of urgent importance. They make the examining consultant think about the ways other evaluators see the problem.

Psychological tests may be needed for one or both parents, or for the children. More often than not, adequate clinical evaluation in sufficient depth leads psychiatrists and other specialists to conclude that such tests are not needed. In other cases, in-depth examination poses questions that only such testing can answer. Clinical psychologists often use tests routinely simply because they are so accustomed to using them. Forensically experienced clinical psychologists probably use the tests more appropriately as an adjunct to the clinicohistorical data. At the outset of the study by any specialist, the attorneys and clients must be told that such tests may be necessary, and how much the examinations will cost.

Some evaluators do not work singly but, rather, function as part of a team. In such cases, one member may see one party and another member another party. A third evaluator may see the children, and a fourth might obtain the data from the significant others. A team approach is not unusual in mental-health examinations, but attorneys may have difficulty determining which of the expert witnesses has primary responsibility. In these situations, conferences among the team members are urgently needed, and all must expect to be called into court if the case actually proceeds to trial. Teams are more characteristic of social agencies than of private practitioners, and many social agencies are reluctant to become involved in medicolegal evaluations.

What data are sought in the evaluation? The referring attorneys will have highlighted the essential issues in contention to the examining expert, but the mental-health professional will probably need to see a larger canvas. When psychiatrists or clinical psychologists are consultants, diagnosis of one or all of the contestants and the children may become a thorny issue. By and large, formal diagnosis has little if any place in reports of custody evaluations unless actual mental illness is discovered that is significant in determining the placement and disposition of the children.

In most child-custody cases the contesting parents are not overtly mentally ill. Although character and personality problems may abound in many of these litigants, no purpose other than muddying the waters is served by making formal diagnoses, which in any case will be used pejoratively in the adversary arena. Psychiatrists and psychologists also are becoming increasingly aware of the disturbing fact that long-ago reports and diagnoses are now being brought forth from data banks in inappropriate surroundings and in inappropriate ways.

Child advocacy, of course, demands protection of the child against whatever harm can be predicted as a part of the evaluation-litigation process. Appending diagnoses to one or both parents will rebound negatively onto the children. The parents will call each other officially crazy, and the children will begin to wonder about themselves as well as their parents. Sometimes specific mental problems can be pointed out in nonpejorative ways so that the courts can be alerted to the need for counseling or other treatment that will affect the custody disposition.

In Court

If the workup has been completed and the reports given to the contesting attorneys and/or the contesting litigants, the child-advocating expert can hope that sensible heads will overcome impetuous and raging ones and that the case will be settled before those involved have to go to court and have someone else settle it for them. No discussion of the expert witness in court in a custody case should omit the point that the child advocate works hard to keep the case from having to go to court at all. If trial is decided despite the expert's best efforts to provide hard data and to convince the attorneys and the litigants, then the expert must assume that he or she will be called into court to expound on the material provided in his or her report and to be cross-examined by the opposing counsel. Assurances can be given that the courtroom experience need not be the ordeal usually dreaded by inexperienced expert witnesses, but nothing is as effective assurance as a good experience. A good experience in turn is the product of a good working relationship between expert and attorney.

At trial, all the material in the preceding chapters highlighting the specific relationship between lawyer and expert witness becomes even more crucial. The two must get together as often and as intensely as possible so that neither is left with any question about the position of the other. Plans must be made regarding every aspect of the presentation of the expert witness's testimony, beginning with the listing of his or her qualifications. Any good trial lawyer will attest to the fact that the best defense against a difficult cross-examination is to prepare as completely as possible for the initial direct examination. In my own practice, in pretrial conferences I usually serve as a devil's advocate for the attorney who calls me as an expert witness. I attempt to determine what a hypothetical expert witness called by the other side might say. This creates a situation in which cross-examination questions may be anticipated and more easily answered.

The most difficult part of a trial for any expert is the cross-examination. After a direct examination by the friendly attorney, who builds up the reputation and professional competence of "his" or "her" witness, the opposing counsel attempts to rip the expert and his or her reputation to shreds. It is understandably difficult for any new or inexperienced expert witness in any field to recognize that the opposing counsel is merely doing his or her job and that attempts to demean the witness should not be taken personally, at least in most cases. Opposing counsel *has the task* of clouding issues previously made clear in direct examinations so that the judge, as the trier of facts, will become confused and/or disenchanted with the whole business. Recognizing this will allow the expert to relax and see the entire scenario more objectively. The basic rule whenever one faces an individual who wants to do battle is *not* to do battle. The bait will be tossed, but the expert must be careful not to rise to it. Nothing can replace experience in this area, but attitude is also extremely important. Perhaps the best approach is to study the experiences of others, as in the mock trial and cases that appear later in this book.

The courtroom task of both lawyer and expert is to convince the judge of the basis for the expert's opinion, and thereby inferentially of its correctness. As pointed out in the previous chapter, the judge may have ideas and questions of his or her own. He or she may ask questions of the expert witness him- or herself. Sometimes those questions reflect the judge's impressions that the comments of the expert witness are unclear or at least require further elaboration. The judge, after all, is the person who must understand the expert witness's testimony completely because he or she has to make a decision in the case. That decision may be based on the expert's testimony or may totally ignore it. Sometimes the judge's questions have nothing to do with the material presented by the expert but, rather, reflect other concerns of the judge about the case or the people involved in it. As with questions asked in cross-examination, if the expert witness does not know the answer, he or she should state that firmly and unashamedly.

Often the judge is preoccupied with some of the realities of the case, such as living arrangements or financial issues. He or she may attempt to get the expert witness to correlate some of these with the psychodynamic, developmental, or other items that might be more important to the mental-health professional. Sometimes the judge may ask questions that are outside of the contested area—for example, about visitation if the issue is custody. Obviously, the expert witness cannot set forth any type of visitation schedule even if the judge would like this; but he or she can discuss whether frequent or infrequent visitation would be beneficial to the children; whether visits should be structured, free, supervised, unsupervised; and so forth. Reasons should always buttress all opinions.

The tasks of the expert witness are manifold and complex, but they are not impossible. Like most teachings, they are also necessary and constructive. Completeness and thoroughness must be the hallmarks of a custody examination, with specific attention to the issues outlined by the adversary attorneys. The more complete and objective the examinations and the presentations of the findings, the more likely their acceptance by the attorneys, the judges, and—inevitably—the contestants in or out of court. If this happens, the expert witness will have fulfilled his or her role as an advocate for the children and will truly have served the children's best interests.

Notes

1. R.A. Solow and P.L. Adams, "Custody by Agreement: Child Psychiatrist as Child Advocate," *J. Psychiatry & Law* 5 (1977):77. © Federal

Legal Publications, Inc., 157 Chambers St., New York, N.Y. 10007. Reprinted with permission.

2. T.A. Rodgers, "The Crisis of Custody: How a Psychiatrist Can Help," *Bull. Amer. Acad. Psychiatry & Law* 5 (1976):138.

3. A.M. Levy, "The Resolution of Child Custody Cases—The Courtroom or the Consultation Room," *J. Psychiatry & Law* 6 (1978):499. © Federal Legal Publications, Inc., 157 Chambers St., New York, N.Y. 10007. Reprinted with permission.

4. J.S. Wallerstein and J.B. Kelly, "Effects of Divorce on the Visiting Father-Child Relationship," *Am. J. Psychiatry* 137 (1980):1534. Copyright 1980, American Psychiatric Association. Reprinted with permission.

5. H.J. Friedman, "The Father's Parenting Experience in Divorce," *Am. J. Psychiatry* 137 (1980):1177.

6. H.H. Foster, "The Devil's Advocate," *Bull. Amer. Acad. Psychiatry & Law* 5 (1976):194.

7. A.M. Levy, "The Meaning of the Child's Preference in Child Custody Determinations," *J. Psychiatry & Law* 8 (1980):221. © Federal Legal Publications, Inc., 157 Chambers St., New York, N.Y. 10007. Reprinted with permission.

5

Dealing with Difficult Clients

The ugliest litigation generally gets uglier as the litigation gets thicker. As time passes and the anxiety levels of the contestants and their advocates mount, overt anger sometimes becomes more pointed. It may be spewed out in all directions without any thought of its consequences. Those consequences, however, affect the angry parties themselves as well as their antagonists and, more often than not, their children. Anxiety among close relatives is more contagious than the measles. Subjecting children already frightened by family disruption to further panic based on the adults' fears about the future is nothing short of heinous.

Thus the question arises, "Is it possible to have contesting parents who are *not* classified as difficult?" Experience has shown that the answer is sometimes affirmative. Usually, however, parents who are fighting for and over their children fall into the difficult category, and they will need special treatment if our goals for them and their children are to be realized. But just what are our goals? First we must establish some areas of general agreement.

The goal of all mental-health experts working in the area of child custody must be to determine the disposition for the child that represents his or her best interests, and to keep the cases out of court, where sometimes arbitrary and always external decisions are imposed on the combatants. This is not to say that those court decisions are not often correct and constructive ones, which make the best out of bad situations. Experience shows, however, that externally imposed decisions that are not worked out with the individuals—or, better, worked through with them in the real sense of that therapeutic term—usually do not work as well as those the parties reach themselves, often with help.

The goal is to work *with* the contestants instead of against them, as they most likely expect every counselor to do at the outset. In their anxiety they are frightened and suspicious of everybody. Sometimes, as we shall see, what frightens them is surprising. But in actually working with the contestants the aim should be to settle issues with and between them and to develop mutually agreeable custody and visitation provisions.

This chapter is adapted from a similarly titled address given by the author during the 1980 Family Law Colloquium sponsored by the Los Angeles County Superior Court, the Family Law Section of the Los Angeles County Bar Association, and the California Chapter of the Association of Family Conciliation Courts.

Obviously, this is nothing new. Even more obviously, the difference between goal and achievement can be considerable, as any custody counselor or investigator can attest. However, the task will be even more difficult if the counselor fails to see accurately the conditions that might underlie the initial difficulties. In order to perceive these most clearly, we must define our terms so that we know exactly what we are talking about. We must ask ourselves, "What do we really mean by 'difficult' clients?"

What, exactly, is difficult? Does the difficulty manifested by the contesting parent stem from a desire for custody of the children? Or does it stem from a desire for revenge against the contesting spouse? Is the difficulty a product of conscious, willful thought and planning? Does the end sought by the consciously, willfully planning client represent a wish for the children or merely a means to another end, such as getting increased financial backing or keeping the house? Does the difficulty spring from an unconscious source, perhaps representing a need for the children that the contesting client does not consciously recognize but only feels vaguely? Situations such as this lead to panic, which, in turn, leads to the quality workers in the field call "difficult." What, in short, are the motivations of the difficult client who wants his or her children and is eager to fight the opposing parent for them—and the devil take the hindmost?

Then again, *who* is really difficult? Is it really the parent, or is it someone working with, around, or behind the parent for reasons of his or her own? For example, does the real difficulty lie with the grandparents or, as another example, with one of the attorneys, who for his or her own reasons feels a need to litigate and do nothing else? A more malignant situation occurs when the expert witness, for reasons of his or her own ranging from ignorance to the need for ego satisfaction, prefers to go to court rather than to keep the case out of court. Clues must always be sought that perhaps some*body* as well as some*thing* else is moving the contestant to be difficult or recalcitrant, even at the expense of the child and his or her own best interests. As mediators, we must determine how best to meet that challenge. Do we meet with the grandparents? Why not? Obviously we ought to meet with the lawyers, as will be discussed later.

Another question, aside from *what* and *who*, is whether the parent is *really* difficult. Is the apparent difficulty mandated by a need for the contesting parent to put on a show in order to placate his or her own conscience, or to please the other people—the *who* behind him or her?

Finally, perhaps the most crucial aspect—and one that is seldom addressed—is whether the counselor becomes difficult by way of chronic countertransference problems or, more simply, of burnout. We in the mental-health professions often create difficulties for ourselves and our clients by operating on the basis of feelings within ourselves that we either do not recognize or think we can shrug off if we do recognize them. As child advocates, we cannot allow this to happen because our burnout adversely affects the decision-making process. We cannot simply tell both parents to go to hell. That will not help the children. Even if a decision is made, the parent to whom the child is directed may be prevented by the counselor's burnout blocks from dealing effectively with his or her own blocks. As mental-health professionals, we simply cannot allow ourselves to become so jaded that we mentally write off certain cases as hopeless when in fact it is we who have become hopeless.

People who work in agencies that deal in nothing but custody problems are in the most acute danger of this type of burnout. Like prison guards or the staffs of state hospitals, they can develop an us *versus* them mentality, unwittingly bucking their negative countertransference and thereby actually preventing possible settlement out of court through conference. Regular rotation out of such agencies, perhaps to other social agencies periodically for several months, is essential. Those counselors need rest and recreation. Fortunately, the bulk of my own practice involves treating psychotherapy patients. If I had done nothing but see custody case after custody case for all the years I have been in practice, I probably would have had my colon removed years ago! That is why I stress that self-examination is essential and fundamental in trying to determine the sources of difficulties in "difficult" clients.

Aside from dealing with what makes either them or us problematic, the best way to deal with all problem patients is to spell out our role with them and their attorneys carefully and precisely. Whenever I enter a child custody case, I adopt the inflexible and nonnegotiable role of child advocate. I explain that role carefully to the attorney who initially calls me, immediately after thanking him or her for referring the case to me. I point out to the attorney that I may not find for his or her client even though that client is paying me for my workup. I also tell the same thing directly to the client, for I certainly see the referring attorney's client, as well as the opposing litigant, the child or children, and whomever else I consider it important to see. This is the basis of my usual verbal contract with the referrer and his or her client—that is, that I function as a totally independent evaluator, free to see all pertinent parties, and that I am necessarily the recipient of all significant material about everyone concerned.

I also tell the attorney that I want to speak to the opposing counsel and let him or her know of my position as well. After my workup is completed, I tell both lawyers my findings and my recommendations and point out the specific reasons that underlie them. In my experience, most lawyers have relationships with their clients that are better and deeper than my own relationships with their clients. Thus the attorneys may be more likely than I would be to convince their clients to follow my recommendations. Of course, I will always discuss these issues with the clients if they wish or if it would be helpful to do so.

The goal in every case is to determine what is best for the children and to effectuate recommendations without having to go to trial. I let both attorneys know that from the outset. Sometimes I get some lip-service agreement from them, and sometimes even from the contestants as well. However, even after proceeding through lengthy discussions with the contestants and their attorneys, if the litigants insist on going to court, I must accede because I have offered myself as a consultant in the case and am committed to see it through. In my experience, however, the approach described here tends to minimize the number of actual trials.

Obviously, both attorneys get duplicate reports. Tactically, these are good levers to apply to the parents, each of whom knows that the other attorney may well call me to appear if he or she does not go along. The good attorney will explain the odds for a favorable or an unfavorable trial decision to his or her client. In most courts those odds are greatly influenced by the reports and recommendations of competent mental-health professionals who back their recommendations with understandable reasons.

In most states the basic standard used in courts affecting the disposition of children in custody cases is the best-interests standard. One often wonders just *whose* best interests are really being emphasized. Definite issues appear in the examination of contesting parents and their children that are of particular import to the examining, child-advocating specialist. Insofar as the parents are concerned, these issues include how the parents view themselves and each other, as opposed to what objective evaluations of each would show, and also how they view their children. Why do they really want them? What clues to their attitudes toward their children emanate from the parents' verbal responses toward and with the children and from their nonverbal communications? What are their attitudes toward the inevitable trauma imposed on the children by taking them to court, especially the attitude of the prime litigator?

Obviously, the mental-health professional is interested in the presence or absence of overt or covert mental illness on the part of either or both contestants and/or the children. As a child advocate, however, he or she is just as interested in the specific reasons that the litigants want the child. The child advocate is also especially concerned about the possibility of a parent establishing a dependent relationship with the child—one in which the parent leans emotionally on the child rather than the child, usually more appropriately, depending on the parent. What kind of role does conscious or unconscious secondary gain (money, keeping a home, and so forth) play in the demand for custody of the children? Oedipal relationships between mutually unconsciously seductive parents and children must also be evaluated with great care.

Child-advocating consultants have learned that, regardless of the supposed use of the best-interests standard, often only grudging acknowledgment is paid to this in and out of court by some judges, some lawyers, and even some experts who—like some officers of the court—unconsciously or even consciously identify with one litigant or the other. That certainly makes difficult clients more difficult. All mediators also must retain a healthy degree of cynicism to know that in all custody cases, parents—despite protestations to the contrary—may not have the best interests of the children at heart. However, it is the mental-health professional's particular job to determine that.

A child advocate will usually follow the principle that a contested child generally ought to be kept where he or she is doing well. If it is necessary for that beleaguered parent to get help in order to continue to do well or even to do better with children who are already progressing well, then the child advocate should make specific recommendations to the court in order to ensure that such help is provided. Advocates for one or the other litigant rather than for the children generally dislike this approach. They may attempt to persuade the evaluator that the children might do even better with the other parent. However, a child advocate usually will attempt to maintain the tenet that, in order to remove a child from an environment that evidently is doing well by him or her, a specific indication for such removal must be demonstrated. Litigation-minded rather than child-advocating attorneys will obviously advise their clients to seek immediate physical custody at the very outset of dissolution proceedings if this principle becomes even more widely followed. Obviously, this can often result in a situation detrimental to the child.

Child-advocating consultants also become aware of the unfortunate tendencies of some courts to "award" "deserving" parents their children, even if the children are doing well where they are. Child advocates will uphold the principle that children are not to be used either to reward good parents or to punish bad ones. The welfare and stability of the children, not compensation for a parent, must be the paramount issue in the decision-making process of the child advocate. He or she will work to maintain a situation or environment that has been demonstrated to do well for the child, or to change it in the least disturbing manner possible if the environment has not done well.

The concept of child advocacy is a conglomerate of many, sometimes subtle facets and considerations; it is the preferred attitude of all mental-health experts involved in evaluating child-custody cases. Although it may go against the grain of litigation-minded attorneys, it is the only approach known to behavioral scientists that guarantees a point of departure clearly defining the best interests of the children rather than the interests of the parents. Obviously, this does not mean that those interests cannot go hand in hand. However, the examiner who functions from the viewpoint of child advocacy must try very carefully to determine where the paths are parallel and where they are not. Where they are not, the path representative of the best likelihood of current and future stability for the children must be illuminated.

Attorneys who work in this field must recognize this, too, and for the sake of their own clients must adopt the same attitude. Many already have done so. Failure to do so often only causes further misery for both their clients and the children. Further difficulties for already anxious divorcing couples create still further difficulties for their panicked children. Child advocacy can and should become the attitudinal hallmark of all specialists in family and matrimonial law. Easing the lot of the children will also ease the lot of even the most litigious parents and will make them less difficult clients for their lawyers and evaluators.

Part II
Mock Trial

6 Bell v. Bell

Introduction

The greatest deterrent against participation by mental-health professionals as expert witnesses in either civil or criminal litigation is their fear of the occasional necessity for participation in a trial. Most mental-health professionals have been conditioned to avoid contacts with lawyers, judges, and the courts. Horror stories about terrible trial experiences have usually influenced these hesitant behavioral scientists. Most of these terrible experiences result from lack of communication between the expert and the lawyer who calls him or her as a consultant. Although it is hoped that effective efforts by behavioral-scientist consultants will result in cases being settled by conference rather than by trial, actual participation in a trial procedure need never be cause for alarm.

As pointed out in earlier chapters, expert witnesses have one function in the legal process: to teach the attorneys and the courts about matters in which the expert witnesses have expertise and the courts do not. In the adversary system that governs the procedures in U.S. and Canadian courtrooms, the opposing attorney has the specific task of preventing the expert's message from getting across if, in his or her opinion, that message might be deleterious to his or her client's cause. How behavioral scientists can work effectively within the courtroom situation to get their messages across is the major subject of part II. No reading, however, is an adequate substitute for experience.

Law students gain trial experience in moot courts and mock trials. These are unlikely experiences for mental-health professionals, who have to enter the adversary arena of the courtroom without similar preparation or background. The American Academy of Psychiatry and the Law (AAPL) is the major organization in the United States and Canada serving as a specialty educational body in forensic psychiatry. During its 1980 annual meeting in Chicago, a number of sessions were scheduled jointly with the American Academy of Child Psychiatry, which met nearby at the same time. The AAPL prepared a mock trial for its members and for the members of the Academy of Child Psychiatry, and the session met with considerable enthusiasm. It was seen by members of both organizations as a valuable teaching tool. All credit should go to Dr. Robert Sadoff of the Department of Psychiatry of the University of Pennsylvania. A former president of AAPL, he has achieved a distinguished national reputation as an educator in forensic psychiatry. In 1975 Dr. Sadoff also helped prepare and participated in a mock custody trial for the annual meeting of the American Psychiatric Association, and this was repeated in the 1976 Symposium on Child Custody for psychiatrists and attorneys in San Diego. That mock trial forms a portion of my *Custody Cases and Expert Witnesses*. That book is a practice manual for attorneys. Thus, in its style, content, and viewpoint, it is directed at a different readership than this book, although the annotated mock trial it contains might well be instructive for mental-health experts, too.

The present mock trial was prepared by Dr. Sadoff with the aid of Dr. Marshall Schechter, director of the Division of Child and Adolescent Psychiatry at the School of Medicine of the University of Pennsylvania. As will be noted in the transcript as well as in the footnotes, a scenario was developed in which each of the two doctor-expert witnesses presented himself in a different manner as well as from a different point of view. Two distinguished Chicago attorneys agreed to serve as the advocates in this trial. Barbara A. Weiner is counsel to the Section on Psychiatry and Law, Department of Psychiatry, Rush-Presbyterian-St. Luke's Medical Center in Chicago, as well as a teacher at the Illinois Institute of Technology-Chicago Kent College of Law. Bernard B. Rinella is the 1981 president-elect of the American Academy of Matrimonial Lawyers, Illinois chapter, and chairman of the Matrimonial Law Committee of the Chicago Bar Association. Serving as judge in this mock trial is Ann Kerr, a distinguished Florida family-law specialist, and a mainstay of the American Academy of Matrimonial Lawyers.

The format and presentation of this mock trial serve the specific educational purpose of acquainting inexperienced or otherwise hesitant mental-health experts with various ways in which they might be addressed in courts throughout the country. As a demonstration of a trial per se, it is highly abridged as a consequence of time restrictions. Many of the abridgments will be pointed out as the trial proceeds, either by the lawyers or the doctors, or in the footnotes. For example, the trial has no real beginning and no ending. There are no opening statements or presentations to the court of the issues involved. Likewise, there is no actual "verdict", although the judge makes remarks indicating the direction of her thinking about the case and its disposition. Again, however, this is done with the specific purpose of letting the inexperienced audience know how the presentations of the expert witnesses influenced her thinking. As pointed out in earlier chapters, although what the experts say is usually deemed important by the court, often decisions are made despite their presentations, and even more often without them.

Very little editing has been done to the original transcript prepared by the court reporter. The flavor of the speech patterns and the question-and-answer pacing and rhythm have been preserved, although some changes have been made to allow for clearer reading of what was once heard aloud. The typography provides clues to the content. The trial questions and answers and the usual procedures are set in ordinary text type. Comments made by the participants as asides or addressed to the audience for explanatory purposes are set in italics. A discussion of the session follows the testimony portion.

Background of the Case

In the usual situation of a custody matter that proceeds to trial and that uses the services of one or more expert witnesses, the experts prepare written reports. These are reviewed by each of the lawyers and, it is hoped, by the judge before the trial or at least before the appearances of the experts. This review gives a fair idea of the approaches and attitudes of the experts, as well as their conclusions and the bases for them. In this case no written reports were prepared because the mock trial took place during two large, simultaneous meetings of two national organizations with active, crowded programs. There was no way to distribute any written material to the audience far enough in advance to ensure comprehensive reading.

In brief synopsis, this fictional but representative case is a custody battle between Jack and Mary Bell, the parents of Barbara Bell. The couple had lived together for three years before their marriage five years ago. The marriage was a difficult one from the outset, more so than the living-together arrangement had been, not only because of the strain imposed on each parent by the unwanted child but also because of increasing sexual difficulties. Jack accuses Mary of having no sexual interest in him, although she has shown considerable interest in other men before the marriage and since.

Jack is currently 30 years old and living with his mother, who has always blamed Mary for the difficulties of the marriage. Jack's mother believes that Barbara would be better off at her home, where she could be cared for by herself as well as by Jack. Jack himself is extremely jealous of Mary and her relationships with other men. He states that he would like to reconcile with her but that she will not consider this. Further, he acknowledges that he spends considerable time during many evenings parked near her house, watching to see which men come and go. At times he looks through her windows in order to observe her sexual behavior with these men, and he expresses concern over the possibility that she is having sexual relations in front of Barbara.

Jack has worked mainly as a construction and maintenance laborer, and he has had an accident in which he fractured his left leg. He became addicted to a narcotic drug that had been prescribed for him as an analgesic during his recovery. Before his marriage he was once jailed for several months after being caught delivering and selling marijuana. He now takes methaqualone in order to sleep nightly. This is a drug that has become very popular "on the street" and has developed almost a cult following because of its reputed euphoria-inducing properties. Jack, however, has participated in drug programs that, he insists, have removed his original addiction to the narcotic. His current goals include returning to school in order to get his high-school diploma and to improve the level of his employment.

Jack was left fatherless by an automobile accident when he was 10. His father had been an abusive alcoholic, and Jack's early history was characterized by numerous beatings, as well as by his observing numerous battles between his parents.

Mary Bell is three years younger than her ex-husband. Her own father was a rigid, unbending Baptist preacher who objected to her relationship with Jack because of the latter's use of drugs. Mary quit high school in the tenth grade, and her father threw her out of the house shortly afterward when she attended a concert with Jack without permission. She then moved in with Jack. Mary's mother, according to Mary, was very passive and completely dominated by the father. Mary has had no contact with her parents for a number of years, and they have never seen their granddaughter, Barbara, the object of this suit.

Mary admits her frequent sexual relationships and also acknowledges that she is not sexually responsive to Jack. She enjoys sex with all her partners except him but is unable to give any reason for this discrepancy. Further, she admits readily that men stay in her home and sleep with her. However, she insists that this behavior is not seen by Barbara because Mary closes and locks her bedroom door. Sometimes Barbara awakens at night and comes to Mary's door, crying. Mary does not respond except to tell her through the closed door to return to bed. Mary acknowledges her annoyance with Barbara's inconvenient crying while she is with her lovers.

Mary's roommate, a female friend, is also sexually active and entertains numerous men. Jack describes both Mary and her friend as promiscuous. Mary works as a waitress, taking Barbara to a nursery school for care during the daytime. She is not at all intrested in a reconciliation with Jack. She describes him as a "peeping Tom" who has outbursts of rage and violence directed at her. He has broken down her front door, has assaulted her, and on occasion has taken Barbara away from her forcibly.

Barbara's custody was granted to Mary at the time of the original divorce action. Because of Jack's violent assaults on her, as well as her allegations that he is still addicted to drugs, Mary initiated a petition to deny Jack his previously awarded visitation with the child. Jack responded by filing a cross-complaint, indicating that Mary was not a fit custodian for his daughter and that he should have custody of the child. Mary believes that

Jack cannot care for Barbara and that he upsets the child when he has contact with her, as he did during the visitations. Thus a case originally involving a quarrel over visitation rights has become a full-fledged custody suit, and that is the issue that is to be tried.

These are the facts and allegations of the case at current issue, purely observational and historical. These facts must be seen as having already been established during the trial, through testimony by the contestants and their own factual or character witnesses, supplemented by investigators from the local child-protective agency who had been asked by the court to investigate the backgrounds of the litigants. What remains is the presentation of opinion evidence, the type for which the expert witnesses have been called. Chapter 7 contains the portion of the trial of specific interest here, which begins with the calling and swearing in of the first expert, Dr. Sadoff.

7

Transcript of the Trial

Robert L. Sadoff

called as a witness herein, having been first duly sworn, was examined and testified as follows:

Direct Examination by Mr. Rinella

Q State your name, please.

A Robert L. Sadoff, S-a-d-o-f-f.

Q What is your profession?

A I'm a physician, a psychiatrist.

Q When were you admitted to the practice of medicine?

A 1959, when I graduated from medical school at the University of Minnesota.

Q Are you licensed to practice medicine?

A Yes. I'm licensed in six states.

Q What are those states?

A Minnesota, California, Pennsylvania, New Jersey, Massachusetts and New York.

Q What is your educational background?

A When I graduated from the University of Minnesota School of Medicine in 1959, I followed that with the general rotating internship at the Veterans Administration Hospital in Los Angeles, California, and I took three years of residency in psychiatry at the UCLA [University of California at Los Angeles] Neuropsychiatric Institute.

I also received a Master of Science degree in psychiatry from UCLA in 1963. Other education was at the Law School at Temple University, from 1963 to 1966.

Q Do you have a specific psychiatric orientation?

A Yes. I'm a forensic psychiatrist.

Q Explain briefly what that is for the judge.

A A forensic psychiatrist, Your Honor, is a psychiatrist in that subspeciality of psychiatry that deals with people who have either mental or emotional problems and who are involved in legal matters, either criminal or civil.

73

Q Are you associated with any hospitals or universities?

A Yes, I am. The University of Pennsylvania and its hospital, Villanova University School of Law, and several other hospitals in the Philadelphia area.

Q Have you lectured on the subject of child psychiatry?

A Yes, I have.

Q To whom?

A To lawyers and to forensic psychiatrists.

Q Have you published any articles in this field of medicine?

A Yes. I have some chapters in books, and I have a chapter in my own book on child custody and child psychiatry, and book reviews of child psychiatry texts and other papers dealing with the problems of children within the law.

Q Do you belong to any medical societies?

A Yes, I do.

Q For the sake of time in this proceeding, we'll skip most of them. But you do belong to many. Do you belong to any specialist societies within the medical field?

A Yes, I do. Primarily the American Academy of Psychiatry and the Law, the American College of Legal Medicine, and the American Academy of Forensic Sciences.

Q Okay. Thank you, Doctor. [to Mrs. Weiner] *Do you want to cross-examine now?*

Mrs. Weiner: *No, not now.*

The Court: *In other words, you're going to accept him as an expert.*

Mrs. Weiner: *Yes.*

Mr. Rinella: *Subject to later cross-examination.*

The Court: *You stipulate as to his qualifications.*

Mr. Rinella: *In some states, including Illinois, you would wait until the entire direct examination was completed before you would then cross-examine the doctor. So, in this matter the entire testimony of the doctor will be taken, and then cross-examination on that testimony will follow.*

The Court: *I'm talking about his qualifications as an expert.*

Are you going to try to question his qualifications as an expert? In Florida, that comes before you decide whether or not you're going to take direct testimony.

Mr. Rinella: *We have a difference in the law. She'll attempt to impeach his credentials when I'm finished with him. Okay? Different states have different laws.*

Q Now, Dr. Sadoff, you're aware that Mrs. Bell has filed a petition to limit visitation, and that Mr. Bell has filed a counterpetition for custody; is that correct?

A Yes. I am aware of that.

Q Have you read those petitions?

A Yes, sir, I have.

Q And you understand them?

A Yes, I do.

Q How is it that you became involved in this case, Doctor?

A You had called me, Mr. Rinella, and asked me if I would examine your client and her family.

Q Have you done so?

A Yes, sir, I have.

Q When did you examine Mrs. Bell?

A I examined Mrs. Bell about three weeks ago for the first time. I spent about an hour and a half with her, and about a half hour with her daughter, Barbara. I followed that by examining Mr. Bell for about an hour, and spent about another half hour talking with Mr. Bell and Barbara. I also examined Barbara alone for about a half hour.

Q And everyone—well, you're suggesting now that you have examined the two participants, Mr. and Mrs. Bell, with the child present; is that right?

A I examined the child in the company of each parent on separate occasions. That's correct.

Q All right. What are your observations of Mrs. Bell, Doctor?

A She is a woman who appears about her stated age, and she is able to present her problems in a clear and relevant manner. She shows no evidence of any thought disorder and she is not psychotic. She seems a bit anxious during the interview, which I would expect under the circumstances. And she also seems to be extremely angry and upset with Jack, her ex-husband, for what she believes he is doing to their daughter.

Q What does she believe he is doing to their daughter?

A Well, she observed him breaking into her home one evening. He was jealous of her and accused her of sleeping with someone at the time, and berated her in front of her daughter. And she believes that that is not in her best interest or her daughter's best interest. She also notes that when Barbara comes back from a visit with him she is withdrawn. She seems more tearful. She doesn't play as much with other people. And on occasion she has wet the bed, although she had previously stopped wetting the bed at age two.

Q Do you feel that she is a stable individual as a result of this examination?

A You mean Mrs. Bell?

Q Yes.

A I believe she is stable, yes.

Q Did you discuss her relationship with her former husband, Mr. Bell, at the present time?

A Yes, I did.

Q What is that relationship?

A At the present time the relationship is a very hostile and negative one. It's very difficult for them to be in the same room at the same time because they tend to argue and because there are so many passionate feelings that they have for each other, especially about their daughter, Barbara.

Q Does this poor relationship that you have described have a bearing on the child's relationship with her mother and father?

A I think it always does. In this case it does because, when she observes their battling, she gets very anxious and very nervous.

I did not take the opportunity to see her with them together because I was concerned about what that might do to her. So I had restricted my examination of her with each parent alone. She seems to be both comfortable and uncomfortable with each parent, depending on the situation, whether the parents had just had a battle or whether there was a smooth relationship.

Q Would this be a natural reaction for a child of 4½ under these circumstances?

A Well, it depends, of course, on the whole atmosphere. It's pretty natural under the circumstances now as they exist between the parents. But one would hope that that kind of thing could be reduced with some form of counseling to the parents, to alert them to the effect that their battling has on their daughter.

Q You also interviewed and examined Mr. Bell; is that correct?

A Yes, I did.

Q And was this in the presence of anyone other than yourself?

A No. I examined him alone.

Q Any diagnostic tests given?

A The only diagnostic tests I gave was a mental-status examination, which I do with everybody that I see.

Q What is that?

A That consists of my observing him, his behavior, his mannerisms, his gait, his manner of approach with me, his dress, and his affective or emotional tone in the course of his telling me various things about his life and his relationship with his wife or his ex-wife and his daughter. I try to learn whether there is consistency in his feeling, or whether there is inconsistency, or what the emotional tone appears to be at various times.

Q What are your observations of Mr. Bell?

A He is a man who is quite anxious and upset over the whole situation. He admits freely that he is a violent person at times, becomes jealous of his wife, and cannot understand her sexual preferences and her difficulties with him sexually. He just has no awareness that his ex-wife can find him sexually unattractive and yet find other men to be appealing. And he has a block in this area which he's not able to reconcile.

Q   Were drugs discussed?

A   We did discuss drugs. He was not, in my opinion, actively on drugs when I saw him. But he did give me a history that he had used marijuana in the past; that he did become addicted to a narcotic after he had broken his leg, but that he is no longer addicted, though he does take a sleeping pill every night. Without that, he's not able to sleep.

Q   What likelihood, if any, is there, as a result of his past drug history, that he may seek harder drugs or become addicted again, in your opinion?

A   Well, my opinion is that people who seek drugs to resolve problems, whether they are broken legs or emotional stresses, may, and more likely than the average person, turn to drugs as a means of resolving conflicts and problems. Since he is still, in my opinion, addicted to a sleeping pill, in the sense that he is not able to sleep without it, at least habituated to it, his use of drugs has not ceased. He is likely, more likely to turn to drugs when things don't go well for him.

Q   You have described Mr. Bell as hostile, angry, and resentful?

A   Yes.

Q   What effect, if any, would that kind of behavior have on his relationship with his daughter when he has visitation with her?

A   Okay. Now, I want to make it clear I have not observed him to be hostile with his daughter. He seems to have a much more moderate tone and attitude with her. However, his hostility toward his ex-wife, his inability to comprehend her sexual life and preferences, and his jealousy of her does emerge. It would have to while she is in his presence during the time of visitation; and when that does emerge, as it did at least on the one occasion described by Mrs. Bell, I think would have a terribly harmful and negative effect on Barbara and her relationship with her mother as well as with her father.

Q   In layman's language, how would you characterize his mental stability?

A   Well, I think for the most part he is fairly stable in his work and his relationship with others. But in his relationship with his ex-wife, I would characterize that as his having serious blind spots which he is not able to understand or to overcome. That would make him much more unstable in his relationship with her, as evidenced by the breaking into the house in a jealous fit, thinking she was in bed with someone else.

Q   Do you think he's trying to get even with his ex-wife by seeking custody?[1]

A   I think that's an element of it, although his presentation to me is that he sincerely believes that his daughter is not in good hands with his wife. He believes she is promiscuous from a sexual standpoint and that she has a bad influence on Barbara.

Q   You have examined the daughter, Barbara, 4½ years old; is that correct?

A   Yes, I have.

Q Briefly, Doctor, what are your observations about Barbara?

A Well, Barbara, when she was alone with me, seemed to be a very warm, sweet child who was able to talk to me in kind of a limited way, because she is only 4½, about her going to nursery school or the day-care center. She was able to talk about some of the things she likes and the friends that she has in her neighborhood. And she really didn't want to talk about the problems that her parents were having.

She does say that she sees her father, and she tends to deny that there is any difficulty between her mother and father, or between her and either parent. She would like, of course, to have her parents reunited so they could all live together.

Q Do you feel she is intellectually her proper age, 4 to 4½?

A I would say so, yes. I don't see any evidence to the contrary.

Q What about her stability generally?

A I found her to be a fairly stable youngster. When we talked about problems that may arise, she does tend to deny, and that's one of the defense mechanisms that I suppose we all use and children use, and it's not abnormal. At least, it doesn't have to be. Taken to an extreme, it could be.

Q Are her stability and her intelligence any reflection on the manner in which she is being raised?

A I would say it would have to be. Her intelligence is about average and her demeanor is fairly restricted. I would say that she is a product of what's happened to her in her life, yes.

Q Is that favorable or unfavorable?

A At this point I don't see it as being either. I think she's progressing, in my opinion, fairly normally under the circumstances. I would not see her as at least requiring psychiatric treatment at the present time, although I believe in situations of this type where there are real problems that children tend to deny or overlook, that counseling could be helpful in terms of making an adjustment, whatever the verdict of the court.

Q Do you know how old she was when her father left the home?

A Yes. She was about 2 or 3 at the time.

Q And, to your knowledge, she has not lived with the father since that time?

A No, only on visitation. She spent overnight there, but she has not lived with him for any long periods of time.

Q Do you feel it would be somewhat traumatic for her to leave her present environment with the mother and move to the father's home with his background that we just discussed?

A I do, primarily because I'm a believer in the continuity-of-care principle.

Q What does that mean?

A Well, this is a very young girl who is only 4½. She spent the last couple of years with her mother, only visiting with her father, and she has made relationships in her neighborhood. She has a babysitter who comes in, by the way, whom I did speak to. And she has friends in the area, and she goes to a particular school. I think to uproot her from all of this environment and from the custody of her mother and the relationship that they had established would, in my opinion, not be in her best interest.

Q I see. You say you interviewed the babysitter? When did you do that?

A I did that after I saw the mother and before I examined Mr. Bell.

This is a woman, Joan Eldridge, who is about 17, a woman—she's—well, she's an adolescent. She's a neighbor who lives down the street a couple of houses away. She comes in after school while the mother works and takes care of Barbara for a few hours every day. She indicates that she gets along well with Barbara, and Barbara shows no problem to her.

Q Did she reflect upon Barbara's relationship with her mother?

A Yes, she did, and she described it as being very favorable, very positive, and she could see no problems from her particular point of view.

Q Now, Doctor, based upon your examination of the parties to this lawsuit and Barbara and the babysitter, do you have an opinion as to whether or not it would be in Barbara's best interest to remain with her mother?

A Yes, I do have an opinion.

Q What is that opinion?

A My opinion is that it would be in her best interest, all things taken into consideration, for her to stay with her mother.

Q Do you have an opinion, again based upon your examination, interviews, and so forth with the parties to this suit, as to whether limiting visitation would also be in the best interest of the child?

A At this time my opinion is that yes, I do have an opinion.

Q What is it?

A My opinion is at this time it would be helpful and in the best interest of Barbara to restrict visitation with her father primarily because of the difficulty between her parents. And until such time as counseling between the parents or for each parent helps resolve some of the conflict, and counseling for Barbara helps her understand and accept the separation and the difficulties involved, I think that restriction should continue. I think that Barbara becomes more disturbed when she spends prolonged periods of time with her father.

Now, I want to make it clear that I believe she ought to see her father. I don't think we ought to terminate the visitation because I think it's extremely important for her to have some contact with him, but not to the extent that she has had because it tends to foster the difficulties between the parents. That reflects in greater anxiety and difficulties for Barbara, evidenced by her behavior after visitation.

Q Doctor, are you being paid a fee for your testimony?

A I am being paid a fee for the time that I have spent on the case and the time that I'm here in court, yes.

Q And who is paying you?

A Mrs. Bell.

Q And what is your fee per hour?

A My fee per hour is $125.00.

Q Would your testimony be any different if your fee were higher or lower?

Dr. Sadoff: *It sounds like an insulting question.*[2]

A The answer, Mr. Rinella, is no, it would not be any higher. And, as a matter of fact, one of the things I insist upon is being paid in advance for the time that I prepared to spend here.

Q Is that your standard procedure?

A My standard procedure is to do that for two reasons. One is I do not work on a contingency basis, and I do not want to be paid any more in case Mrs. Bell gets a favorable opinion from the court. But, even more important, I would like to be free to say whatever I need to say under cross-examination, even if it hurts your particular case, without worrying whether or not Mrs. Bell will pay me after it's over and in case she loses.

Q Thank you.

A You're welcome.

Cross-Examination by Mrs. Weiner

Mrs. Weiner: *Some of this we are going to shorten. Some of the background questions that the attorney would ask before getting to the really meaty questions will not be done either in the cross or in the direct in the interest of time.*

Q Dr. Sadoff, do you have any special training with children?

A The only training I had was during my residency period, when I spent a full year of my three years in child and adolescent psychiatry.

Q And, as a matter of fact, during that residency period did you train under Dr. Schechter?

A Yes, ma'am. I'm proud to say that I did.

Q So you are not board certified in child psychiatry?

A No, ma'am, I'm not.

Q In your private practice, do you treat any children?

A I do not treat children, no. But I do examine them for particular legal matters.

Q But you do not have an ongoing treatment relationship with any children; is that correct?

A   Not any children under the age of 13. I do treat adolescents on occasion and enjoy that.

Q   Since you are not involved in the treatment of any children, have you kept up with the recent developments in literature in child psychiatry?

A   I have not. It's really been enough to keep up with the vastly growing literature in forensic psychiatry.[3]

Q   So then, Doctor, you would not hold yourself out as someone with a special expertise in dealing with young children; is that correct?

A   That would be correct. I do not have special expertise in dealing with young children. Just regular expertise. [Laughter.]

Q   Could you give me a broader or better description of the time you spent along with Barbara? What did you do during your evaluation of her?

A   Well, she sat in a large chair and I sat in my chair, which I usually do when I see adults. We talked a little bit. I asked her questions. She answered them. She seemed cooperative. She was willing to draw some things for me. She was willing to answer questions about wishes that I asked her, and she was able to tell me about her school, her life, what she does all day, and friends that she has, and her relationship with her mother, and when she goes to see her father. But that's about—those are the kinds of questions I asked.

Q   Did you engage in play therapy with her?

A   No. I don't do play therapy.

Q   Do you think the kind of examination you engaged in was really adequate to get an understanding of the feelings of a 4½-year-old?

A   I believe that what I did was adequate for me to get an understanding of Barbara in this particular case, yes.

Q   And preparing for this case, did you have the occasion to talk to the pediatrician, Barbara's pediatrician?

A   I did not talk with him, no.

Q   Did you have an occasion to talk to someone from the day-care center, the nursery school where Barbara attends?

A   No, I did not.

Q   Did you interview the paternal grandmother; Jack's father—Jack's mother?

A   No, I did not.

Q   In your discussions with Mr. Bell, did you have the indication that his mother would play an important role should he have custody of Barbara?

A   From my discussions with him, it was clear that his mother would be the one to take care of her while Jack was working. That's right.

Q   Didn't you think it would be important, should that issue come up, to have some understanding of what the grandmother would be like?

A   I thought I had some understanding of her from my discussions with her son. And I think it would be—look, all the information you can get would be helpful. So I suppose that would be helpful, too.

Q Well, Doctor, since we were considering talking about either denying visitation to a father or changing the custody from the mother to a father, don't you think it's important to interview all the important people who would be actively involved in the child's life?

A I think it would be helpful. I don't think it's essential. There are time restrictions in which you have to do it. There are fee restrictions. There is only so much time and I felt that under the restriction of time and available budget that I could examine and evaluate those important people that I could do in the time I had.[4]

Q So you didn't consider the paternal grandmother important enough to talk to, although you did talk to the teenage babysitter who spends a couple hours with Barbara each afternoon?

A Well, she, I think, is at least as important as the paternal grandmother, especially now because she is with Barbara, whereas the paternal grandmother is there only infrequently when Barbara goes to see her father.

Q But you didn't contact the nursery school where they spend eight hours a day with Barbara; is that correct?

A No, but I did talk to Mrs. Bell about Barbara's function in school and her progress, and that all seems to be very satisfactory.

Q Doctor, in your testimony about continuity of care, is it your view that generally a child at this age should stay with the mother because of her age?

A Well, if you're talking about a daughter staying with her mother, I think that's more frequent. I think that continuity of care really doesn't have anything to do with the mother. It has to do with the psychological parent,[5] and in this case this happens to be the mother. I would suppose, under the same circumstances, if Barbara had spent two years with her father, the continuity of care principle would work in your favor.

Q When you were meeting with Mr. Bell, was it your impression that the only time he is violent is in relation to dealing with his ex-wife?

A That's all the history that I got. I don't have any other evidence to show that he's violent in other areas, except by history when he was younger and he had a number of fights.

Q By younger, you mean a teenager?

A Teenager in school, yes.

Q But it was your impression that with his daughter there was quite a warm relationship? There was not any violence indicated; isn't that correct?

A Well, there are two separate questions that you asked me. One was when you asked me if there was a warm relationship; one was if there was any violence. I didn't see any violence and, for the most part, there seemed to be a fairly good relationship. I'm not sure it was as warm as what I observed between mother and Barbara.

Q The mother never complained that the husband was violent with the daughter, did she?

A No, she did not.

Q Her major complaint was she was upset about him breaking into the house and spying on her; is that correct?

A Those are her two major complaints.

Q And she did not issue any complaints about the kind of care that Barbara received while she was with her father and grandmother, did she?

A Not specifically, except for the behavior, the attitude of the child after she returned from such visitation, which, in her mind, reflected problems of being with her father.

Q Isn't it quite common for children who are in a divorce situation to exhibit acting-out behavior when they return to one or the other parent because of split loyalties?

A Unfortunately, Mrs. Weiner, it is more frequent than I'd like to see, primarily because parents are not properly counseled on how to take care of their children in such circumstances. But it's all too frequent, and I don't think it has to be that way.

Q So the behavior that Barbara exhibits is not really particularly unusual for a child in a divorce situation; isn't that correct?

A Not unusual, but it does reflect the difficulties of the situation.

Q Did Mr. Bell tell you that he was involved in a drug-treatment program?

A He told me that he had been. I didn't get the impression that he is currently involved in one.

Q Did he also state to you that he believed his wife was on drugs?

A Yes, he did.

Q Okay. Did you have any indication whether she was on drugs or not?

A I asked her and she denied it. And I had no observations to indicate that she was.

Q You suggested that it would be appropriate to limit visitation more, although you felt that Barbara should be able to see her father. Don't you think it would be detrimental to her to limit it at this point, because she might feel that she is being punished as a result of the court actions of her parents?

A That's one speculation. I don't know that that would be her feeling about it. I didn't get that from her when I examined her. My major concern is her reaction to what's happening to her, changing the status quo, which has led to a very difficult problem which I believe is not in her best interest.

Q Did Barbara mention any fears of her father?

A She only mentioned a fear that her father might harm her mother.

Q But she was not afraid of being harmed herself?

A No. She did not express that fear.

Q When you met with Barbara, she talked about her mother having people sleep over; is that correct?

A   That's correct.

Q   Do you think that is detrimental, for a little girl to see frequent male visitors in the home?

A   I think it can be, depending how it's handled. Certainly if there are any overt on open sexual relations between her mother and these men in front of Barbara, that would be a terrible thing and I would be totally against that. I'm assured that this does not happen. The other aspect of it is if it is harmful for Barbara even to see a number of "uncles" floating through the house from time to time. I think that that can be, again, harmful, depending on how it's handled, because of identification problems, because of her lack of understanding of what this means. If the mother takes the time to sit down with her and explain what this means and how it affects her life and helps her, it may be that Barbara can handle it without too much of a problem. I think that this kind of thing would be one of the things I would stress in counseling sessions for Mrs. Bell.

Q   Doctor, you said that Barbara sometimes has nightmares; is that correct?

A   Yes. That's correct.

Q   And during this time she goes and pounds on her mother's door and the mother will not open the door; is that correct?

A   That's when the mother has a boyfriend in the room she doesn't want to expose to Barbara.

Q   But, during that period, many times the daughter is having a nightmare, and the mother, in order not to expose her to a sexual partner, cannot respond to her daughter's needs; is that correct?

A   I think that's true, and I would certainly counsel her against that because I don't think that's helpful for Barbara.

Q   So you think that is clearly detrimental to Barbara?

A   I think it has been. I talked to her about it, and I think she's going to make some amendments in her life-style so that she does respond more quickly to Barbara's needs.

Q   But in talking to Mrs. Bell, she made it clear that she did enjoy and planned to continue her sexual activities; isn't that correct?

A   Yes. But she also indicated after we talked about it that much of this will occur outside the home now.

Q   If it occurs outside of the home, then who will take care of Barbara in the middle of the night?

A   Well, there is a woman who sleeps there, who lives there, who will be there, or perhaps the babysitter can sleep over, or Barbara's mother.

Q   Leaving Barbara with a 17-year-old babysitter?

A   Well, I don't think she is going to sleep all night overnight. She may engage in sexual activities in the shank of the evening and then perhaps come home to sleep.

Q It's your impression that Mary Bell enjoys quickie activities rather than a deeper relationship. Is that your impression, Doctor?

Doctor Sadoff: *If that's not objected to, I'll object to it.*

A I couldn't speak from experience.[6]

Q Doctor, just one final question. If someone contacted you and asked for a referral to an outstanding child psychiatrist in your city, isn't it likely that you would refer them to Dr. Schechter for treatment?

A It's not only very likely, but he is my first choice.

Q Fine. Thank you. I have no further questions.

A Thank you.

Mrs. Weiner [to Mr. Rinella]: *You want to redirect?*

Mr. Rinella: *One minute. I'm going to have to try to rehabilitate this mashed witness.* [Laughter.]

Redirect Examination by Mr. Rinella

Q Do you believe it is absolutely necessary to have a background in child psychiatry to render an opinion or the opinion that you rendered today?

A I would not render the opinion without the kind of child-psychiatry background that I know Dr. Schechter has, if I did not feel that I was at least giving an opinion based on competent medical certainty. So the answer to your question is that I feel that I can do it or I wouldn't be here.

Q Your orientations are different; is that correct?

A Yes, they are.

Q And what benefit, if any, does the forensic orientation have over the psychiatric orientation?

A Well, the forensic orientation, I think, allows us to evaluate the adults and their total relationship outside the family, and with agencies and with their legal problems, as well as their relationships with their children within the family, to give a total and comprehensive evaluation of the family dynamics and of the problems of the parents in order to render an opinion.

Q Are you familiar with the tender years doctrine?

A Yes, I am.

Q What is that?

A Tender years doctrine indicates that a young girl ought to be cared for by her mother unless there are indications to the contrary, that she would be an unfit mother.

Q Do you believe in that doctrine?

A I believe in it to a certain extent. But I think it gets abused. So I would prefer to go on the basis of a newer concept in law that states that each parent has equal opportunity to have custody of the children, and that the issue may be one that has to be ajudicated in this particular type of forum.

Q And it's how you arrived at your opinion; is that correct?
A Yes, I did.
Q I have no questions.
Mrs. Weiner: *Just one further question, Doctor.*

Re-Cross-Examination by Mrs. Weiner

Q Really, as a forensic psychiatrist you just feel you are better prepared to deal with the legal issues that interface with psychiatry; isn't that correct?
A Well, I think when you say, "just feel that way," I think that gets to be too restricting. I believe that child-custody problems and family dynamics are part of the total medical-legal system in which we work, and I feel very comfortable working within that system with my background in forensic psychiatry.
Q Couldn't another general adult psychiatrist have made the same evaluation you would have made, even though they are not qualified in forensic psychiatry?
A Well, of course you just asked a very important question which I could talk about for a couple of hours. But I know the court's time is restricted, and I would tell you that the answer is no. I think the value of forensic psychiatry is that we do take into consideration evidence and collateral information that general psychiatrists sometimes ignore, or else the general psychiatrists simply believe what the patients tell them because the person that they are examining is a patient and not a person who's coming because somebody else has sent them.[7]
Q Okay. We'll now call Dr. Schechter to the stand. [Witness excused.]
Mrs. Weiner I'm going to go through his qualifications a little bit more briefly in the interest of saving time. At least some of his qualifications. He's so much more qualified than Dr. Sadoff that—[Laughter.]
The Court: Strike that from the record.

Marshall D. Schechter,

called as a witness herein, having been first duly sworn, was examined and testified as follows:

Direct Examination by Mrs. Weiner

Q Doctor, would you state your name, please?
A Marshall D. Schechter, S-c-h-e-c-h-t-e-r.
Q Could you tell us what your occupation is?

A Yes. I'm professor and director of the Division of Child and Adolescent Psychiatry at the University of Pennsylvania and, therefore, a physician licensed in the state of Pennsylvania.

Q And you are board certified in adult psychiatry?

A Yes.

Q Are you board certified in child psychiatry?

A Yes.

Q Do you have any other board certifications?

A I'm certified also in adult psychoanalysis as well as child psychoanalysis.

Q Have you ever published anything in the area of child psychiatry?

A Yes, I have.

Q Approximately how many publications do you have?

A Between sixty and seventy.

Mrs. Weiner: *Now, normally I would go through some of his publications. Also, generally in qualifying a witness, I would go through his whole educational experience, but in the interest of saving time, we are cutting that out.*

Q How long have you been practicing child psychiatry?

A Thirty-two years.

Q And in your practice, do you also see adults?

A Yes, indeed.

Q Have you treated adults?

A Yes.

Q And have you treated families together?

A Yes.

Q Doctor, did you have an occasion to visit the Bell family?

A Yes, I did.

Q Whom did you see during this examination?

A I spent an hour each, with Mr. Bell first and then Mrs. Bell, an hour each with Barbara and each of the parents. Then an hour with Barbara alone, an hour with the paternal grandmother, and then approximately an hour with the teacher and the head of the nursery school.

Q Did you also have the occasion to do any testing with any of these people?

A The testing that I did as far as—

Q Besides the mental-status exam.

A The mental-status exam obviously with all of the people involved. But we did a Denver Development Screening Test with Barbara and then plotted her, in effect, in some of the developmental aspects on a synoptic chart in child development.

Q Could you tell me why you decided to do the Denver Development Screening Test?

A   There had been a series of questions derived in the history from Mrs. Bell that, perhaps, in some parameters Barbara seemed to have been either regressed at times or, perhaps may not have progressed satisfactorily to age-appropriate behaviors.

Q   What were your conclusions as a result of that test?

A   The testing is that Barbara essentially, at the time of the testing, functioned well at about the 5-year level.

Q   So she was a little bit ahead of herself?

A   Yes.

Q   Could you describe to us what you concluded about Mrs. Bell?

A   Mrs. Bell?

Q   Mary Bell, the mother.

A   The mother. Mrs. Bell seemed to me to be really quite antagonistic toward the examination which I had requested. Like Dr. Sadoff, I had the opportunity of visiting with both parents. But she seemed very antagonistic toward the notion of being examined by me, especially regarding any kind of question vis-à-vis her daughter. She seemed suspicious of the direction the questions were taking, and certainly resentful of any questions that dealt with her personal relationships of a meretricious sort with anybody other than Mr. Bell before.

Q   Did you explore with her her husband's charge that she had been involved in drug usage?

A   Yes. She said that she had not been involved with any drugs recently. And there certainly was no evidence during the time of the interview that she had any current use of drugs.

Q   Could you describe for us what the interview was like when the two, the mother and the daughter, were together?

A   That was a most interesting kind of a thing because, during the time of the interview with the mother with Barbara, in contrast to the time that I had just two days before with Barbara and the father, Barbara was clingy. She was whiny, she was complaining. And, incidentally, I did this exam the same time during the day so as to avoid any kind of question of undue fatigue in the child or other difference from each of the interviews. She certainly was not physically ill, but she gave every evidence of being a regressed, demanding child. And one of the most interesting aspects of that interview was the difficulty not only in separating from mother, as she did easily when father was with her, but the fact that throughout the interview Barbara used baby talk, in contrast to the language development that she displayed when together with the father.

Q   Could you describe what you found after interviewing Jack Bell?

A   Mr. Bell seemed to me to be a rather forthright, somewhat anxious, but much more well-put-together individual than Mrs. Bell. I found that his interests in terms of Barbara were very sincere. His major element of concern,

I think, was that, indeed, his daughter was potentially going to be mistreated while living together with mother. This evoked in him a considerable replay, if you will, of many of the kinds of situations that he went through himself as a child with an alcoholic father.

Q When Barbara and her father were together, what kind of behavior did Barbara exhibit?

A Barbara, first of all, displayed a considerable amount of affection for her father. As I indicated, her speech was age appropriate and perhaps even somewhat advanced. She separated easily from father when he was in the room with her and came with me to the play table where we then drew a number of pictures and did a number of tests, including the Denver. During that particular period of time, whenever she finished a production, she gleefully went over to the father to demonstrate what it was she had done. It seemed to me there was just a very close and warm relationship between the two of them, and he responded correspondingly to her signs of affection to him.

Q What did you conclude after talking to Barbara alone?

A That, too, was an interesting kind of thing because a couple of things came out that I thought were really pertinent to this particular case. One of them was as we did the mental-status exam. Included in the mental-status exam, certainly with children as we do with adults, we raise the question about many aspects of fantasy life, dream life, and so on. And what she reported to me was that she was having continued dreams of nightmarish quality that involved being chased by witches. And this was something that she reported as being present practically every night.

The concern she had also was that, at the time of awakening with the frightening dream, in which apparently, according to the mother herself as she had reported to me, sometimes there is sleepwalking and some talking during the sleep; that when Barbara, herself, talked about the awakening in fear, and then going to her mother's room and knocking on the door trying to get some solace, mother, with the door locked, would frequently send her away and say, "Go back to your room and go back to bed. I don't want to see you," which then increased Barbara's anxiety.

The other aspect that seemed to me to bear on this kind of relationship between daughter and mother was the fact that when Barbara was playing with the dolls that I had set up as a sort of family situation, which I do routinely with children, Barbara insisted on placing mother together with a man by the name of Mike in the bed, and herself outside of that particular setting.

Q Doctor, is it your view from your training that it would be difficult for someone who is not an expert in child psychiatry to be able to observe these things without engaging in play therapy or in the type of evaluation that you did?

A   Yes. It would be very difficult.

Q   You mentioned that you talked to someone from the nursery school. Whom did you speak to?

A   I spoke to the teacher in her particular class, as well as the director of the nursery school, who was a separate person from the teacher.

Q   And did you get any impressions from them?

A   Yes.

Q   As to how Barbara was doing in school?

A   Yes. Barbara is generally doing well in school. However, since she has been in this particular nursery school for almost a two-year period now, they have noted that there have been innumerable times that mother drops her off at nursery prior to going on to her own job, where Barbara again is very clingy, very demanding, crying considerably, and that crying lasts for considerable periods of time. There have been occasional times when they reported that Barbara was dropped off by her father. And under those circumstances Barbara seems happy and able to separate well.

Q   Did they also report that when Mrs. Bell picks up Barbara that Barbara seems changed from the way she is during the day in the nursery school?

A   Yes. Again there is a very interesting kind of change in Barbara's approach in some of her functions, including her speech. When mother picks her up, oftentimes there is again a return to some of the crying behavior, the whininess, and with this also the return to baby talk.

Q   You had the occasion to contact Barbara's pediatrician. When you talked to Dr. Roberts, what did you learn?

A   As a routine, I not only get the report from the pediatricians when I do an examination on children, I also get the records from the obstetrician and the hospital where the children were born. One of the things that came out of the pediatric records, which then I questioned Dr. Roberts about, was the fact that during the approximately four years that he has been involved with Barbara, on a number of occasions there were bruises on Barbara's arms and legs, which the mother explained as related to her having fallen, as children would tend to do. On close questioning, Dr. Roberts had some concern as to whether or not these might have been induced by somebody else.

Q   Did the pediatrician say whether Mrs. Bell kept her appointments regularly and brought Barbara in for all her shots on time?

A   The time was somewhat difficult. Generally speaking, he said she had appeared somewhat late at times, but generally did bring her in.

Q   Okay. You also talked to the paternal grandmother, Jack's mother, Mrs. Bell?

A   Yes.

Q   Could you tell us what you concluded after talking to her?

A   Mrs. Bell is a very warm, maternal, kindly disposed individual to children. She volunteers, incidentally, at one of these grandparent programs for mentally retarded children and really has a great concern about—

Mr. Rinella: *Objection.*[8]

The Witness: —has a great concern about children and certainly her granddaughter, who is her only grandchild. I felt that she had very clear ideas about rules of upbringing, the discipline the children needed to have. She certainly seemed to have a great concern about her son and what he has been put through through the divorce period and subsequently.

Q   Was she aware of her son's problems with the drugs and his sometimes violent behavior?

A   Yes. She was actually the one who, during his teenage period when some of this did occur, had referred him to the local mental-health community center that they had in their community. And then subsequently she has been aware that he has been back on this and has been attending the drug-treatment program of their community-mental-health center.

Q   Did you talk to anyone at the community-mental-health center?

A   Yes, I did. I was very much concerned about this report, not only because of the addictive history but also because of the possibility that the sleeping pills might be seen in this particular direction. Interestingly enough, the reports from the community-mental-health center validated what I saw during the interview, and that was that Mr. Bell was seen as really developing quite well. His direction both in terms of occupation and of further education were clearly seen as valid, and his motivation was good toward bettering himself. They did not feel that he was addicted at this point to any drug.

Q   Do you have any impression of what the life-style would be like for Barbara, should she live with her father and grandmother?

A   Yes. I think that it would continue, to some degree, certainly with the nursery school that seems to be doing very well with her. The grandmother, I think, is somebody who, partly because of the woman's very firm and solid religious convictions, would include a religious background and a discipline for Barbara that would include the very chief discrimination of right and wrong.[9]

Q   Is it your understanding that Mr. Bell and his mother live only about two blocks from where Mrs. Bell presently lives?

A   Yes.

Q   So they are in the same area?

A   They are in the same area. The capacity, therefore, to keep up with friendships in the neighborhood would be good.[10]

Q   Did you reach any conclusion about whether Mr. Bell should get custody of his daughter, Barbara?

A   It seemed to me from the warmth and affection betwen the two that, yes, I did feel that he should get custody.

Q Doctor, wouldn't it be unusual to suggest that a little girl of 4½ years of age be put with her father?

A No. It's not unusual.

Mrs. Weiner: *It is in Illinois.* [Laughter.]

Q In making this suggestion, do you anticipate that Barbara will, at some point, have problems in terms of sexual identity, her own sexual identity?

A No, I don't. Quite the contrary. In all the work dealing with father's role with the rearing of children, it is the fathers who seems to have the major aspect in identifying the femininity in the female child.

Q Are you familiar with some recent work by Judy Wallerstein and others that has shown that children who go with parents of the same sex seem to do better in the divorce situation?

A Yes, I'm aware of that work.

Q But it is your conclusion anyway that Barbara would probably do better with her father?

A Yes.[11]

Q Is much of your conclusion based on the role of the grandmother?

A No. That certainly has played a significant amount in terms of the decision. However, the major aspect was the relationship between Barbara and her father.

Q Do you think if Barbara went with her father that the father would be able to act in a more mature manner towards his ex-wife?[12]

A Yes.

Q And, therefore, the possible spying and maybe somewhat violent behavior would be eliminated or at least drastically reduced?

A Yes. That's my impression.

Q If Barbara were to remain with mother, do you think she would continue in this regressive behavior that you have described?

A Yes. I think that's much more likely that that would occur.

Q Why do you think she is regressive with her mother and not with her father?

A The mother, it seems, periodically has a considerable amount of antagonism toward the invasion of her own privacy and her own style of living that Barbara represents. I think that there is an antagonistic, hostile relationship between the two, which the presence of Barbara seems to stimulate considerably.

Q And the mother expressed to you in her interview that sometimes she resented having the daughter and that this limited her freedom; is that correct?

A Indeed, yes.

Q So it is your conclusion that Barbara would do best with her father; is that correct?

A That's correct.

Q If custody were to be changed, what sort of visitation should the mother have?

A It would be my impression that the mother ought to continue, obviously, to have visitation. But that those visitations ought to be limited to the daytime with no overnights, unless there was a specific restriction against having a gentleman within the home. That's somewhat difficult, if I might just continue this for one moment, because there is another roommate at home who has her own sexual involvements which she certainly ought to have the right to have. And there was no way that I could understand the court limiting that other person within the home's activities.[13]

Q So it is your view that for Barbara to be exposed to the continuing sexual activity is detrimental to her?

A At this particular point, yes, indeed.

Q Okay. I have no further questions of this witness.

Mr. Rinella: *Is this the same case we rehearsed?*

Cross-Examination by Mr. Rinella

Q Incidentally, Doctor, you testified that you were Dr. Sadoff's professor in medical school; is that correct?

A No. During his residency.

Q Was he a good—

A Excellent.

Q —resident?

A Excellent.

Q Did he learn a lot?

A I believe he did from me as well as from everyone else?

Q Do you feel that he's an expert in psychiatry?

A Yes.

Q And you've mentioned on direct examination that it would be difficult for a person who is not a child psychiatrist to observe the things that you noted. But do you think that Dr. Sadoff has that skill and ability, having been trained by you?

A No. I don't think he has. He didn't spend the extra amount of time to qualify to become board certified, which would require at least another year of training.

Q How many years of training has he had in child psychiatry, to your knowledge?

A Just the one, which was basically in adolescent psychiatry as well as child. If I remember correctly, the vast majority was with adolescents, not with younger children this age.

Q How many years are required to become board certified in child psychiatry?

A It requires two or three years of general psychiatry and then two years of child psychiatry on top of that.

Q He is one year short of certification; is that correct?

A Being eligible for certification.

Q I see. Now, this loving grandmother, as you portrayed her, where did she go wrong with her son, Doctor? Why is he a drug addict? He was unemployed, according to my notes, for some period of time.

Mrs. Weiner: I object to the characterization of his being a drug addict.[14]

Mr. Rinella: **Q** He did take drugs; is that correct?

The Court: I understand your objection and I note it. I think that it's not important to strike it from the record, though.

Mr. Rinella: **Q** He does seem to have a violent temper. He does act as the peeping Tom, by his own admission, observing his former wife's behavior and conduct sexually. Where did the mother go wrong?

A I can't answer that. I have no idea about the child rearing that went on at that time, nor the influence of the alcoholic father, and even the possibility that there may have been some direct child abuse that perhaps created some organic mental problems in the son dealing with violence.

Q So that he may, in fact, have some organic mental problems; is that correct?

A That's certainly possible. None of the exams that I did or that I heard Dr. Sadoff report would suggest that. However, the drug-treatment program, which is a very thorough one, certainly has not looked into that area because of suspicion.

Q I see. But there are specific examinations which can be given to test for that particular problem, are there not?

A Yes.

Q They were not given to him; is that correct?

A That's correct.

Q What is your impression of his behavior relative to his former wife in the presence of the daughter Barbara?

A I'm sorry. I don't understand the question.

Q Well, the specific example that was mentioned was that Mr. Bell broke into the, Mrs. Bell's residence and took the child. You recall that?

A Yes.

Q And there was a pulling and tugging of this child back and forth. Do you feel that this is rational, reasonable behavior on the part of Mr. Bell?

A Under the circumstances of constant provocative behavior on Mrs. Bell's part, it would seem to me that one could understand this, yes.

Q But—could understand it. But do you feel that it is the proper solution to the problem?

A I don't know how to answer that. I really don't know.

Q He has recourse through the courts. You're aware of that?

A Yes, indeed, and that's what I understand we are doing right now.

Mr. Rinella: *One for him.* [Laughter.][15]

Q But he saw fit to break into the home, as the evidence would suggest, and take the child, snatch the child, so to speak; is that correct?

A I don't think I would characterize it as a snatching. I certainly would suggest that under the provocative situation that he was in, the anger was present. And in these kinds of angry outbursts, one does act at times somewhat irrationally. One would say the same thing is true from Mrs. Bell's standpoint under these circumstances.

Q She did not act in outward anger, to your knowledge, in any of the instances that we are aware of; is that correct?

A Except in this one instance of the break-in and then subsequent court suit that we are into right now.

Q Well, you consider that as anger, the fact that she tried to take her cause to a court to have a court rule upon the visitation?

A Well, if you remember, sir, the original appeal was that of discontinuing the visitation entirely. And then that got modified to then changing some of the —shortening the visitation.

Q Let's go back to Mr. Bell's behavior. You're indicating that he takes things in his own hands. He can become violent; isn't that correct?

A I indicated only under those circumstances that we have described in that one circumstance. There was no other indication at any other time in his adult life within the past five years that we have had similar kinds of experiences with him.

Q Only as it relates to his former wife; is that right?

A That's right.

Q Do you feel that the fact that he was at one time addicted to drugs has any bearing on his potential custody or having custody of Barbara?

A No, I do not.

Q Do you feel that he is cured at this time?

A It certainly would appear that's—if not cured, well on his way, according to other experts.

Q Do you have any other reports from any of the experts here with you today?

A No, I don't.

Q Do you have any records with you at all of any of your interviews?

A Yes, I do.

Q And you have them with you today subject to my examination?

A Yes, sir.

Mr. Rinella: *We'll skip that now, but ordinarily I would want to examine them carefully. Now, this next question is playing right into your hands.*

Q What about the oedipal complex? This girl is only 4½ years old; is that correct?

A That's correct.

Q Is there any possibility that this possibility may exist a few years from now if she's, in fact, going to be living with the father?

A No. I expect a normal resolution with certainly the balance being there with the grandmother's character. During that period of time one would expect it to resolve normally.

Q The grandmother is in her fifties?

A Yes.

Q Do you feel she'll be able to cope with a teenage girl in another ten years?

A She certainly is a vigorous lady whose family history suggests that there is longevity as part of this particular family.

Q Don't you feel, Doctor, it would be better for the natural mother to raise this child as opposed to a 60 or—the grandmother of the child, given the circumstances in a normal situation?

A In a normal situation, yes, that certainly would be of help.

Q And you're considering this abnormal?

A Yes, sir.

Q Is that correct? Because of Mrs. Bell's somewhat promiscuous conduct?

A That's certainly part of it.

Q But you are overlooking, aren't you, Mr. Bell's history of some violence as it relates to her alone?

A No, I'm not overlooking that. I still think that there is enough to warrant a more thorough psychological-psychiatric evaluation of Mrs. Bell because we are concerned, I'm sure, as are counsel, with the best interest of the child, the kind of upbringing that we would expect from either parent in terms of not only custody, but the visitation and so on.

Q Doctor, you have been divorced, have you not?

A Yes, I have.

Mrs. Weiner: I object. It's irrelevant.

The Court: *It's already in.*

Mr. Rinella: **Q** Are your children living with your former wife?

The Court: Now that goes too far.

Mr. Rinella: *I raised this point obviously to try to portray the fact that all mothers are not bad. It's a nasty thing to do, but I'm just saying that for the purpose of this demonstrating we might try to get it in. I would not do it otherwise.*

Q You're aware that Barbara has lived with her mother from birth until the present time; is that correct?

A Yes, sir.

Q And you're also aware that Mr. Bell left, I think, when the child was about 1 or 2 years of age.

A She was between 2 and 3.

Q All right. And we had talked in particular about continuity of care, the fact that she has been with the mother from the onset of her life until the present time. What this suit suggests is that she would be taken from that home into a home that she is unfamiliar with; is that correct? Into the home of Mr. Bell and his mother?

A I would find it very difficult to answer that because I think that your premise is that she is unfamiliar with that home. And she is certainly familiar with that home, visiting twice a week there.

Q Are you now saying that Mr. Bell had regular visitation with the child?

A Yes. That was my understanding.

Q Not according to my facts. But for the sake of argument, your—you feel that she would be comfortable in that setting?

A Yes.

Q Do you feel there'd be any psychological damage to her if she were removed from her mother's home?

A No.

Q Even though she has lived there and resided there, this continuity of care is, in your opinion, not as important as Dr. Sadoff had testified?

A Well, I think that here is where I tend to differ with my colleague, in that the continuity of care implies a certain quality of care. And the quality of care that she was receiving with the mother, to me, has been deficient. That quality of that kind of continuous care by the father and the grandmother more likely would be in the best interest of the child, and salutary in terms of her psychological development.

Q You're indicating Mrs. Bell was annoyed when you interviewed her; is that correct?

A Yes, sir.

Q Isn't that a natural reaction?

A I would expect so.

Q You're indicating, likewise, that the child was more comfortable, as I understand it, with the father than with the mother?

A Yes.

Q Isn't it also a natural reaction, when the child had not lived with the parent on a full-time basis, to be more loving and affectionate with the parent that the child has not been on a regular basis?

A No, sir. Quite the contrary, in my experience.

Mr. Rinella: *You're saying, "Don't go any further, Rinella!"*

Q   Do you feel that you're a biased witness, Doctor?

A   No, sir, I don't.

Q   From my observations and from my vantage point here today it appears there are no saving graces as far as Mrs. Bell is concerned as a mother.

A   That may be your observation, not mine.

Q   Do you feel that she is, in fact, a good mother?

A   I think there are many positive things between mother and child.

Q   What are they?

A   The care that the mother has taken, as I indicated, with her bringing the child to the pediatrician regularly, albeit late sometimes; that she does take the child to the nursery school and it's an excellent, one of the best in the city.

Q   The school is, right?

A   Yes. She does employ this lovely young lady as a babysitter, and I think that in this sense she has attempted to maintain some kind of close and warm relationship with Barbara.

Q   Is there any relationship between the child's educational and emotional stability and the mother's rearing?

A   Could you be a little bit clearer?

Q   Well, you indicated the child was an intelligent child and seemed to be stable; is that correct?

A   No. I didn't indicate that she was stable.

Q   What did you say?

A   I indicated, rather, that there was a fluctuant quality in her current age-appropriate behaviors. That that quality seemed to be influenced periodically when together with mother.

Q   Now, you interviewed this child for what period of time?

A   I saw the child for essentially two hours, one each with each of the parents and then an hour separately by herself.

Q   Did you spend that much time with the parents?

A   Yes. Spent an hour each with each of the parents separately.

Q   You are a child psychiatrist, is that correct?

A   Yes, sir.

Q   Do you—you also indicated that you have worked with adults; is that right?

A   I continue to work with adults.

Q   What percentage of your practice is with adults?

A   It's about 50 percent.

Mr. Rinella: *I'm sorry to hear that. Normally I would have done more homework.*

Q   So that you—well, strike that.

I have no further questions.

The Court: I have one question.

Doctor, from a developmental point of view, isn't it true that Barbara is reacting normally to her father at this state in her life?

The Witness: The answer is yes.

Discussion

Dr. Sadoff: We have to stop at 12:30. We do want to have questions from you, but each of us wants to give a very brief statement about what we attempted to do. I hope we did it successfully.

First of all, we wanted to show that there was a difference between a forensic psychiatrist's testimony and a child psychiatrist's testimony. My particular bias in this particular type of case, a child psychiatrist really does a better job and probably ought to be the expert of choice when very young children are involved. The child psychiatrist, unlike the forensic psychiatrist, who may not be trained or may not have the current experience in working with children on a regular basis, has the expertise to delve deeply into the dynamics of the child. After all, we are talking about the best interest of the child. Our hope is that more child psychiatrists, many of whom are here, will be more comfortable in becoming involved in legal matters, because I know there is a great anxiety among most of us about doing this kind of thing. And the fact that you're all here indicates that this does occur.

Clearly, we wanted to raise the strengths of the forensic approach as well as the weaknesses within this type of a situation. And I hope that they were clearly brought out. The forensic psychiatrist can use collateral information, though the kind of collateral that I chose to use was not the same kind that Marshall did. His was geared primarily toward the child, her schooling, and so on.

One thing I did not do that I probably would have done if this were a real case, and I had had instructed funds, would be to talk to the grandmother. And I probably also would have got more information about the father's drug treatment. But Marshall did that, and we chose to have this rather extreme dichotomy established for illustrative purposes.

Did you want to say something, Marshall?

Dr. Schecter: Just a couple of words about how I see the expert, whether it be forensic psychiatrist or child psychiatrist, dealing with counsel.

It seems to me that we start out with an initial kind of a contact where we make a decision as to whether we ought to be part of the case or not. And I think that that's a time that is absolutely vital for us to make some kind of internal decision, but then very clear decision with counsel as to whether we are going to take on this particular matter.

Secondly, it seems to me that the next step along the way, irrespective of the information that we derive in any of our examinations, is to share it with counsel. We must share with that counsel not only our impressions but also get from counsel what the laws are of that particular community and state that you're involved with as it may pertain to this particular case, and what the rules of evidence are in that particular community. It becomes an important question, then, to derive along with counsel what the opposition might bring up, and to help counsel and to be helped by counsel about the cross-examination material that you may be subjected to.

Now, the thing that Mr. Rinella brought up, and I think very appropriately was quashed by the judge, is certainly something that we can expect if we are to be discredited. That is the job of cross-examination, to help discredit the witness to a certain degree. Therefore, things dealing with our private lives and with personal kinds of matters may, indeed, be brought up as germane to the case. The bias element that Mr. Rinella was talking about is a valid concept.

It seems to me the other thing that I just want to emphasize for you all is that the important issue that we are dealing with is the cross-sectional review we have of a developmental status of the child. We recognize that these things are not static, and that over time, particularly in the custody cases, we may have to suggest to court, even though it may be more costly, that the decision of this moment may be subject to review later on, depending on the developmental status of the child and other circumstances that may influence development.

Dr. Sadoff: Bernie or Barbara?

Mrs. Weiner: I have a number of comments.

Bernie and I were at a real disadvantage. Normally, the attorneys would have the doctors' written reports in front of them before they would go into court. Therefore, we can use them to know what to expect and for impeachment purposes. So this demonstration was not very accurate in that sense. I do want to urge more child psychiatrists to get involved in this process. It is really essential, particularly with young children, that the child psychiatrist become involved. And I think once you do become involved, you will see that it is not as bad as it's been painted. It's up to you to get straightened out by and with the attorney from the beginning about what you are expected to do, what your fees are, and that he will spend time with you preparing the case.

I think one of the things we really wanted to bring out in Marshall's testimony is that not only did he interview the major parties, but he then turned to the grandmother, who would clearly be a major party, should custody be switched. He also talked to the pediatrician and was interested in school reports. I think that's absolutely essential. And that really makes a difference between making a good case and a bad case.

I think there are very few people who get on the stand who have published sixty articles and are the head of Child and Adolescent Psychiatry at Penn. That should not scare you off because you have not published. I think the thing that's important is that you have trained and worked with children and therefore would be sensitive to their needs. Traditionally, one of the problems has been that adult psychiatrists have looked at the problems from the adult's perspective. In other words, if the mother loses custody of Barbara this is going to cause the mother to fall apart. We really need a lot more emphasis on what's going to happen to Barbara, not what's going to happen to the mother.

When you write a report for the court, you really should do it in an organized fashion. Put in the beginning what you were asked to evaluate and what your conclusions are so that the judge doesn't have to read through fifteen pages.[16] And then I would set out whom you saw, for what length of time, what other reports you considered, etc., and then go back and support your conclusions, as we did in the examinations here.

The other thing about the reports is that you really should not use psychiatric labels unless there is a reason. For example, if the mother is a schizophrenic or the mother is a manic-depressive who needs treatment, then that should be in there. But putting in characterizations about their personalities has no real relevancy to what the outcome is going to be. It is only going to be detrimental because it's all going to come out in the court. The kids might become aware of it and it really—it doesn't benefit anybody unless, of course, you're saying the mother is a schizophrenic and, therefore, she shouldn't get custody and, therefore, she needs treatment.

Dr. Sadoff: Thank you. Bernie?

Mr. Rinella: There's only one point I'd like to raise, and it's objectivity. I think you got an example here today of two different approaches from expert witnesses.

Bob was more flexible. He admitted in certain instances that there was another side to the case. As far as Marshall's concerned, he was an advocate more than an expert. In my opinion he did an outstanding job, and nobody would take him on one-on-one. No lawyer with brains, at least. But the point is that he was advocating, in my opinion, and I think a judge may hold that against him to a degree. He was too forceful. He was too rigid, too unbending. Judges and lawyers think differently than doctors, and I think he discredited himself to a degree because he was so rigid and unbending.

Dr. Sadoff: Thank you, Bernie.

Now we are going to hear from the judge, before we turn it over to the audience, to have her comments.

Mrs. Kerr: I don't believe that it had anything to do with Marshall being unbending, but I think, because of my experience in the Florida courts, I still would not have taken custody of the child away from the mother. I know this may be awfully frustrating for the child psychiatrists in the group. But judges are very slow to change custody and they are very concerned about continuity.

They almost never will change custody when it starts with a visitation problem, especially when the father was at fault from the point of view of causing all kinds of upheaval. They usually hold that against the father and ordinarily will. If they are convinced by the child psychiatrist, then they might do the following:

I would leave Barbara with the mother for a period of six months for further evaluation. I would restrain the father from any further violence to Mrs. Bell and I would restrain him from any further surveillance of Mrs. Bell.

I would direct that Mrs. Bell deliver the child directly to the grandmother's home each weekend, so that in the event I was going to have to change custody of the child to the father, then I would be able to have the child have a continuous, building relationship with the grandmother and with the father. So I would leave her there every weekend from six o'clock on Friday until six o'clock on Sunday.

I would restrain the mother from having any contact with any males in the home while the child was living with the mother. She can have her weekends off to do whatever she wanted to do. And if her roommate was going to have men sleeping over, the roommate would have to go if the mother wants to keep custody. And that sometimes is a very good test of what the mother's going to do too.

I would direct them to undergo counseling and evaluations on a continuing basis with Barbara for a six-month period, and I would have another report before the court in six months.

So that I wouldn't totally dash the father's hope, but, hopefully, could educate the mother toward having a good relationship with the child. [Applause.]

A Voice: Another report from whom?

Dr. Sadoff: I assume the applause is for Judge Kerr, and I wish that some other judges that I have faced would have the wisdom and the balance that you have. That's the kind of judgment that's balanced and not polarized. It takes into account the needs for further counseling and observation, and I think the best of both of your testimonies.

Mrs. Kerr: Regarding the question, as far as the further counseling is concerned, you'd have to know who the good agencies in your town are. I would not make the mother go back to Marshall because Marshall is not a treating psychiatrist and because he has definitely taken a side. I certainly would not send her to Bob Sadoff either. Not because I'm not impressed by his abilities, but because of the fact that he has taken a side.

In our area we might use the Family Service Association, which has a sliding-scale fee situation so that they can't use the excuse of not being able to afford the counseling. Sometimes the courts have their own counseling programs. I have to say that I'm not very impressed by some of those programs. I would just have to use the program that I knew in the community was the best and try to make it something that was economical.

Dr. Sadoff: All right. We don't have much time, and I want to call on Mel Goldzband.

Mel Goldzband is one of the ablest experts in child-custody matters, and has written a book recently which, in part, also contains a mock trial that we had in San Diego several years ago for AAPL. I hope you'll be brief but cogent.

Dr. Goldzband: Succinct, as those who know and love me, is my middle name.

I just want to make a few comments purely on a pedagogical basis. This is an educational session directed mainly at people who do not have a great deal of experience with child-custody testimony and child-custody legal procedures. This is the purpose for which we are all here.

I must say as I do in every child-custody symposium and every situation that deals with child-custody trials, that the fundamental purpose for each of us as psychiatrists to get involved in custody cases is to work like hell to try and prevent them from coming into court. They are dealt with better either in the consulting room or in the attorney's offices, via some other situation which does not necessitate bringing the case before even as competent a jurist as Ann here, who makes good decisions but, nonetheless, provides a tremendous amount of agitation and anxiety for all concerned. That's the first thing we must remember.

Bernie already commented about the fact that Bob gave some points and Marshall did not. And Marshall already commented about the marital status of the examinee. But I would like to comment about the marital status of the *judge*, and of the feelings of the *judge* before this case is tried.

Each attorney should have the obligation of teaching "his" expert witness about the judge before whom that expert witness is going to appear. And knowing the judge and knowing the tangents that bounce off of this judge at particular angles is a very important thing for both to know.

Dr. Sadoff: Thank you, Mel. Succinct.

Richard, I take it you have a question for the judge?

Dr. Rapaport: Richard Rapaport. Yes. I'd like to ask the judge to say how much the expert witnesses influenced her decision as opposed to precedent influencing it.

Mrs. Kerr: I think that the expert witness—it depends on the judge. As we heard earlier, you have to know your judges and know whether the judges think that they are junior psychologists themselves, whether anything that they are going to hear is going to impress them at all, or whether you're making a record just for future use because actually appeals of custody cases don't usually work out very well. You do have to know the judge, and each judge has a different approach to custody cases. Basically they do not like to move children around because they have so many contempt hearings. When the other person who's been fighting for control gets control, they are very hard on visitation a lot of times, and there is just a constant war if you move the child. And that's how most judges view it.

So they will listen, but the first time they usually don't bite. Now that's how it is in Florida. I can't tell you on a national level how it is.

Dr. Sadoff: Thank you, Ann.

I want to thank our guests, certainly Ann Kerr, Barbara Weiner, Bernie Rinella, Marshall Schechter, and all of you for participating. Thank you.

Notes

1. Mrs. Weiner and Mr. Rinella each explained to me that, in Illinois at least, it is deemed poor technique and practice to object in these types of cases, when one or the other lawyer, or the witness, says or does something controversial. It is felt that objecting would draw attention to something that might better be left alone, and that the result of the objection might open up a can of worms.

In other jurisdictions, attorneys are less hesitant to object. In this instance the opposing attorney might wish to call the court's attention to the leading nature of Mr. Rinella's question. Obviously, Mr. Rinella would like to "lead" as much as possible so that opinion evidence from Dr. Sadoff will be brought out as negatively toward the opposition as possible. Mrs. Weiner and other Illinois lawyers are content to file this away and try to demolish it later if they can. Other lawyers elsewhere would object, often simply for the tactical purpose of breaking the examining lawyer's concentration, style, and rhythm.

All witnesses must learn to stop talking—in midsyllable if need be—if they hear opposing counsel start to say anything. Then the witness must learn to sit back and let the lawyers play their tactical games. Those games usually have little to do with the witness. They have far more to do with the adversaries.

2. Dr. Sadoff is quite right; it is very insulting. However, it is important to note that the question is asked by the friendly attorney, not by opposing counsel. This implies the wish to deprive opposing counsel of the opportunity to ask about the expert's fees, the practice of "buying opinions," and so forth. The inexperienced witness should realize that in most cases tried without juries, custody cases included, lawyers usually do not bother with this crudity because the judges are sophisticated enough to recognize the ploy for what it is.

Dr. Sadoff's comment, of course, was directed to the audience simply to point out the educational value of this exchange. In a real trial he would have expected the question, because it would have been discussed in the pretrial conference held with the attorney; and he might have suggested that the attorney calling him ask this question.

3. A simple answer would have been better and obviously less defensive. However, because of Dr. Sadoff's wide courtroom experience, he is attuned to Mrs. Weiner's strategy and is aware that "her" witness has child-psychiatry credentials that he lacks. His poise, however, is instructive, as is evident from the exchange that follows.

4. The scenario for this mock trial calls for these omissions and also demonstrates how a good expert witness explains these. Of course, the situation really points up the need to obtain as much information as possible. If there are restrictive time and financial limitations, written reports may be obtained from, for example, the pediatrician, the nursery school, and so forth by the lawyer. The expert should instruct the lawyer to get these if they have not already been obtained. Of course, when possible, nothing beats first-hand interviewing, as will be noted in Dr. Schechter's testimony.

5. The *psychological parent* is the person to whom the child relates most closely as the individual who has provided him or her with the most stability, warmth, and other aspects of nurturing. It may be one of the biological parents, or it may be someone else entirely. The concept is widely used and was discussed at length in Solnit, Freud, and Goldstein, *Beyond the Best Interests of the Child* (New York: Free Press, 1973). It is further reviewed in the more recent *Divorce, Child Custody and the Family,* by the Committee on the Family of the Group for the Advancement of Psychiatry.

6. Again, the lack of objection by the friendly attorney must be pointed out. Dr. Sadoff's aside is appropriate *as addressed to the audience* in a mock-trial setting. Likewise, his real answer is very apt. The inference made by Mrs. Weiner is toward Mrs. Bell, not toward Dr. Sadoff, although a less experienced witness, in his possible, unfortunate identification with the party "for whom" he or she is testifying, might take umbrage and become rattled. The experienced witness testifies *about* rather than *for;* and in this ugliest of litigations, it is expected that attacks will be made on the litigants by the opposition. However, those are not necessarily attacks on the expert witnesses, who must learn not to take them personally.

7. Dr. Sadoff, whose history in forensic-psychiatric education is long and distinguished, here makes an open pitch for more forensic-psychiatric education. This, of course, would be highly valuable; but as of now forensically inexperienced but otherwise competent general or child psychiatrists will need to fill an increasing gap. Thus it is necessary for those forensically inexperienced psychiatrists to work closely with the attorneys who call on

them so that the attorneys can teach them what to expect and what is needed to work in their turf.

8. Mr. Rinella obviously sees the increasing weight of the opinion evidence presented by his opposition; and even though it may be risky in his jurisdiction as to form, he sees the need to interrupt the steadily encroaching flow and inexorable rhythm of this damaging testimony. The objection was made for the record and was not responded to by the court. In other jurisdictions the court would respond, and then Mr. Rinella would have to explain his move, perhaps pointing out that Dr. Schechter has already answered the question by his first sentence.

As will be seen later, Dr. Schechter's tendencies to be a highly advocative witness will eventually adversely affect the effect he is trying to make. This is a crucial lesson.

9. Again, the advocating by Dr. Schechter becomes transparent as he waxes glowingly over the grandmother. This material is valuable, but it would have more positive value were it developed by specific, pointed questions about her, her character and her likely role. Without such questions, the impression is gained that Dr. Schechter is "making a pitch".

10. This too, represents advocacy. Dr. Schechter's gratuitous comment answers a question not yet asked, albeit obviously it was being approached.

11. Like Mr. Rinella's earlier questions to his witness about fees, this is a good example of the best defense being a good offense. In pretrial conferences, the attorney and expert should explore all the aspects they can that would be harmful to their case. Obviously, the expert witness should be acquainted with current literature, and he or she must warn the lawyer that the opposition might refer to this to buttress its case.

12. This and the following are certainly leading questions, and in many jurisdictions they would lead to objections as such by the opposing attorney.

13. Now we are back to Dr. Schechter's advocative posture. He brings in uninvited a complicating party, for whose presence no previous basis has been laid. Further, his comments about the court border on presumption, and it is surprising that the judge makes no comment here.

14. Trial attorneys describe rhythms in varying types of testimony. For example, in direct examination by the friendly attorney, the pace is slow and measured. This allows as much material and opinion evidence as possible to be developed by the expert witness. In contrast, the rhythm of cross-examination serves a different purpose, and for that reason the tempo of the questions speeds up. The examining lawyer wants to trap or confuse the witness, or else he wants to home in on a particular subject. Here Mr. Rinella senses vulnerability when it comes to discussing the grandmother. Mrs. Weiner uses one of her rare objections here because she recognizes this and wishes to break the rhythm. In any event, the experienced witness learns to set and maintain his or her own pace in answering direct or cross-examination questions.

15. Mr. Rinella can afford to relax a little here and inject some humor, even self-deprecating humor. He has succeeded in demonstrating further the witness's defensive unwillingness to "give points" to the opposition. That defensiveness can have disastrous effects in a trial, regardless of the viewpoint or the stellar credentials of the witness. Dr. Schechter might well have acknowledged the immature behavior of Mr. Bell, just as he pointed out Mrs. Bell's provocative behavior. Again, the basic lesson is that all of the advocating should be left to the lawyers.

16. The subject of psychiatric-legal reports is a complex one, and many forensic psychiatrists would disagree with Mrs. Weiner in one respect. They would urge the writers of reports to organize them carefully and logically, and to do so in such a way that the reader will want to digest all fifteen pages. Most judges and attorneys, like so many mystery-story readers, automatically turn to the end in order to see the conclusions and recommendations., It is up to the expert to make sure that everything in the report is understood by the referring attorney or judge.

**Part III
Case Studies**

Part III consists of summaries of actual cases in which I have participated. They were selected because of their particular educational aspects. I feel that I learned a great deal from each of them, and each seems to illustrate a specific set of circumstances to serve as a good springboard for general discussion.

As I point out throughout these cases, in no way am I presenting my own work as exemplary. In fact, often I elaborate on how I may have been quite wrong in given situations. Likewise, my own reports are not presented as models for everyone to follow. The writing of medicolegal psychiatric reports is a topic that deserves a book of its own, as was determined during a symposium on this topic presented by the American Academy of Psychiatry and the Law in 1978.

Although the somewhat flowery style that unfortunately characterizes much of my report writing bothers me somewhat on rereading, I made a conscious decision not to rewrite any reports for this book because to do so would distort the actual presentations made during those cases. Of course, all the names except mine have been changed in order to preserve confidentiality.

8 *H* v. *H*: An Ideal Case

Even in those situations characterized by marked vituperation between the parties, settlement by peaceful and nontraumatic means is often possible. In this particular case, the cooperation of the adversary attorneys was essential. Notably, the cooperation of the petitioner's attorney who initially contacted me was very active; that of the respondent's attorney was quite passive. In fact, the respondent's attorney never contacted me except indirectly through the petitioner's lawyer—always, however, agreeing with the point of view expressed in my correspondence.

Following his remarriage some time before, Mr. H, the petitioner, sought the advice of an attorney with whom I had previously worked closely in a number of cases, criminal and civil. Mr. H told the attorney that his ex-wife was seriously mentally ill with an obsessive-compulsive neurosis, formerly diagnosed and treated briefly by a psychiatrist. Mr. H expressed many fears that his wife's illness was still evident and that it was going to affect their only child, then 4 years old. He complained that the child's extreme shyness and "backwardness" were likely manifestations of a developing neurosis, and he wished to file a motion for change of custody. Custody had been awarded to the wife at the time of the divorce more than a year before, and the husband had not contested that decision because his naval career and single life would have made it impossible for him to assume responsibility for the child.

The petitioner's attorney contacted me by telephone and discussed the case briefly with me. When I agreed to accept the case on the condition that I would be able to see all the parties involved whom I deemed significant, he told me that he, too, felt that this was the correct approach. However, the respondent's attorney, knowing that psychiatric data were to be the heart of the deciding matter, had already arranged to work with another psychiatrist. I knew the other psychiatrist well. In fact, he had been one of my residents in training at the local medical school where I had, for a time, supervised him in his own psychotherapy of patients. Furthermore, I had taught him forensic psychiatry in my seminar for the residents. I felt that he was more than capable of providing adequate help in this situation, and I told this to the referring attorney. However, he still wanted "his" psychiatrist to have a look. I agreed to become involved as long as I had *carte blanche.*

A few days later I saw the petitioner for the first time. I explained to him the same things I had expressed to the referring attorney. Mr. H told me that it was his understanding that all parties would see me as I wished, just as they had agreed to see Dr. Y, the psychiatrist hired by the respondent's attorney. I also explained to him my role as a child advocate despite my having been hired by his own attorney, and I explained that it was quite possible that my findings would not be helpful to his cause. I spelled out to him the possibility that I might recommend that his ex-wife retain custody, and he understood this.

Following my initial interview with the petitioner, I sent the following letter to both attorneys.

Sam Smith   John Jones
Attorney-at-Law   (and)   Attorney-at-Law
[Address]   [Address]
San Diego, California   San Diego, California

Gentlemen:
    Many thanks for agreeing that I serve as one of the psychiatric consultants in the child custody matter between Mr. H and his former wife, Mrs. H-1. I appreciate the confidence expressed in me via this choice, and I shall be pleased to work with you in an attempt to seek a solution to this controversy which is in the best interests of the child, Melina H.
    The purpose of this note is to let you both know the point of departure I use in these unfortunate situations. Each of you, of course, appropriately serves as an advocate for each contending party. I must serve as an advocate for the child, and I assume that Dr. Y, the other psychiatrist you have chosen for this effort, sees himself the same way although I have not communicated with him. In fact, I will not communicate with him unless I have both of your permissions to do so, although my own impression is that a much more meaningful report may emerge from both of us if there is intercommunication or cross-fertilization of ideas. I would be very grateful if the two of you would communicate and determine if Dr. Y and I should confer prior to the submission of our individual reports.
    Also, I would like to serve notice upon each of you that I probably will ask the two of you to meet jointly with me after I have completed my work with the other parties involved. I may have recommendations and findings which will need to be clarified so that they are completely and entirely understood by all of us. This may allow for further out-of-court conferences which we may hope will eliminate the need for an in-court hearing and judgment. In any case, however, it is important for all of us to maintain very open contact prior to and following the submission of the report. In child custody litigations, it behooves all of us, psychiatrists and attorneys alike, to attempt to ease and deal effectively with the necessarily hurt and likely vindictive feelings usually seen. The feelings of the child are, however, the paramount issue involved in the situation, and it is hoped that these can be protected. Please let me hear from you about this so that I may proceed accordingly. I shall not contact Dr. Y until I receive clearance from both of you, except for sending him a carbon copy of this.
    Thank you for your consideration and courtesy in this matter.

Very truly yours,
Melvin G. Goldzband, M.D., F.A.P.A.

The petitioner's attorney called me a few days after receipt of this letter. He told me that he had spoken with Attorney Smith, and both of them agreed with my point of departure with the sole exception that the respondent's attorney did not want me to communicate with "his" psychiatrist. I arranged follow-up appointments with Mr. H, and I contacted Mrs. H-1 as well. There was never any problem regarding cooperation of any of the parties. Mrs. H-1 signed a release form that allowed her previous psychiatrist to communicate with me about his contacts with her about a year and a half before. He responded to my request for information with the following note.

Dear Dr. Goldzband:
    My initial visit with Mrs. H-1 was [date]. Her husband had initiated the visit, and she accepted the idea of a psychiatric evaluation because they were both concerned about her preoccupation with cleanliness. I felt that Mrs. H-1 was manifesting acute signs and symptoms of an obsessive compulsive psychoneurotic. Our initial meeting was good, and Mrs. H-1 was very accepting of therapeutic invitations and was favorable to continued meetings. In essence, we met on a weekly basis and focused on patient's phobias and ambivalence about the marriage. I last saw her [date] and at that meeting patient continued working on her phobias and a meeting was scheduled for [date]. She called [date] to cancel. I felt she worked very well in therapy and saw her increasing awareness and growth; when she called to cancel the appointment, the concept of future therapy was left open. I felt my responsibilities as her therapist terminated at that point until she made future contact. I received a call some months later from her husband, in essence inquiring about her competency as a mother. I acknowledged the fact that she had worked with me in therapy, but such questions would be a breach of confidentiality and I did not feel I could be of help to him, and his questions regarding competency were more within a legal rather than psychiatric realm.

Yours truly,
Dr. X

My own workup of the case consisted of a series of interviews with both contesting parties, with the child, and with relatives. It took a number of weeks, and at its conclusion I submitted the following report to the petitioner's attorney:

Mr. John Jones, Attorney-at-Law,
[Address]
San Diego, California

Dear Mr. Jones:
    Thank you very much for referring the child custody matter of Melina H. to me. I saw your client, Mister H, in my office initially on [date] and again on [date]. Following my work-up with the entire family, I saw him

again on [date], during which time I discussed my findings and my recommendations with him. I also saw Mrs. H-1 in my office, initially on [date]
and again on [date]. Furthermore, I saw Mrs. H-2, in a private interview on
[date], and on [date]. I saw Mr. and Mrs. C. Mrs. C. is the older sister of
Mrs. H-1, and Mr. C. is a former co-worker of Mr. H, who actually introduced him to his first wife, Mrs. H-1. On [date] I evaluated Melina H.
She was brought to the office by her mother for the interview.

Over and above my own clinical findings, I administered similar psychological tests to Mr. H and his first wife. The test used was the Minnesota
Multiphasic Personality Inventory [MMPI], a highly validated, highly stan-
dardized screening test given to several hundreds of thousands of individuals in the United States and Canada. I used this to validate and buttress
my own clinical impressions which were, by the way, seconded by the tests.
[I have generally discontinued routine use of screening tests such as the
MMPI because my own experience has been that with effective presentation of clinical data, there is no need for buttressing. Obviously, if a *clinical*
situation arises wherein psychological tests are indicated, they should be used
forthwith.] I also communicated with Dr. X, a San Diego psychiatrist who
had seen Mrs. H-1 in psychotherapy some time ago. I understand that
another psychiatrist has been involved in this current child custody evaluation. I have not communicated with him regarding this matter nor have I
seen his report. However, I have discussed this case with the Probation Officer assigned to it, and she told me that my own findings were similar to
those of the other psychiatrist and that my impressions were quite similar to
those that she herself had gained of the matter.

During his two interviews, Mr. H discussed his own past history as well
as his history of the marriage. He described his first wife as a woman who
deceived him in many respects regarding marriageability. He says that she
lied to him about her age (she was much younger than she had stated to
him) and that she had absolutely no background or capacity for marriage.
He wanted her to live with his mother in order to learn some things about
marriage. In fact, he took her to Texas where his mother lived and where
they got married. He described his wife's subsequent germ phobia symptoms, and he described the difficulties that these made in their life. He
could bring no friends to the house. She would be constantly washing
everything he touched and washing everything in the house all the time. No
one could bring shoes into the home. He says that when they went out she
would not even be able to use a public toilet but instead would squat along
the roadside. Finally, he was able to find a psychiatrist of Greek extraction
to whom he sent her for treatment. However, it was only about a month
and a half after he sent her that he decided to leave.

In contrast, Mrs. H-1 defends herself admirably. She acknowledges
that she has always been very fussy about dirt, and she also acknowledges
that she would not tolerate her husband's friends in their home. However,
she described them as "pigs" who were always drunk and disorderly. There
is a great deal of resentment toward Mr. H for having married her and immediately abandoning her by going out to sea, leaving her with no support
or encouragement. Her older sister was living in Hawaii at the time of their
marriage, and she had no one in San Diego to whom she could turn. Her
husband always deprecated her, her "foreign ways" and her accent. On
several occasions he struck her, and she described one episode in which he

threatened to take her out to the desert and kill her. As regards the child, she describes her as a clever and delightful girl who is perfectly normal in every way. They go out to play at the neighborhood recreation yard, and Mrs. H-1 takes Melina H to her sister's home quite frequently so that the child can play with her two young male cousins. Likewise, there are several other children in the immediate area with whom she can and does play. Mrs. H-1 states that there are many children passing through their home and that there is no problem regarding this at this time. She plans on sending Melina H to pre-school.

The current Mrs. H-2 strikes me as a level and sensible individual who attempted to describe Melina as a girl whom she thought might have had problems in the past. However, these had not ever really been noted specifically by her, although she thought that she and her husband might be able to provide more advantages for the child than the child would obtain via living with her mother. She says that the child often is shy and hangs back, but that her *own* daughter, by bringing her into her *own* circle of playmates, has done a great deal for Melina who no longer acts quite as shyly.

Mr. and Mrs. C describe Mr. H as a very aggressive and overbearing individual who demands a great deal from everyone. They see him pushing the little girl into premature independence via his expectations. At times, they feel that he does not allow her to be the little girl that she is, and that often he rough-houses with her as if she were the little boy that he always wished for. Mrs. C described her younger sister as the spoiled baby of the family. She said that there were no indications of any developing obsessive-compulsive neurosis during her childhood or adolescence. In fact, she was a rather spoiled adolescent who was interested only in having a good time and in looking pretty. She was popular, and she agrees with Mrs. H-1 who acknowledges that she had considerable freedom for a Greek teenage girl in her homeland.

Finally and centrally, the session with Melina H was deliberately designed as a "stress interview." My specific function with the child was to determine whether or not she was adversely affected by the mother's obsessive-compulsive neurosis and whether or not a similar pattern was developing in the child. The answer is definitely in the negative. Co-incidentally, it was garbage collection day when I saw Melina H, and she had prepared the office garbage together, dumping wastebaskets and playing a great deal with this material. Also, I had prepared the office plants for Melina H to water. I had done so in a specific and highly symbolic way which might be expected to provoke a great deal of anxiety in an obsessive-compulsive child. I had her water the plants in the toilet bowl! This proved to be no obstacle whatsoever for the little girl who cheerfully carried on her light and charming conversation during this entire period. Incidentally, her mother was there observing this during the entire time, and it might be expected that she, too, would become exceedingly anxious during those types of procedures. There was no anxiety noted in Mrs. H-1 during this episode.

My clinical conclusions are that Melina H is developing into a normal young girl who has a good and deep relationship with her mother. I see no reason to break it because there is no indication that the relationship is actually or potentially harmful to the child. I discussed this recommendation with Mr. H, and I urged him to continue the weekend visitation with the child. He is concerned that his doing so might cause more problems than blessings for the girl. I urged him to continue seeing the child and taking her into his new family because she had a good relationship with him and with the family, and I felt that continuing this would be helpful to her. However, I pointed out a number of instances in which I felt that he had expected a great deal of the child, and in fact, might be doing the child some harm by "looking at her through a microscope" for indications of illness. He agreed that this might be so, and agreed that he ought to accept the child as she was and for whom she was. He discussed problems he and his first wife are having regarding visitation. These appeared to be manifestations of residual rage the two of them felt toward each other and I urged him to contact the Conciliation Court of the Superior Court for custody counseling. I urge that counselors there see both Mr. H and his first wife so that their resentment toward each other will not spill over into the relationships they make (and sometimes break) over their daughter.

Mr. H appeared to accept most of my recommendations, although he became markedly anxious when I was especially confrontative regarding his attitudes and orientations toward the child. I think, however, he has the capacity to integrate this material and even to utilize it for the purposes of changing into a more easy going person with her. I certainly hope that he does, and I again urge that he avail himself of the opportunity for custody counseling at the Conciliation Court.

Once again, thank you for referring this case to me. I hope that my findings and recommendations are helpful to all involved in it.

Very truly yours,
Melvin G. Goldzband, M.D., F.A.P.A.

Upon receiving my report, the petitioner's attorney called me to say that he was not at all surprised at my findings and that he had discussed the possibility of a negative report from me when he first saw Mr. H. The attorney told me that there had been some suspicions on his part that the accusations of psychiatric illness were overstressed by the petitioner because of a number of factors, not the least of which was the original award of custody to the wife.

I never did talk with the respondent's attorney. Likewise, I never spoke with Dr. Y, except informally at a psychiatric society meeting a few months after the disposition of the case. As it turned out, there was no real need to speak with anyone. The petitioner's attorney sat down with the petitioner and discussed my findings and recommendations. It may be recalled that I had also talked with Mr. H about these issues before writing the report to his lawyer. Although Mr. H was ostensibly agreeable to the recommendation that Melina H stay with her mother and that he contact the conciliation court for counseling about custody and visitation problems, the seconding of these recommendations by his own attorney provided a real force that led to the decision to drop his motion to change custody.

It must be stressed, however, that in many cases adverse findings do not lead to decisions to drop the proposed court battles. Sometimes the degree and depth of bitterness are so great that the petitioners cannot accept the realistic prospects of defeat in court, and they insist on continuing their crusades. They fail to recognize the neurotic components of this grossly overdetermined behavior, and often considerable ventilating is needed before they can begin to recognize it—if then. In this particular case, multiple factors were at work. Two psychiatrists, hired by opposing attorneys and each working totally independently, reached identical conclusions, as did the investigating probation worker—and, perhaps most significantly, as had the petitioner's own attorney.

Regardless of whether or not my final session with Mr. H was considered counseling or therapy, I believe that it was helpful. It allowed for considerable expression of feeling on his part and for supportive interpretations of his feelings and wishes on my part. This process permitted his own attorney to deal with the problem of the negative reports realistically, which in turn allowed Mr. H to accept the situation realistically.

The Doctor as Advocate: A Lesson in Anxiety

Most psychotherapists avoid taking their own friends into treatment. Doing so destroys friendships and possibly even destroys the friends because of the therapist's lack of objective and dispassionate judgment. Personal involvements based on deep feelings can be dangerous when they emerge and become insinuated into treatment or medicolegal cases.

This chapter describes a situation that, by rights, should not have occurred but did occur because of my own meddling. Charitably, my actions might best be described as inappropriate, but bad examples can be as instructive as good ones.

Both the petitioner and the respondent in this case had been well known to me for nearly fifteen years. The husband especially became quite close to me and to my family following the couple's separation and eventual divorce. He is an active member of the community, outstanding in his profession, and capable of using his remarkable skills to create and expand a thriving business organization with contacts and contracts the world over. The aggressiveness he was able to harness in the business arena was nowhere in evidence in his close relationships, however, and the deterioration of his marriage was painful to watch. He was unable to assert himself effectively either with his wife or within the framework of the emerging divorce settlement, which was worked out for both parties by one lawyer, another old family friend. Instead, he was beset with feelings of guilt and ambivalence about his own role in the failed marriage. The wife, in contrast, struck out angrily, using the contemporary jargon of the feminist movement against her husband. She eventually moved out of the house, leaving him with their three children. Only the eldest, aged 10 at the time, was biologically theirs. The two adopted youngsters were a girl, then 8, and a boy, nearly 3. Each of the two younger children was adopted at the age of 5 months.

Like other friends of the husband, we were occasionally involved in efforts to find adequate housekeepers, to bring him and the children to our home for "R and R," and so forth. As close as we had been before, we became even closer. He followed my advice and sought professional counseling to help him through the rigors of the divorce. However, the counseling relationship was short-lived. After more than a year, the interlocutory decree provided joint and equal custody of the children, with physical custody to be held by the father. Joint custody, as pointed out elsewhere in this book, although theoretically a valuable instrument, rarely works in practice because the basic goodwill needed by both parents is usually lacking. It often serves unwittingly as an invitation to more muscle flexing by the less satisfied parent. (See part I, chapter 3, for a further discussion of the problems of joint custody.)

The husband reared the children successfully, often struggling through crises that usually seemed humorous only in retrospect. His ex-wife lived nearby and often telephoned the children, and the children saw her frequently. Her relationship with her daughter grew closer, but her feelings toward the two boys were never warm. They were always tinged by expressions of hostility toward men in general, expressions that had, in fact, also been verbalized to me (though not *at* me) in conversation when I happened to see her. What was most apparent, however, was her penchant for getting at her ex-husband by constantly shifting her wishes and demands about having the children visit her, stay with her over weekends, and so forth. This became even more transparent after the husband remarried (the ex-wife has never remarried), when his household was greatly expanded by the addition of his new wife and her three daughters. The husband was apparently unable and unwilling to set firm limits to the visitation patterns, and the situation was creating considerable stress in his new household. Plans made for trips, for instance, always seemed to be set askew by the ex-wife's demands for the children at those times regardless of previous arrangements. The husband rationalized his obvious passivity (and probable unconscious, guilt-induced ambivalence) by saying that he felt it was important for the children to maintain their relationships with their mother.

Finally, his ex-wife, using the same attorney who had handled the original divorce action, filed an order to show cause requiring modification of visitation:

> The oldest child is now emancipated. The two younger children, now 13 and 9, wish to spend time with both parents. This is feasible and desirable. In the circumstances now existing, the father refuses to consent to this arrangement. I request that custody of the two minor children be awarded to me with reasonable visitation with the father, respondent. . . .

The husband sought the aid of another attorney, and a response was filed. In it the husband stated that over the past three years his desire to permit increased visitation by the mother

> . . . has caused a situation in which my former wife has seen the children virtually every weekend and has had constant contact during the week. The net result of this expanded visitation has been a developing lack of continuity. I find that my former wife has been using visitation as a method of improving her relationship with the children at my expense. . . . My former wife has always been using visitation as a way of portraying me as an ogre, while calling upon the children's love and sympathy. I do not wish in any

way to limit my former wife's relationship with our children. I do, however, feel that it is necessary to draw some lines as to the extent and nature of this relationship. . . .

In a letter to his attorney the husband expanded his thoughts:

My own personal belief is that kids have to live somewhere full time, with proper visitation from the other parent. So, I guess my own gut reaction is that I should have the kids full time or not at all. After six years of being both father and mother most of the time, the thought of losing my kids scares the hell out of me. . . .

As it does so often, the maneuvering dragged on for months. During that time considerable stress was placed on my friend and his families, original and new. I spent much time with him, trying to encourage him and assuring him that the ideas and actions of his attorney seemed quite appropriate. I also tried to get him to recognize his overreactions to the maneuvers of his ex-wife and her attorney.

One day my friend told me that his ex-wife's attorney had proposed that a psychiatrist be appointed to evaluate the children and determine what might serve their best interests. When he told me which child psychiatrist was selected, I was pleased because I had known and liked the man for years. This psychiatrist was well qualified in his field, but I was surprised that he had accepted this task because he had always told me that he assiduously avoided child-custody proceedings. The psychiatrist's interview with my friend was a catastrophe; the psychiatrist took considerable umbrage at the father's contention that he had served as both parents for many years, and at his resentment over his ex-wife's attempts to get the children. I was told that a number of harsh and sarcastic comments were passed between them. This was unfortunate and unseemly, but it must be understood that the psychiatrist was having his own personal problems. He had recently divorced, and he too had custody of his children. One must wonder what he unconsciously saw of himself—and rejected—in my friend. But such speculations can play no role in the legal process. What did play a role was the psychiatrist's report, sent to each attorney and reprinted here in its entirety.

Dear Sirs:
    I have completed a psychiatric evaluation of the Wright children's custody issue, and submit my findings.
    My opinions were formed after spending six hours with Mary Wright, Frank and Sarah Wright, and David, Kim and Bruce. I have paid attention to everyone's feelings and desires, but a commitment to serve the best interest of the children has been my first priority.
    I suggest that Kim and Bruce be granted their wish to make their mother's home their principal residence. This is in accordance with their

clearly stated wishes, and it is entirely consistent with their mother's wish.

While it is true that their father and stepmother provide an accepting and loving home for Kim and Bruce, the children eagerly want this chance to be closer to their mother. Neither their decision nor my opinion should in any way be construed to reflect unfavorably on anyone, as it is clear that all adults involved are conscientious parents, devoted to their children's best interests.

I would hope that the visitation arrangements could be worked out in a flexible and casual manner, and furthermore, that this entire matter could be resolved quickly, amicably, and informally.

Very truly yours,

Regardless of its conclusions, this is an inadequate report. Limited to conclusory statements with no bases, it cannot help the court in its decision-making process. Certainly, for a man who had always verbalized his unwillingness to become involved in litigation, this report must be seen as paradoxical because it mandates participation. It certainly cannot be admitted into the proceedings by stipulation; it demands interrogation and cross-examination. Nonetheless, it was sent as it was, with the predictable result that my friend nearly collapsed from fear that his case was lost.

At this point love overcame good judgment, and I determined to mount my white charger and save the day. I told my friend that I would communicate with his attorney, whom I did not know, and would offer some ideas that the attorney might find helpful. The following letter to the lawyer was the result.

Dear Mister _____:

Perhaps it is inappropriate, even impertinent for me to write to you regarding this matter. After all, I have not been asked. Besides, my knowledge of all parties in the Wright child custody case extended back fourteen years, and I have been through numerous crises in the Wright household. My role there was as a friend, albeit one with particular training and background. This is the role I am assuming at this time, too. I can hardly be considered by anyone involved here as a distant, cool, solely clinical observer. I have seen too much over the years to be detached about the Wrights, and I have felt too much along with everyone concerned. However, no one can deny that I have some special qualifications to express my opinions in this matter—asked for or not. I have seen a large number of individuals involved in custody litigation, and have written and lectured extensively on this subject. Therefore, I think I must be considered as more than just an interfering busybody. I have weighed very carefully what I have written here, and the end result, although still lengthy, stems from several drafts and stringent editing. I have assiduously tried to step outside of myself and look at what I have said, trying to be as objective as possible. I cannot state whether or not I have succeeded, but I doubt that any psychiatrist would dispute the relevance of most of the points I have made here.

I am submitting this specifically to you because you are representing the person closest to me now. If you feel there is any merit in the material I am presenting here, I hope that you share it with _____, Mary's lawyer. I have not been in touch with her or with her lawyer since the current litigation began, and I fear that it would be seen by them as an even greater intrusion than this one if I communicated directly with them.

It is best if custody disputes are settled outside the adversary arena. Bringing the fights into court often creates further traumas for all concerned, especially the children. They are the people most in a "no-win" situation. Regardless of how they are treated, regardless of whether or not they are interviewed about their "choices" (which may not be real choices, after all), and regardless of the decision, they lose. Doubt and guilt often plague them for years, and often this becomes the nidus for future psychiatric disturbances. I can only hope very hard that a courtroom battle can be avoided for their sakes, and for the sakes of Frank and Mary as well. Of course, the mutual decisions reached in such a situation would have to reflect the real best interests of the kids. I have some thoughts about that.

In a sense, I went through the Wrights' divorce with them, especially with Frank. I have been a close friend of the couple. We had all shared a great deal of our lives with each other, and I could not really say then that I was closer to one than to the other. However, when the divorce action *per se* started and Mary moved out, Frank and I became increasingly close. I can attest to the serious, sometimes agonized concern he had for the children and their welfare during those difficult times. We were often together with him and the children, and we observed them all closely. Frank's ups-and-downs with various housekeepers were shared with us until he was able to find someone who could steadily and dependably oversee the needs of the children. On occasion, I would see Mary, usually coming across her casually in a store, in an auto repair shop, etc., and we would talk briefly. Despite the brevity of these contacts, I never felt enmity from her toward my wife or me despite our continuing and increasing closeness to Frank. In fact, my impression was that she often portrayed much sorrow and regret that her life and her relationships with former friends had changed. However, she would always verbalize, rather defensively I thought, her happiness at being free. To her, freedom from a domestic existence was paramount, and she saw herself as a liberated woman who no longer was enshackled by her submerging role of wife-mother. She would verbalize about this at length, and within these verbalizations would be demeaning remarks about the children and their constant demands upon her which no longer would seem so depleting to her. There were also many remarks reflecting her resentment toward men generally, and it was surprising that she would include David and Kim within that framework. I specifically recall wondering at Frank's allegations that she had verbalized such hostility toward him and the two male children just because they were male, and then wondering at what I had heard from her, myself, after Mary verbalized those same feelings to me! On one occasion, I was concerned about what appeared to be considerable preoccupation on her part, a state which led to her responding only tangentially to my own greeting or to the other, small-talk remarks I made to her. I last saw her several months ago, in a line in a cafeteria, and we spoke briefly but warmly. She gave me a hug which was appreciated and reciprocated. We were glad to see each other, and I hope we always shall be.

In my opinion, a number of factors need to be weighed here. The most obvious one centers about the fact that when Mary left originally, she verbalized that she did not want the children or the responsibility for them, thus leaving their care to Frank who worked hard providing this for them. My observations indicate that he has done a good job with them, now aided by his current wife whose care and attention toward the children are quite genuine. Perhaps I should point out at this time that I had known Sarah Wright, too, long before her marriage to Frank—in fact, prior to her divorce from her first husband. I know her excellent capacities and abilities as a mother, and I also know the children she has reared so well.

We must be very careful here not to point accusing fingers at Mary because of her unwillingness at the time of the divorce to continue her role as a mother. Nonetheless, it is very important to try to determine what has led to her change of heart now. Why has she now determined that she wants custody of Kim and Bruce at this time? Why now, and why not last year or next year? In my practice of psychotherapy, I have learned to seek reasons for changes occurring *when they do* because they often highlight other changes or stresses in the individuals' lives.

My knowledge of Frank and Sarah, and of the way that they have been leading their lives with their children, indicates to me that there have been no upsetting or jolting changes occurring within their household to cause them or the children to seek changes in custody status now. I do not know what has been going on in Mary's life, although I have the impression that she is living alone and that she may be feeling the need for more companionship and love. Certainly, those needs are hardly abnormal! We all have them. I would wonder, however, about the appropriateness of having them fulfilled by children who, themselves, are hungry seekers after love and attention for themselves. Perhaps mutuality of love and caring will be good for all concerned, but I wonder about the need to alter the living situations of all the children in order to achieve this. If Mary feels a need for more from her children—or, if they feel more of a need for more from her (and I believe that they must feel such a need as compensation for longstanding feelings of unconscious rejection since the divorce), I am sure that these needs can be fulfilled via increasing Mary's visitations with the children. Frank's household, with its large number of children who seem to do very well with each other (with one exception to be discussed subsequently), ought to provide the baseline for the existence of the kids, especially for Bruce who is pre-adolescent and who needs increasingly the presence of close, significant male figures. Insofar as I am aware, there is no significant male in Mary's life. In fact, she probably harbors the same negative feelings toward men that she expressed to me some time ago, even if they are no longer as floridly expressed. In his current home, Bruce has his father and his older brother. Even if David goes away to school, his presence will still be felt in the household where he has become quite a significant, even adored figure. He will be spoken of positively and will be missed if he goes away, thereby keeping his semblance at home. This will hardly be the case at Mary's. As I saw it, her relationship with David over the years has been tenuous, and it rarely appeared warm or productive. If Mary has developed a need or a wish to gain increased closeness with Bruce, and Bruce, of course, has a longstanding need for demonstrated acceptance from his mother, they both should have that need fulfilled. Mary should be able to see more of Bruce. Her visitation privileges should be increased and she should be encouraged to spend much more positive time with him. However, the boy's needs for strong and significant, close male figures are now greater than ever, and taking him away from his current household for more than extended visits will be potentially harmful to him. There is nothing I know of in the relationship between Bruce, Frank and Sarah which is not positive and productive. The boy appears to be doing exceedingly well.

This is not quite the case with Kim, whose relations with Frank and Sarah have become quite stormy. Of all three Wright children, Kim was always the closest to her mother; after all, she was the only non-male. Her relations within the current Wright household are difficult because of many adolescent stresses with their impetus toward independence (and their concomitant advertising that independence is the last thing wanted!). Sarah's own daughters are all quite accomplished, and there is considerable competition within the household, leading to much jealousy on Kim's part on the bases of insecurity and consciousness of lack of status.

As a behavioral scientist, I would think that the stresses upon Kim in her current household ought to be the subject of clinical investigation and evaluation, and that therapy ought to be instituted so that she need not feel as she does about herself. I would predict that her running to Mama will not solve these problems of self-image, especially for a 14-year-old girl who is turning into quite an attractive young woman. She will soon have dozens of boys flitting about her. What effect will this have on Mary if she maintains her feelings toward men and their roles as sexual predators? What effect will this have on the relationship between Mary and her daughter who will relish the male attention her mother sees as so problematic? I would predict that if Kim goes to live with her mother, that relationship will become even stormier in the end than the one from which Kim now wishes to run. Perhaps she ought to try the relationship with Mary if she is insistent, but in either event I would recommend meaningful and deep counseling for the girl. If she does not have this, I fear that the eventual rupture of the relationship with Mary may be irreparable, a situation I am sure Mary would want to avoid at all costs.

Finally, as regards Kim *and* Bruce, their mutual relationship must be evaluated. It is a poor one, with much resentment toward the boy by his older sister. She thereby identifies strongly with her mother. Sibling rivalry is seen in most families but is generally offset insofar as effect is concerned by good and deep relationships with parents. In contrast, the effect upon Bruce of his living with two women who have expressed or who do express hostility towards him would be very harmful to him. What feelings does Kim have about her having to take care of Bruce after school, until her mother will be coming home from work? What feelings does Bruce have about his sister taking care of him in that setting? All of these points must be weighed very carefully.

Unsolicited as they are, these are some of my feelings, fears and concerns about this pending custody litigation. I hope that the contesting parties will be able to sit down and make determinations which will be satisfactory to some degree for everyone, with as little jostling of the children as possible. I hear that Frank will see fit to let Mary be with Bruce and Kim as much as they all need to be with each other. I hope that Mary will recognize the need for Bruce to remain very close to his father at this increasingly stressful time in his pre-adolescent life. I further hope that

Mary will see the need for therapy for Kim if Kim insists upon living with her or not, so that her self-image will be strengthened to the point at which she no longer feels threatened by the competition she faces in her current household and which she will face all of her life.

If I can be of any help in this hurtful and difficult matter, I shall be pleased to do whatever I can. Please remember that I speak at this time as a friend of long standing to both parties, and that I am most convinced that each ought to lead long, happy and productive lives with ever-closer relationships with their children whose love they each need—and who need each of their love. Thank you for your consideration and your courtesy.

Very truly yours,
Melvin G. Goldzband, M.D., F.A.P.A.

My friend's lawyer received my unsolicited letter with grace and courtesy, and his client began to feel a little relief. This was short-lived, however, because he was soon faced with an evaluation by the probation department. My friend feared that they would also submit a negative report, just as had the psychiatrist, for reasons that appeared to be highly personal and subjective. With emotional support, he was able to follow through. Both attorneys also furnished the probation worker with copies of the report of the appointed psychiatrist and of my letter as well (my friend's lawyer had sent a copy of my letter to Mary's lawyer right away), as well as letters from the children's pediatrician and from the youngest child's learning-disabilities therapist. By now it was only the youngest child about whom the storm raged. The eldest was never in contention, always wishing to remain with his father, and the girl had acted out so much against her father and his new family that it was deemed advisable for her to move to her mother's home, at least on a temporary basis. This provided considerable relief for everyone after a very stormy period.

The interview with the probation worker went smoothly enough, and her report was quite favorable to the idea of my friend retaining physical custody of his children. Finally the case found its way into court. It was heard over a three-day period that proved grossly traumatic to just about everyone involved. Interestingly, it was decided that the psychiatrist's report would be ignored, and he was not involved in the case further by the ex-wife's attorney. My own letter was not admitted into evidence per se but it formed a significant part of the basis for the probation worker's report and was quoted liberally within her report.

The court determined that the following measures must be taken.

1. Petitioner is awarded the care, custody and control of the minor child of the parties, Kim Wright, born _____, with the right of reasonable visitation reserved to respondent.

2. Respondent is awarded the care, custody and control of the minor child of the parties, Bruce Wright, born _____. Petitioner shall have visitation with said child at the following times and places:

a. Alternate weekends, commencing 5:00 p.m. on Fridays and ending Sunday at 5:00 p.m.
b. On the remaining weekends, one day commencing 5:00 p.m. and terminating at 5:00 p.m. the next day.
c. On Tuesdays and Thursdays commencing after school and ending 9:30 p.m. that evening. Said visitation shall not interfere with the minor child's homework, and petitioner is specifically ordered to encourage the minor child to complete all homework assignments during said visitation.

3. That the parties are mutually restrained and enjoined from discussing with the minor child, Bruce Wright, or discussing in the minor child's presence, any questions pertaining to visitation or child custody.

4. That the parties are mutually restrained and enjoined from speaking in a derogatory or disparaging manner of the other party in the presence of the minor child or commenting upon or discussing with the minor children the lifestyle of the other parent.

5. That respondent shall arrange an appointment for psychological counseling for the minor child, Bruce, and to include family counseling for the respondent and his present wife. That said counselor shall provide reports to the Court and _____, attorney for petitioner, within three weeks of the date of commencement of counseling and periodically thereafter.

6. That the visitation schedule heretofore established shall be reviewed by the court upon the court's receipt of the above mentioned psychiatric reports.

7. That the respondent shall consult with petitioner regarding the health, education, and welfare of the minor child, Bruce, but that respondent shall have final decisions after first giving fair consideration to petitioner's views in these regards.

8. That respondent shall pay to petitioner as and for the support and maintenance of the minor child, Kim, the sum of $150.00 per month commencing _____, and continuing until such time as the minor child reaches the age of eighteen (18) years, is sooner emancipated, or until further order of the court.

9. That this court shall continue personal jurisdiction in this matter until further order of the court.

This case exemplifies the traumas imposed on all the participants, even those who stimulate the actions in ways that often seem self-destructive. Certainly many people invite litigation in unconscious attempts to stimute external controls over their own fearsome impulses. This is one reason people may press hopeless suits: the petitioners need the courts to stop them. From the tragedy of this case, however, there have been some beneficial results. My friend and his second wife have become closer than ever; their marriage was strengthened in the cauldron. The adolescent daughter appears to be making an excellent adjustment, and she often appears spontaneously at her father's home for informal and relaxed visits. Counseling with a highly competent child psychiatrist has resulted in increased fluency in the relationship between the youngest child and the family; and the child's own activity and learning level have been stimulated markedly.

For personal reasons, of course, I am pleased that the case turned out as it did. I must admit that my own ego was satisfied by everyone's responses to my self-invited role. Nevertheless, it was a gross error on my part to intervene as I did. Earlier, perhaps, I should have communicated informally with my friend's attorney, even though I knew that he was being informed by my friend of our talks together. But that, too, might have been unwarranted meddling. Like most professionals, I pride myself on my estimations of my own judgment and prudence. However, these traits sometimes fail in the heat of emotional situations. Anxiety is contagious, especially when it emanates from people emotionally close to the recipient. In this case, it infected me. All of us who work closely with people in need and in conflict must become increasingly aware of our own capacities to be moved by them and to have our own objectivity swayed, even when they are not, as in this case, people already close to us.

10 The Psychiatrist as Liaison

A psychiatric cliché states that patients really present very few problems—*but the families*! Despite their training and understanding of family psychodynamics and interrelationships, all counselors can become frustrated by interfering families. All the illogical internal conflicts between family members may be funeled through the person who is the ostensible subject of a medicolegal examination, with further illogical behavior as a result.

This case represents such a situation. Dr. Jane Doe, a young physician and daughter of two physicians, had married another physician, Dr. John Doe. The couple had three sons. As an only child, Jane had been especially close to her parents. As often happens, this had led to difficulties because the parents were very controlling, demanding, and clinging. Jane's mother retired from her own medical practice when she and her husband moved to San Diego a few years ago, but the father, Dr. Smith, continued working in his specialty, developing a large and lucrative practice. Jane and her husband finished their medical-school training in the midwestern town in which they were both reared. They came to San Diego for further specialty training, each in a different field. (They chose San Diego, of course, because Jane's parents were there.) Jane's training was delayed by her pregnancies, and the husband began to practice while the wife restarted her specialty training. The marriage had been foundering for a long time, and the crowning blow was struck when the wife developed a relationship with another doctor at the hospital where she was pursuing her training.

The impending and actual breakup of their daughter's marriage was a shock to the Smiths. The mother became severely depressed; the father ranted, raved, and attempted to manipulate everyone. Accustomed to giving orders, in his anxiety he did so even more than usual, ordering his daughter to stop seeing the other man and to return to her husband, and ordering the husband to take her back. As might be expected, everyone ignored the orders, which only increased in volume and intensity. As the mother became increasingly morose in anticipation of the loss of her grandsons, the father became every more bellicose. When his daughter's husband saw an attorney for the purpose of filing a divorce action, the father decided that something must be done about the situation. He thereupon stopped me in the hallway of a hospital one day and, over coffee, told me about his impressions of what had been going on, all the time pointing out how he had tried to tell everyone the right thing to do. Finally, he told *me* what to do: I was to see his daughter and talk some sense into her. Thereupon she would give up her crazy romantic attachment and would return to her husband—and, of course, to the bosom of her own parents—along with her prized children.

I agreed to see Dr. Jane Doe only if *she* wanted to talk with me, and I told Dr. Smith that I would set up an appointment with her only if *she* would call me and tell me that she wanted this. She dutifully called me, and I saw her for four sessions. She really did not want psychotherapy as I saw her needing it—that is, as a process of introspection and a recognition of a need for change in the way she operated. The changes I refer to here are not related to her romantic attachments but rather to her clinging, parental attachments. She and I talked about her obvious (to me) feelings of need for her parents, which she denied, and about her likely resentment toward them, which she also denied. In part that resentment had been reponsible for her destruction of her marriage, which her parents had seen as ideal. I saw Dr. Jane Doe as full of rage and as a severely dependent, manipulative person. She had learned early in life that she could move her parents into any position of advantage to herself, and that they were always available to bail her out of whatever problems arose for her. The concept of growth through therapy did not interest her, but we parted amicably. I encouraged her to call me if she ever decided that she wanted to look into herself for her own sake, not for that of the marriage or her parents.

As might have been expected, I heard nothing until six months later, when Dr. Smith stopped me again in the hospital hallway. Following his daughter's cessation of appointments with me, he had avoided contact with me and had even discontinued referring patients to me. Dr. Smith asked me if I knew about his daughter's beginning psychotherapy with Dr. Z and about her recent suicide attempt. This was all news to me, and I told him so, accenting my positive feeling about his daughter's seeing as competent a therapist as Dr. Z. Characteristically, the father asked me to see his daughter again because the suicide attempt was so upsetting to all of them. He was very much afraid that the upcoming divorce hearings and the husband's motion to gain custody of the children would be too upsetting to his wife. The unspoken but obvious concern was that the grandchildren would be spirited away and not seen again if the husband gained custody. I told Dr. Smith that I would be pleased to help in any way I could but that, if his daughter already was seeing a competent psychiatrist, I certainly could not interfere in the situation.

Jane Doe called me the next day, but I told her that I would have to clear up some details before I saw her. I called Dr. Z and told him about the confusing issues that, totally unsolicited, seemed to be spinning around me. Dr. Z was still seeing his patient and planned to continue seeing her for some time to come. He was very concerned about the possibility of having to be drawn into the litigation. Aside from the distasteful aspects of that situation, he especially realized that serving as an expert witness for this patient might well jeopardize the therapy relationship. He jumped at my suggestion that I might serve as a liaison, functioning as an independent examiner of his patient and then serving as the expert witness. Dr. Z agreed to meet with me after I had finished my evaluation of his patient and to comment on my conclusions as freely as he could without destroying confidentiality.

I called Mr. Y, Jane Doe's lawyer, and told him of this plan. He was enthusiastic and agreed to call the opposing attorney to seek his approval as well. The opposing attorney, Mr. X, an old friend of mine, called me himself to discuss this novel approach. I believe he agreed to this plan more out of friendship for me than out of respect for the necessarily inviolate quality of the therapy relationship, although he was well able to appreciate that necessity.

I saw Dr. Jane Doe for five sessions for the purpose of independent evaluation. During that time she continued to see Dr. Z uninterruptedly, as she had following her suicide attempt several weeks before. After my sessions with her, I consulted with Dr. Z. It was apparent that we were in substantial agreement about his patient, about her beginning new growth, and about her capacity to function as a good mother despite the obvious psychopathology. The husband's attorney called me to set up a deposition to be taken in this matter. We arranged it, and I called Dr. Jane Doe's attorney, Mr. Y. He was not available then, and he never responded either to that call or to my two subsequent calls.

In contrast, Dr. Jane Doe's father, Dr. Smith, called me several times, usually at home in the evening, to ask for assurances that I would testify favorably about his daughter. On one occasion his wife called me in tears, pleading that I *must* see that her daughter retained custody of the children because she would die if her grandchildren were taken away. The following day, I called Dr. Smith about his wife's panic and suggested that she might benefit from seeing a psychiatrist during these exceptional times. He minimized that need, characteristically asserting that he could handle her just as he had handled everything and everyone else. He would give her some tranquilizers, he said. I ought not to worry about his daughter's attorney, either, he continued, because he was in constant contact with him and had succeeded in keeping him off my back. When I protested that it was desirable for me to meet with that lawyer if I were appearing as an expert witness in his case, Dr. Smith insisted that I leave the whole thing to him. Another call by me to Attorney Y also met with no response, a real testimonial to the strength of Dr. Smith's assertive and domineering personality.

Thus, without any consultation with the attorney or preparation by him, I appeared at the prescribed time and place for the deposition. Ordinarily I would not appear in court or at a deposition without a prior conference with the referring attorney. The only familiar faces at this deposition were those of Dr. Jane Doe and her *opposing* attorney. I was introduced to her divorcing husband, Dr. John Doe, and—finally—to her attorney, Mr. Y. I was surprised that Dr. Smith was not present. The deposition transcript was as follows:

Examination
by Attorney X

Q   Would you state your full name, please?

A   My name is Melvin G. Goldzband. The last name spelled G-o-l-d-z-b-a-n-d.

Q   You are a medical doctor with a specialty in psychiatry?

A   That is correct.

Q   Where are your offices?

A   3242 Fourth Avenue in San Diego.

Q   Doctor, you've had your deposition taken before, have you not?

A   Yes, I have.

Q   You've also testified in Superior Court proceedings here in San Diego?

A   That's correct.

Q   You are completely familiar with the deposition process?

A   Yes, I am.

Q   Are you presently treating Jane Doe?

A   I'm presently seeing Jane Doe. I am not treating her as much as I am observing her. There is another psychiatrist who is engaged in the process of treatment with her.

Q   Who is the treating psychiatrist?

A   Dr. Z.

Q   How did Jane Doe happen to be referred to your office?

A   Well, Jane Doe was originally referred to my office this past summer. She was referred to me, basically, by her father, who knew me and with whom I worked in many cases at General Hospital. He asked me if I would see her because she was upset and depressed.

Q   So, your first office visit from Mrs. Doe was on [date]?

A   That's right.

Q   How many times have you seen her thereafter?

A   In June and July, I saw her for a total of four sessions. She came back to see me again the first of December, and from the first of December, I saw her, including yesterday, for a total of five visits. That's plus the four this past summer.

Q Do the duration of those visits with Mrs. Doe vary?

A No, I see her for about 45 minutes each time.

Q Have you taken a complete history from her as to prior psychiatric consultations?

A This past summer, I talked with her about her history.

Q Had she seen a psychiatrist, another psychiatrist before she saw you on [date]?

A Yes. There was a time in the Bay Area, in San Francisco, that she saw someone, but briefly, and there was no follow-up therapy.

Q Do you recall or does your history show the year that she saw the psychiatrist?

A No—

Q —in the bay area?

A I don't have that information.

Q But from your history, that was the only previous psychiatric consultation she had?

A So far as my knowledge.

Q Did the history, prior to her seeing you, record any hospitalization of any type relating to an emotional or mental distress or disturbance?

A Prior to June, no.

Q When Mrs. Doe was in to see you in June and July for these four sessions, what was the nature of the problem that she was having at that time?

A Mrs. Doe was upset and confused, concerned over the deteriorating relationship with her husband and a possible relationship with another doctor, as well as concerned over the relationship with her parents who were, in turn, quite concerned about her; and this seemed to be going round and round. This is what led to her coming to see me.

Q Did you form any opinion during those four sessions in June and July as to an identifiable condition or problem that she had?

A Yes, I did.

Q What was that opinion?

A Well, on the basis of the four sessions that I had with her at the time, the opinion that I formed was really that of a somewhat immature dependent girl who was symptomatically depressed and frightened over losing the source of dependency that she had always counted on.

The relationship with her parents is a very tenuous one, and the relationship with her husband had deteriorated. There was really no countable-on relationship with the other man with whom she had been attempting to develop a relationship; and she was by and large, feeling upset and very abandoned, not knowing exactly which way to go.

I thought at the time that it would be a wise thing for her if she would consider psychotherapy because, it seemed to me, for a person of her intelligence and discernment and background and apparent capacity and ability, that this kind of behavior represented something that ought to be corrected and could be.

Q What was your recommendation to her at the time—that she seek psychotherapy?

A That's right.

Q Did you actually make specific recommendations to her at that time?

A I told her that she seemed to be very, very ambivalent, that she had a lot of mixed feelings about coming to see me and the idea of really getting involved in the therapy situation. I told her I really didn't think it would do anyone any good for her to come without really making a commitment that that's what she wanted to do, and that I would be around and would be available if she would want to come and see me.

But only on that basis; not on a finger-in-the-dike kind of situation, but in a fairly intensive treatment setting.

Q Do your records indicate as to whether she did in fact pursue psychotherapy?

A She did not in fact pursue psychotherapy with me.

Q Do you know whether she pursued it with anyone else?

A Yes, she did. As I understand it, she was subsequently referred to Dr. Z, who is a psychiatrist in La Jolla, and, during this past fall, began seeing him.

Q Do your records reflect when she began to see Dr. Z?

A No.

Q Was Dr. Z a referral by you?

A No. My understanding—and I must point out that my understanding of this initially was from her father, whom I saw at General Hospital following my return to San Diego from a trip the end of November—that she had been referred to Dr. Z by a psychiatrist whom I believe Dr. John Doe turned to for help and advice in regard to the situation. I think, on the basis of my recollection, this was some time in August.

Q When you speak of psychotherapy on a continuous relationship, first, what do you mean by psychotherapy?

A Psychotherapy is a process whereby a person learns to look into himself or herself to determine where and what the situations are that cause them to get in repeated trouble with themselves or with other people. It is a process which is based on the development of a relationship between the patient and psychotherapist, who becomes the target and repository of a lot of feelings that the patient has, that the patient is probably not even aware of having.

The function of the psychotherapist is to deal with those feelings, to show the patient where those feelings come from, that they actually exist and that they are governing the way he or she is leading his or her life, and that it is possible to find out the origin and the sources of these feelings that keep getting them into trouble so that they won't have to keep operating on the basis of them anymore.

Q In the case of Mrs. Doe, how often did you feel she should engage in psychotherapy?

A Well, when I saw her in the summer, which is the time that I suggested she ought to have psychotherapy, I thought that she ought to be seen fairly intensively, at least on a couple-of-times-a-week basis. I thought she had the capacity to look into herself at least to that degree.

Q Is there a medical word that defines the condition that she had at that time?

A At the time that I saw her, she was depressed. She was anxious or scared or somewhat disorganized in terms of what she was really doing and what she thought she was going to do. My impression at the time, clinically, was that I was seeing symptoms—by that, I refer to the depression and the anxiety—of a person who basically manifested a personality-trait disturbance, a very passive, dependent personality, a person who feels a real need to have sources of dependency and without them really couldn't function well and would transfer, in her case, dependency wishes, longing and needs to her parents, to her husband, to somebody else, perhaps to her profession, and so on.

Now, finding that all of them were at best very tenuous sources, she became very anxious and was becoming depressed. At the time, I was more impressed by the general run of the personality than I was by the actual anxiety and depression, and we talked during that time about the tendencies to have to depend on one or another situation.

Q What was the occasion that caused Mrs. Doe to come back to you on or about the first of December?

A Once again, this was brought about by the intervention of her father, whom I saw, I guess, the day before. I had just returned to San Diego on the night of the twenty-ninth, and I went back to work, I suppose, the following day.

At General Hospital, the day after that, as I said before, I saw her father, who told me what had happened, told me that Dr. Doe had gone into psychotherapy with Dr. Z, and that she had been becoming increasingly depressed and that there was an attempted suicide. I guess it had been about ten days or so before that—and that he was quite concerned and alarmed and would I please see her.

So I said, "sure," and he picked up the telephone then and there in the office at General Hospital where he and I were talking and tried to get hold of her. I don't think he was successful at that time, but later in the day he did; and he said something to the effect, I suppose, "Go see Mel Goldzband tomorrow."

Q So, thus comes the December one appointment?

A Yes. That's right.

Q Is the reason that you've only seen her five times since December 1, because she's still counseling with Dr. Z?

A Yes, that's correct. My relationship with her is a kind of a special phenomenon. I am not her therapist. She has started in psychotherapy with Dr. Z. I knew that she was going to be involved in all of this legal hassle over this next-several-month period.

I knew also that she needed psychotherapy; and the two are really diametrically opposed in terms of a psychiatrist dealing with a patient.

Q Excuse me, Doctor. In what respect do you mean thay are opposed?

A All right. Psychotherapy cannot be carried on in a vacuum. People have to continue living their ordinary daily lives, work and function during the time that they are seeing a psychotherapist and delving into themselves.

Life does not stop during the time that people are investigating themselves, but there is a particular kind of special relationship that is formed with a psychotherapist. He becomes a very particular person in that patient's life. A psychotherapist does not get involved with the life of the patient in any way outside of therapy. If he does, then the relationship, which is a highly specific type of relationship, is unalterably changed from that which is necessary for the performance of psychotherapy.

That relationship has to be a particularly—and I hate to use the word because it is kind of a cliché—but it represents a kind of a feeling that you have a particularly sacred kind of one, an untouchable kind of a relationship. But the patients—and here, I'm speaking of all, not just Dr. Doe, but all patients who are involved in depth psychotherapy—must have the feeling as well as the knowledge that that relationship is not going to be altered, that that person to whom he or she is opening himself or herself up is not going to divulge anything that is going to be going on, that it's purely and completely confidential, and that there could be no breach of that contractual relationship that's formed between the two of them.

Part of that contractual relationship is an absolute mandatory trust. So, knowing that she is in psychotherapy, knowing the pressures that are going to be upon her by virtue of the legal hassle which she is going to go through, I offered to serve as a kind of consulting psychiatrist, an observer psychiatrist; someone who would, for the purposes of the legal evaluation, report impressions, diagnoses, situations, so as not to jeopardize the psychotherapy in which she was finally becoming involved.

Q Is it true then that you basically have formed your impressions without consultations with Dr. Z?

A No. I talked with Dr. Z. I certainly would never have seen her without contacting him and asking him if it would be all right. He was very agreeable and, in fact, relieved that my role would keep him away from this litigation.

Q All right. So, your impressions are influenced by your discussing with him also?

A My impressions are based upon my contacts with Dr. Doe and my talks with Dr. Z. My talks with Dr. Z are not detailed. My talks with Dr. Z are very generalized. My talks with Dr. Z really are based upon a kind of pattern in which I give my impressions, based upon what I hear from her and how she is responding in the relationship with me.

He then usually confirms this and perhaps may amplify this just a little bit—but generally, without getting into the specific psychodynamics, the specific material, the specific verbalizations that she is giving in psychotherapy, which he really cannot do if she is going to see him as a trustworthy person.

Q Was an attempted suicide by Dr. Doe consistent with your impressions formed last June and July?

A As I said, the girl was running around like the proverbial chicken without a head, in all directions at the same time. She was getting increasingly panicky because she felt that she really had very few people, or decreasingly few people to lean on, to count on.

By virtue of that and by virtue of the increasing feelings of loss of sources that she could lean on or count on, it is not only feasible but expectable that a depression will arise. Depressions arise, and depressions themselves give rise to all kinds of behavior, suicidal included. There is a whole gamut, a whole spectrum of behavior.

Q All right. So, the depression, though, was predictable from your impressions of her situation in June and July?

A Yes.

Q It is only the severity of depressions which would be hard to measure, unless you had a constant association with the patient?

A That's right.

Q Have you, in forming your impressions at the present time, had some contact with the Smith family other than the fact that there was a referral by Dr. Smith?

A Well, I had known Dr.—the Drs. Smith—both parents of Dr. Jane Doe are physicians—for some years, on a social basis. Dr. Sam Smith, her father, had often referred patients to me for psychiatric evaluation and treatment. I knew them on that basis.

Is that what you are—?

Q Well, I'm curious as to whether you have, as a result of forming your history or attempting to arrive at your impressions of Dr. Doe's condition, whether you have also discussed the problem and gathered some background history from the Smiths?

A Yes, I was called on several occasions at my home, usually by Mrs. Smith, during the latter summer after Dr. Doe had stopped seeing me; and she was—she kept asking the question, "Well, what can we do? What can we do?"

I said, "Well, we"—and this was repeated over and over again throughout the telephone call—"we can't do anything. It really depends upon your daughter. Nobody is going to step in and collar her or prevent her doing whatever she wants. She's a free agent. She has her constitutional rights and can operate whatever way she wants.

"See needs therapy, and I have laid this on the line with her, to her, and she had to have it but nobody can drag her to it." Meanwhile, Mrs. Smith was getting increasingly upset, and I told her that her reaction was something that might be pretty harmful in the long run, because with a person as overtly dependent upon her as her daughter, the daughter really only has to shed a tear and she, as a very overprotecting, hovering mother, would come running.

There is really no growth promoted this way. She would be really much better off trying to get her involved in a psychiatric-treatment program, than once again—and I use the same metaphor—than just trying to put a finger in a dike. This was—

Q Do you—?

A This was basically all. It was repeated several times, I imagine two or three times, over the telephone.

Once at a party, where I happened to meet them, they took me aside and we talked about the same thing.

Q In arriving at your present impressions as to Dr. Doe's condition, have you relied on any other sources other than your consultation and discussions with your patient, her prior history as outlined and contained in your files, and your discussions with her family and your discussions with Dr. Z? Are there any other things, other than those that I've mentioned, that I should know of?

A No, there are no other sources.

Q Do you have an impression at the present time as to her present emotional and mental condition?

A Yes.

Q Please tell me.

A I think it can probably best be summarized by saying—if I can use the vernacular—that she's kind of putting herself together.

I saw her yesterday for the first time in four weeks or a month, or something like that. The previous time was December nineteenth, and yesterday was the seventeenth of January. Before the December nineteenth session, I had seen her on a, give or take a little, weekly basis. On the nineteenth, I told her to just wait a couple of weeks, give me a ring, and come in.

I was considerably impressed by the difference with which she presented herself to me yesterday, the way she talked, her mood, and even the nature of her verbalizations. There was a considerable regaining of confidence. This is an ongoing procedure.

I would say she felt considerably more secure in her own thinking in regard to her own conclusions about herself and about her relationships with her children and her parents. She did not give me the impressions, as she had before, that she was so very, very insecure and doubtful about her own role in this regard. She seems to have been developing a renewed identity, one which I think, obviously, is the result of ongoing psychotherapy.

Q Do you have a recommendation as to the course of treatment she should continue with for a full recovery or full reestablishment of her emotional self?

A Oh, I would urge that she continue in the present course of psychotherapy with Dr. Z.

Q You think that's a very important aspect of her—

A Absolutely. I think it is mandatory.

Q When you say "mandatory," what would be the consequences, perhaps, if she discontinued psychotherapy?

A Well, I've given up predicting a long time ago; but I think that, with a person who has the kind of passive-dependent personality-trait disturbance that this girl has manifested for so long, that she can certainly regress once again, and could be overtly dependent and anxious once again.

Q Have you had an opportunity to meet the three boys or three children?

A No, I haven't seen the children.

Q You do understand, though, that there are young boys, 11, 9, and 7 approximately?

A Yes.

Q Do you feel or is it your impression at this time that she could cope with three young boys of that age?

A According to the information that I have from both Dr. Doe and from Dr. Z, she seems to be coping with them. She seems to be dealing with them quite realistically, as an adult and as a parent.

She sees herself assuming a parental role, one in which she applies a good deal of firmness and expectations of the kids, lets them know what she expects of them and what they can really expect of her. She tells me, and Dr. Z confirms this, that by and large her relationship with the kids is really much less anxiety-laden than it has been before.

The relationship with the two younger children, apparently, has never been much of a problem. That is, the older boy was more problematic. There was apparently a great deal of hostile feeling expressed by him toward her and towards his maternal grandparents; and this had in the past been a problem. I say "in the past" because, according to what she tells me, it is much less of a problem.

She has, over the past few weeks, been dealing very consistently with him, not taking a great deal of the provocative behavior, setting limits; and not expecting that he is going to love the limits that are being set for him but expecting him to tolerate them and operate within her framework in dealing with the kids.

Apparently this is working, and there is considerably less acting out on the part of the older boy with her.

Q When you say there is "considerably less," this is her relating the incidents to you?

A To me, yes, and what I get from Dr. Z.

Q You never personally have observed—

A I have not seen the children. I would not even recognize them if I would see them on the street. I don't know who they are. My information is from Dr. Doe and from Dr. Z.

Q If her depression states were to return, would she be able to emotionally cope with children of this age?

A Well, if she becomes seriously depressed, she probably would have difficulty in coping with the children. I see people in my practice who are depressed. I see a lot of depressed mothers and a lot of depressed fathers, too, for that matter. They have to expend a great deal more energy than otherwise in dealing and coping with their daily responsibilities, among which are included their families, their children. They can or cannot, depending upon, number one, who they are and what they are in terms of the actual fiber they are composed of; number two, the depth of their depression; and number three, the kind of help that they have in the situation in which they are involved.

If she becomes seriously and severely depressed in such a way that there is a real regressive withdrawal and a suicidal intent again, obviously I think there is going to be difficulty in dealing with the children.

Q I would assume if there is serious withdrawal and suicidal intent, this will be detrimental to the children also?

A Well, I think that obviously kids are raised better in nondepressed households.

Q Am I correct now in assuming that your prescribed treatment for her for the future would basically be the continuation of her psychotherapy—

A Absolutely.

Q —and that other than perhaps what is necessary for an appearance in this court proceeding, if necessary, your continued treatment of her would greatly diminish or terminate completely?

A Yes. I don't see myself playing any kind of a role in her treatment situation.

Attorney X: Thank you very much, Doctor. I have no further questions.

Examination
By Attorney Y

Q As I understand your testimony, perhaps somewhat summarized, you are of the opinion that Mrs. Doe's condition has improved significantly since you saw her the first time, is that correct?

A That's correct.

Q I—

Attorney X: Excuse me for just a moment. Since we may be using this deposition, I take it the usual stipulations do not apply.

Attorney Y: Right, right. What Mr. X is saying, translated, is that objections are not reserved until the time of the trial. Am I correct?

Attorney X: That's correct.

Attorney Y: **Q** Have you discussed with Mrs. Doe her concern with the children's present relationship with John Doe?

A Oh, yes. She's talked with me about that to a considerable extent.

Q Has she expressed any concern with John Doe's lack of discipline of the children or permissiveness?

A She expresses it in a number of ways. She contrasts her own mode of behavior with the children and the kind of expectations the kids have of her with what she feels they have from their father. She takes pains to point out the fact that her husband has bought a large home, quite near their own home, in which there is plenty of room for all of them, and in which each of the children has his own room; where there is a large swimming pool and the kind of situation which would certainly be pleasing to any kid.

In contrast, she sees their home as one in which more discipline is exerted.

Q By "their home," you mean her home?

A Her home. That which she had previously shared with her husband and children, in which the two younger children need to share a room, which she thinks is a desirable situation because they have to, as she says, learn to live with each other and get along with each other; in which there is no swimming pool, which she sees as advantageous because she does not like the idea of kids having a swimming pool around when there isn't a supervising parent there during the day, but which she feels, probably correctly, the children don't like as much.

According to her, her husband is buying the children and, by virtue of this, the children are hedonistic, as children are, and will certainly enjoy and approve this type of life more than a more disciplined one.

Q Do you feel that she has mature and realistic attitudes with respect to her relationship with her children?

A I think that this is certainly developing. I was struck, for example, by something that she told me yesterday. Just as an example, if I can give this, apparently there was some discussion about the kids; about divorce, custody, and judges; and so on and so forth.

I forgot the exact situation as to how it was brought out, but the older child—the oldest boy said that their father had instructed him that he is to say what he thinks is the best thing.

Q For himself?

A Yes. If he's asked, he's to speak his mind and to think—to say what he thinks is best for himself; whereupon Mrs. Doe, picking this up, said to him, "That's really putting quite a load on you," and that it really isn't reasonable that a ten-year-old boy has the capacity to make such an irrevocable decision; and that's what judges are for. That's why there are these procedures, to which they are going to go; and that, really, he shouldn't feel that he is placed in such a situation where he has to make this kind of decision, which he is really not capable of making; thereby relieving, I think a good deal of potential guilt.

There is a whole gamut of psychiatric literature about children in divorce and custody cases who are asked, "What do you want to do?" Of course, you see, this is a real pressure placed upon them, and later on they find themselves suffering a great deal by virtue of guilt feelings they developed when they were to pick between parents, and so on and so forth. Of course, this is a terrible responsibility to place on a kid. [For further discussion of this issue, see part I, chapter 4.]

I was particularly impressed with the way that she handled this, when she said to him, "Sure, you are always to say, you know—speak your mind, but this decision really can't be yours and it has to be the judge's. It has to be the process's."

Q Do you believe, Dr. Goldzband, that Mrs. John Doe presents any danger to the children if she were to have custody of them? I mean that, by her conduct, would she subject the children to any danger?

A Oh, no. I don't think she would harm the children.

Q Based upon your response to a question by Attorney X, am I correct in assuming that you believe that Mrs. Doe has the capacity to assume custody of the children at this time?

A I think she can.

Q Do you have any reason, Dr. Goldzband, to believe that her condition would not continue to improve as it has if she were to continue her present psychotherapy with Dr. Z?

A I have no reason to assume that it wouldn't.

Attorney Y: That's all.

Attorney X: I have one or two additional questions, Doctor.

Reexamination
by Attorney X

Q It is your opinion, I take it, that she apparently would not physically harm the children?

A That's correct.

Q If the children were to experience a situation with her where she went into a withdrawal type of depression again, though, it is your opinion that that would be harmful to the children?

A Well, I think the situation in the past was that she would go into that kind of withdrawal and get on the phone and call for help. She would say, "Somebody come over and take care of these kids," and, of course, the implied wish was to "take care of me," as well.

The welfare of the kids was really not jeopardized in that because the situation was that there was always help for them.

Q But were you aware, Doctor, that when she would withdraw, there would be a physical withdrawal, that she'd go to bed and pull the covers up over her head and refuse to do anything?

A Oh, yes, yes.

Q The children would often have to call and request help. Were you aware of that?

A My impression was that she called.

Q Have you anywhere discussed with her the fact that the children had to make the calls?

A No.

Q Would that change your opinion at all?

A Well, I have no reason to assume that this type of behavior would raise its ugly head again, and if she continues in an ongoing intensive psychotherapeutic relationship with Dr. Z, I think that that kind of symptom can probably be seen as past history.

Q But if the symptom did reoccur—that is, the deep withdrawal—it would be a harmful situation to the children?

A Oh, I don't know. I'm certain that it wouldn't be pleasant for them. How harmful it would be in terms of any emotional trauma—is that what you are referring to?

Q Yes.

A That kind of thing, I—I really don't know. They've already seen it.

Q Do you think if they are subjected to it again, it wouldn't be as harmful as the first time around?

A I'm sure that it wouldn't be pleasant, but I don't know how harmful it would be. I don't know what would come of it, for instance, in terms of an effect on them in the future. I think more than enough effect has already been made.

I think that it could lead to anxiety on the part of the children who need to be dependent upon her or upon somebody. That's just as Dr. Doe's situation this past summer, that the sources of anxiety are drying up—pardon me, I meant to say that the sources of dependency are drying up, and this leads to anxiety.

Q But it is your testimony and your feeling that the continuation of psychotherapy is absolutely a must in her case?

A   Yes.

Q   If she discontinued the therapy, you would have reservations about whether she should have the custody of the boys?

A   If she discontinues the therapy prematurely, prior to its completion, yes.

Q   All right. But at the present time, we are talking about an ongoing, rather continuous therapy; is that correct?

A   Yes, that's correct.

Q   If she were to discontinue that at the present time—

A   Yes.

Q   —then you would feel doubtful about whether she should have custody of the children?

A   Indeed so.

Attorney X: I have no further questions.

Attorney Y: I have no further questions.

All examples, bad and good, can teach us something. This particular case is especially interesting and provocative because of the interrelationships between the participants. San Diego is a large city, although at the time of this case a few years ago it was not as large as it is today. In this city, then, the professional community was still relatively close-knit, and a number of doctors knew each other fairly well. In the huge eastern cities this situation might well be different simply because of the greater numbers and because of different life-styles. However, the more professionals tend to call on each other, the better they tend to know each other. The cross-currents created by their interprofessional and friendly relationships can lead to problems.

In this case it obviously would have been much better had I not known any of the family and, in all candor, had I not been the recipient of a number of case referrals from Dr. Smith. Predictably, those referrals have totally dried up. I still see him in the hospital, however, blustering and bawling out patients and staff alike, oblivious to the swath of irritation he cuts. He prefers not to see me when we pass.

The destruction of my relationship with Dr. Smith might seem paradoxical because the case was actually decided in favor of Dr. Smith's daughter, Dr. Jane Doe. She received physical custody of the three children, and Dr. John Doe was granted liberal visitation rights. Nonetheless, social relations usually suffer when professional noses are poked into family business.

Follow-up in this case is especially interesting. After her divorcing husband's motion for custody was denied, Dr. Jane Doe continued to see Dr. Z in ongoing psychotherapy for about a month. She then discontinued treatment unilaterally. She resumed seeing her previous boyfriend, who had dropped her just before the suicide attempt; and this relationship led to increased friction between her and her oldest son. The boy began to spend increasing periods at his father's nearby home. Soon he was joined by his younger siblings, with no apparent objection from their mother. About a year after the original custody decision, the father's attorney introduced a new motion for custody of the three children, which was granted without contest.

I have no data to support any amplification of this situation. In retrospect, it appears that the mother's desire for the children was perhaps not as great as originally thought, nor was any potential desire stimulated by the psychotherapy, as might have been expected. Also in retrospect, my role appears to have been colored a great deal by the manipulations of the family members—the grandmother who needed the grandchildren, the grandfather who needed to control everyone within reach, and the daughter who sacrificed her children in order to prove that she actually had control over both of them.

On the bright side, this case offers another phenomenon to be studied— the use of a psychiatrist as a liaison between the needs of the court and the attorneys, on the one hand, and the needs of the treatment psychiatrist and the patient on the other.

The use of a mental-health professional as a liaison in court is a new concept, unfamiliar to most jurists and attorneys, and even to most behavioral scientists in many parts of the country. My experience has been that many attorneys and judges recognize the need for confidentiality in therapy relationships. They also recognize that enough data can be obtained by this method for pertinent and potent direct and cross-examination. The procedure has been eminently successful. The use of liaisons ought to increase and become rapidly accepted. It holds much promise for allowing the client to maintain a good, ongoing therapeutic relationship, which will benefit the client and the client's family as well. In child-custody cases the best interests of the children demand the optimal mental health of the parents.

11 Right and Not So Right

The old story is told of the village sage to whom all disputants came for resolution of their conflicts. In one case, on listening to the first claimant, the sage nodded gravely and said, "You're right." When the claimant's adversary protested and then told his story, the sage nodded just as gravely and said to him, "You're right." At this, the sage's long-suffering wife could tolerate no more. She burst out at her husband, "How can you tell him that he's right, and then turn around and tell the other man that he's right?" The sage thought about this for a moment, nodded even more gravely, and said to his wife, "You know, you're right!"

If only it were that simple for the decision makers in custody cases—or for the expert evaluators. This chapter discusses one such case. It is especially notable for the seemingly adversarial psychiatric reports, in which one expert said to one party, "You're right," and the other said the same to the adversary. As it turned out, and is often the case, both psychiatrists could not be right. However, their differences were more apparent than real and were based on the fact that not everything was known to the first consultant, who had seen only one of the parties.

This divorce action had been finalized some years before, and the custody issue had been decided. The ex-wife had physical custody, but the two small boys who represented the issue of the marriage often visited with the father who, unlike the wife, had remained in San Diego. Extended visits were held during the summer, and during this particular summer the father decided that he simply was not going to send the boys back to his former wife, who had remarried and was going to live in the Canal Zone. Although the father had long thought of suing for a change of custody, he had never done so until this time. The reason for his timing was never clarified, but it may have had something to do with the Panama Canal crisis, brewing then. That situation might have made the father feel that this represented a favorable issue and a favorable time for him.

The father contacted an attorney, who determined that a psychiatric evaluation of the father and both boys would be very helpful to his case. The attorney contacted a local psychiatrist who was experienced in custody determinations but was unable to schedule the case. Instead, the psychiatrist turned the case over to a young associate, a woman who only recently had finished her psychiatric residency and who had little forensic psychiatric experience. As can be seen from her report, her capability is not in question;

but the results, as in every investigation, are only as good as the information provided to the investigator.

To Whom It May Concern:

Mr. Arturo Martinez has requested an evaluation of the psychological health of his two sons, Robert and Scotty. He expresses much concern over their emotional and physical welfare. He believes that the emotional and physical problems he has observed are caused by their environment and the nature of the relationship with their mother, who currently has custody of the boys and lives in either Virginia or Panama (Central America). The boys have been here in San Diego with Mr. Martinez since May 25, 1979, for their regular visitation. Mr. Martinez wishes to obtain custody, which he believes to be in the best interest of both Robert and Scotty. To complete this evaluation, I worked with Mr. Arturo Martinez for two hours, with Scotty Martinez for 1¼ hours, with Robert Martinez for 1⅓ hours, observed the three of them together for ⅓ hour and also referred them for psychological testing.

Robert Martinez is an 11-year-old white boy, and Scotty Martinez is an 8-year-old white boy. Both boys were born in San Diego to Arturo Martinez and his ex-wife, Alice. Arturo and Alice were divorced in 1974, and Alice remarried at that time to a man named Pat, who is in the Navy. In 1976 Alice and Pat moved to Iowa for a year, taking with them Robert and Scotty. In 1978 the four of them moved to Virginia. For this current visitation Arturo was given a Miami, Florida, address to contact Alice in case of emergency, but Arturo has been told that she and Pat have moved to Panama, Central America. The boys confirm that there were plans to move to Panama. Arturo expresses concern about both boys' "nervousness" and lack of spontaneity and friends. Scotty brings with him six asthma drugs and Robert two asthma drugs every time they visit him in San Diego. Neither of the children have any asthmatic symptoms during any visitation and Arturo states that two pediatricians have recommended totally discontinuing these potent drugs for the boys. He is further concerned about Scotty's night fears, which terrify him so much that he will not sleep in a room alone. Arturo states he has bought the boys bicycles, fishing rods and a typewriter which have been sent to Virginia, but which the boys say they are unable to use, because of lack of opportunity for the bicycles and fishing rods, and the typewriter because Pat needs it. Arturo says he provides most of the clothing for the boys because they come for visitation so poorly dressed. He pays $200.00 per month regularly for child support. His visitation privileges include two months every summer and every other Christmas, and he is required to pay one-half of the necessary travel fare, but generally pays all of the fare. Arturo feels that Alice and Pat have a low-priority attitude about the child-rearing responsibilities that they currently hold legally. Another example he gives is that he wishes to pay for at least one-half of the cost to send Robert to an orthodontist, but the mother refuses to either take Robert or to pay anything toward orthodontic care. Arturo is worried about the boys' lack of friends and their isolated lifestyle.

Robert Martinez is a 11-year, 8-month-old boy who presents himself in an extremely polite way, shaking hands as he greets this examiner and anyone in the office. He is very clean, well dressed in shirt and slacks. His hair is so neatly combed back it is noticeably out of fashion for his age group.

He is wearing glasses, and appears just pre-pubertal. His eye contact is good and he sits quietly, without moving about. His affect is normal in amplitude and range. His mood is mildly depressed. He has a rather serious demeanor, and is very respectful of adults. At times he would smile, and when told he had a very nice smile, he commented that never in his life had anyone told him that. He seemed sad, and on questioning agreed that his feelings often are sad ones. His speech is clear and coherent and shows a bright intellect. He shows no evidence of a thought disorder. He lacks spontaneity in his interactions and seems guarded and withdrawn. When questioned he responds that he is very lonely.

Robert relates the events in his life in a matter of fact way. He says he attended school in San Diego while living at his father's house through the third grade. His mother married Pat before he began fourth grade and they moved to Iowa. He said that Pat has children also from a previous marriage, but he has never met them. In Virginia they live in a two bedroom apartment. Pat is in the Navy and his mother works in a pizza restaurant. They have no pets. When asked about family activities he says they once went to an amusement park and sometimes he plays catch with Pat and Scotty. He denies ever going to picnics, ball games, bowling, skating, to the park or any other place than the one amusement park. The family does attend church on Sundays. He also says he has been to a couple of movies, his favorite being "Star Wars." When asked about family fun on weekends, he says they go to church and then do the laundry.

Robert describes his mother as being nice and "not that strict." She kisses and hugs him at night before he goes to sleep. Mother does not cook dinner as she is usually "working, resting, or doing laundry." Pat does the cooking. Pat is described as "nice, more strict." He says that mother and Pat argue sometimes with loud yelling (about once a week) and it particularly upsets him if it is about him. Sometimes they argue about how strict to be with the children. Robert says he hasn't been spanked in a while, but sometimes does get spanked either with a hand or a belt. Sometimes he is punished with allowance deductions (allowance is $2.50/wk.). Robert says he gets A's in school except for C's in physical education. He takes no lessons outside of school, and has no involvement in organized nor neighborhood sport activities. His non-school activities include reading, doing homework, and watching TV. His favorite TV shows are "Mork and Mindy," and "Battlestar Galactica." He reads space stories, animal stories and Snoopy. He says his family has no family friends. He himself has no friends. He has never had a friend to his home to play, eat dinner or spend the night. When asked what he would change if he could in his family he could not think of anything. When asked to give three wishes at first he said he had none, but with encouragement says: (1) to have all the comic books he wants, (2) for Scotty and himself to be free of asthma, (3) for his father's ear to be better. When asked to draw a house, tree and person he attempted the drawing and then restarted, drawing very precisely and in minute detail in ink pen (he was given crayons) which he later colored. He says the picture is about a 12-year-old boy named Frank who is going to a ball game with his family (mother, father, brother, and sister) who are all waiting for him in the car (Frank was slow in getting ready). When asked to complete the bird fable about the mother, father and baby bird, he begins, "mother bird yells at the father bird to go get the baby bird," and completes the story by having the baby bird rescued by neither parent, but by a squirrel. When playing a game of acting out emotions Robert chose to act out the following emotions: nervousness, surprise, laughing at a joke and sadness. On proverb interpretation he abstracts well, but personalizes the proverb in a pessimistic way. He says he wishes his parents were not divorced, which is common among children in his situation. He expresses no preference as to which home he would prefer to stay in, as he says if he would ever express that opinion it would be like hurting one of his parents. Immediately following this discussion, he says it is more fun here because his father is less strict and they can go places together, and that he doesn't get "hollered at" so much. He says he understands that his father wants him to live here because his father loves him so much.

Psychological testing showed an age normal intellectual status, social knowledge and judgment, but that Robert feels high amounts of disapproval and control from people around him, making him feel threatened and afraid to do anything "wrong." On testing, as in clinical evaluation, he showed very overcontrolled emotions. On projective testing he made references to violent acts by someone crazy or drunk involving beating and killing.

Scotty Martinez is an 8-year-old boy who has plans to celebrate his birthday after his appointment. He described his life with his mother and Pat as a happy one, and pointed out immediately that once they went to an amusement park. He finished second grade this spring and earned the highest grades possible except in music. He likes to play soccer during school recess but doesn't play at any other times. He says that a couple of times he played with a girl who used to live in the same apartment building until she moved. He says he has never visited a friend, nor ever had a friend home to play, to eat dinenr or to spend the night. He says he would like to have friends. Scotty says usually he plays by himself during the week because Robert has to stay in and do homework, only being able to play outside on weekends. He watches TV and his favorite show is "Bugs Bunny." His favorite movie was "Star Wars."

When asked to tell about Pat and what he is like, Scotty replies, "He likes to go out with my mom—maybe sometimes with all of us . . . once we ate dinner on the ship with him. He likes us if we are good boys and we listen to him." Scotty says that sometimes Pat helps him with homework or plays checkers with him. Scotty's household chore is to take out the garbage and if he doesn't do that he might get punished verbally, or with allowance deductions. He says if he were to break something he might get spanked with a hand or a belt.

Scotty says he is very frightened at night and is unable to sleep alone, at home he sleeps with his brother and here he sleeps either with his brother or in his father's room. He has recurrent bad dreams about an angry monster that eats people and carries a long pointed steel sword. Sometimes in these dreams "poppy" (Arturo) protects him. He says he is afraid that someone will beat him up in the night.

He says the saddest thing in his life is that him mom and poppy are divorced. Scotty mentioned many times in the interview that it is fun to be here with his father, that it is happy here, that he likes to be together with Robert and poppy, and that he likes going places together.

Scotty is also very well groomed and neatly dressed. He can best be described as a "charmer." He is exceptionally polite for his years, and is very cooperative. His eye contact is good, and his kinetics betray some anxiety, which is to be expected. Most children his age would lose concentration and seek out the toys in my office, but Scotty sat and talked, behaving in some ways like a reserved adult. His speech is clear and coherent. His affect is normal, and his mood is friendly, but serious. His vocabulary and understanding show an above-average I.Q. When asked what he would have if he could have three wishes he says: (1) a motorcycle when he is old enough, (2) a lot of money to buy food for the poor and (3) to have his mother and father not fight any more. When asked to complete the fable about the mother, father and baby bird he says the baby bird faints. The mother and father bird forget about their baby bird, remembering him only later. Stranger birds rescue the baby bird and return him to the parents. The parents make a new nest and then "take good care of him, and gave him medicine, and in two days [he] was strong again." Scotty's drawing of a house, person and tree is outlined in pen and crayon then carefully shaded in with colors. It is a cheerful picture and Scotty tells a story about the boy in the picture, named John, who is nine years old and is ready to go outside and play soccer with four friends. John's mother and father and 11-year-old sister Sandy are all home, inside the house, making food to eat in the fireplace. Scotty's letter and numbers are very carefully and correctly printed.

On psychological testing Scotty performs some of the I.Q. subtests (social understanding) in the 130 I.Q. range, yet his abstract reasoning is below average. On projective tests he shows a need for stability and certainty. He shows overcontrolled emotional expression, and there is some question about the presence of an underlying depression. He made strong references to interpersonal hostility and violence, especially to wives being beaten or killed. It is not clear if he feels the hostility or is exposed to it in his environment. His projective testing fits in with the dreams he speaks of in clinical interview. The monster with a sword is a male figure, most likely a father figure. These dreams are more common and expected in a boy child about the age of 5, but at Scotty's age represent some fear of physical or emotional injury.

Arturo Martinez is a Costa Rica-born man who just turned 64 years old. He is a retired fisherman and ship cook. He owns outright his 3 bedroom home and has another home he rents for income. He is retired from work since 1976 because of a shoulder injury for which he receives disability and he also receives social security and a pension. He was first married in the forties and had five children. The five children are all grown and live in California. His first wife died in 1961 because of an embolism. In 1965 he met Alice in Costa Rica and they married and had two children, Robert and Scotty. Arturo was actively employed as a fisherman then, and says in the days when the boys were little they were cared for by his youngest daughters when he was out to sea, describing Alice as a "neglectful" mother from the start. He says that he and Alice argued mostly about parenting issues, mainly about whether or not to use physical punishment on the boys. Arturo says he doesn't believe the boys needed to be spanked so frequently. Arturo thinks there is a possiblity that he may remarry again, and has a girl friend (41 years old, with no children of her own) who lives in Costa Rica, and who would come to live in San Diego if they decide to marry in the future. Arturo's last physical examination was less than a year ago and he is in good health. He says he drinks no alcohol, although he used to years ago while aboard ship. He does not smoke. He has never had any legal difficulties nor any history of psychiatric problems. He values highly his religion (Catholic) and attends church weekly. He also values work, work for earning one's way in life, and truth. He is a kind, warm man, who seems to be quite conscientious. On two occasions in my office he washed the dishes in our kitchen while waiting for his children, to help out since he had drunk some of the coffee. It was at first difficult to understand his speech since he speaks both Spanish and English in a broken way. His concern seems to be for his boys, and not a grudge against his ex-spouse as is often seen in child-custody cases. Arturo could best be described as "the salt of the earth" type of person.

Summary and Recommendations

1. Robert is a young man who is intellectually bright and performs well in the world, but he has a lack of emotional development. He is abnormally uninvolved with a peer group, and noticeably lacks any friends or interests outside of school work. He is insecure and fearful of making any mistakes, and is not likely at this time to take the risk of forming any close relationships with friends or others unless he feels more acceptable to the people around him. It does not mean that people around him have encouraged him to experience people, activities, or pleasant things in life. He is isolated and lonely. When not in San Diego he takes asthma medications for some past episodes of wheezing. It is well known that asthma has a strong emotional component, and it is not possible to know if it is San Diego's temperate climate or if it is the more expressive accepting emotional climate in his father's home that makes the medications unnecessary here.

2. Scotty is a very bright young boy who lacks the playfulness of a normal child. As with Robert, he lacks friends and the normal experience of socializing and activities. Scotty is a fearful child which reflects his fears of an insecure environment. One could speculate that he has been exposed to a great deal of anger and hostility in his environment, and it seems that he may have been exposed to physical or threatened physical abuse between his mother and a man. He does not perceive his mother as protection against the world, or the things he fears. He does however, equate in the bird story the giving of medicine as a way of receiving something from parent figures. This would reinforce his emotional need to have asthma as a way of surviving emotionally, as children need some attention, and will get it even in negative ways if there is no other way.

3. Scotty would most likely benefit from psychiatric intervention, and it may be that he will do poorly without it. Both boys need a very secure, loving environment where interactions are open and more emotionally free. They both would benefit from encouragement to find friends and spending time with them in play at home and in normal child activities.

4. Arturo Martinez seems very capable and motivated to provide this kind of environment for the boys and would provide a good male model for them both. He seems to naturally encourage them to be involved in the type of activities that they need, such as physical activities, family outings, and things such as fishing. He already recognizes and spoke of the issues of the boys needing friends. He has time to supervise them and be with them since he is retired. His love for them is obvious.

5. It is extremely unfortunate in this case to not also have available the opportunity to evaluate the home, and the relationship of the mother and

Pat with each other and the boys. This is not possible and one can only make estimations of what it is like for the boys by the reflection of the home through the psychological evaluations of the boys. It is not possible to say with certainty then, that one home is better than the other. It is only possible to say that the boys both have psychological and social difficulties that need home and professional intervention and that Arturo seems able to provide this. Nothing can be said as to whether or not it can be provided with Pat and Alice with some intervention and family counseling.

6. It would be helpful to have a field study of the home of Alice and Pat, although this may be difficult with their residence being in Central America.

7. It would be harmful to the boys to have any less contact with their father than they already do, and the effect of the recent move by the boys' mother to Panama and the availability of Arturo to the boys should be investigated.

8. It is my medical judgment that the boys, Robert and Scotty, would do well living with their father, and with the help of psychotherapy for Scotty.

Respectfully submitted,
_____, M.D.

The recommendations made by the doctor bear special attention. It should be emphasized that she did not recommend placement of the boys with the father over the mother. She was quite correct in her restraint here. Her conclusion was that in her opinion the father could do well by the boys, and they could do well with him.

The mother had no idea that a suit for change of custody had been instituted in San Diego. Only when the boys did not arrive at the Canal Zone Airport on the previously arranged-for plane did the mother learned about this. She called her attorney in San Diego the following day, and he arranged for a hearing to be held when the mother was able to come to San Diego. At that hearing the father's attorney presented the psychiatric report. He thought that this represented a fait accompli, but the mother's lawyer objected because it had not been reviewed. On review, when certain facts regarding the background of the case were brought out—situations apparently unknown to the initial examining psychiatrist—the judge determined that a new and complete review of the situation was needed. He called for an investigation by the probation department, and he stated that he wanted a new and different psychiatric evaluation of all parties, not just the father and the two boys. The costs of all of this were to be borne by the father.

Usually the judge gets what he or she wants in these cases. Both attorneys and their clients agreed, although it was recognized that there might be difficulty in scheduling all the needed interviews in the limited time spent by the mother and her new husband in San Diego. In fact, the new husband had not come to San Diego; he was unable to get leave, so the children's mother came without him on the first plane available to her. Complicating the problem was the fact that the summer was ending, and the children needed to be enrolled in school. Was this to be in San Diego, where they were then staying with the father, or in the Canal Zone, where the mother had arranged for registration in a local parochial school? The judge asked the petitioner-father's attorney to call me and to ask me to perform the necessary examinations. When the restrictive schedule was explained to me, I refused to accept the case because I felt that I probably would be unable to see all the principals as much as I might feel they should be seen. I knew also that even if I could, I would not be able to prepare a report in time for the next hearing, set only ten days away.

When the attorney called the judge to tell him that I had refused the case, the judge called me. I was highly flattered by his request, but I repeated my refusal to him. He recognized my reasons and asked me how much time I thought I would need. I told him that I simply could not give him an answer because I did not know what would turn up in the interviews as they proceeded. Besides, I had a fairly full appointment schedule of ongoing psychotherapy patients, and my commitments to them obviously came first. The judge called me back two hours later and said that if I would arrange to start seeing the family whenever I could, he would set the hearing for whatever date I could meet. I could not refuse such an offer, so I proceeded. With appointments at odd hours and on Saturdays and Sundays, everyone was able to be seen. The probation-department worker also demonstrated considerable willingness to be flexible and accommodating in her own scheduling, and we were eventually able to complete our assigned tasks. She and I communicated several times by telephone during this period, and we informed each other of the trends developing in our separate investigations. She quoted some of my comments in her report; and, as will be seen, I referred to her in mine. My report to the court follows here.

The Hon._____, Judge,
The Superior Court,
San Diego County Courthourse,
San Diego, California 92101

In Re: The marriage of Martinez
      Case No._____

Your Honor:

I am especially grateful to you for the confidence you expressed in me via referring this case to me, especially following our telephone communications regarding the need for haste and my inability to fulfill that need because of the dictates of my schedule and the time required to evaluate all of the pertinent parties to this tragic child custody case. Both attorneys have been most cooperative, and I have been the recipient of communications from each of them. Mr. X has spelled out the arrangements and has seen to their execution. Mr. Y has supplied me with materials referable to this case, including the earlier psychiatric report by Dr. _____; reports by Dr. Z, the pediatric allergist currently treating both boys; and the declaration of the father, Mr. Martinez. Mr. Martinez also gave me a copy of an earlier report by Dr. Z. Aside from all of this, I was able to speak briefly, via telephone, with the counselor at the Conciliation Court, and I also met briefly with the probation officer involved in the investigation of this case. She accompanied Mr. and Mrs. Little to my office yesterday when that couple had found that the boys had not been made available to them to be picked up by them in order for them to bring them to my office for their interview with me. Finally, you were kind enough to forward a copy of the order elaborating my role in this case.

Aside from reviewing all of the above, I saw Mrs. Little in a private session of double-standard length on [date]. She came to see me again on [date] when her husband had a session with me. He had been able to catch a MATS flight from Panama and, via a circuitous route, reached San Diego over the weekend immediately preceding that date. Also on that same day I saw the father, Mr. Martinez, for the first time, also in a private session in my office which lasted 45 minutes. He returned for his scheduled appointment on [date], but he arrived 25 minutes late so that our second session was somewhat truncated. He brought both boys to my office for their interviews with me the next day, and I spent about a half hour each with them.

It is probably most convenient to divide this report into two sections; the first will be the description of my contacts with the parties, and the second will be my conclusions and recommendations. It is probably best to proceed with my discussions of the parties in the order in which they were seen.

Born 37 years ago in Costa Rica, Alice Little (the former Mrs. Martinez) came promptly to my office on all occasions and appeared to relate openly, freely and unguardedly. Well-groomed and attractive, she appears healthy and complains of no physical discomforts. The mental status examination *per se* is generally negative and indicative of no signs of overt neurosis or of frank psychosis. The general emotional tone of her communications is often colored by the expected ongoing level of hostility she feels toward her ex-husband, but she is aware of that feeling and she discusses it openly. Pointedly, she speaks at length about her strict enforcement of the rule she set up with her sons that they communicate often with their father, and even when she expresses her suspicions that he is seeking custody for nefarious reasons including financial, she acknowledges that her ex-husband does, indeed, love the boys.

She describes her family as poor but quite striving. She is the ninth of a sibship of eleven, and she attended only through the sixth grade. When she was 15, her father died of cancer, and her 76-year-old mother was operated in June for "female problems." Mrs. Little was 23 when she married Mr. Martinez in 1965; they had met in Costa Rica, Mr. Martinez's family home as well. He was 53 at the time and the father of four children, one of whom had already married. Mr. Martinez's first wife had died. Mrs. Little lived with him and his two younger children in San Diego, to which place he had brought her following the marriage. Mr. Martinez had worked for many years as a cook aboard tuna craft operating out of this port. Mrs. Little states that her husband had kicked the two older boys out of his home, and she also says that Mr. Martinez is claiming falsely that she did not rear the remaining children but that the job was actually done by his daughter. She says that he has accused her of many things including promiscuity and drinking, but that these have been proven false (this is confirmed by the probation worker, who discussed the earlier allegations and the earlier workup).

Mrs. Little claims that she eventually decided to divorce her husband because he was an abusive alcoholic. He was extremely jealous and would always spy on her. Their first separation was in 1974, and the divorce was finalized in 1976, after attempts to reconcile because of the children. The divorce promoted considerable conflict within her because of the religious beliefs which are so important to Mrs. Little, still a devout Roman Catholic. One of her sisters is a nun, and she states that the entire family is very religious. When he attempted to choke her, Mrs. Little felt that she could no longer continue living with her husband.

She met her present husband after her separation, at a party she attended with her sister, and she married him five months after her divorce was finalized. Mr. Little is a chief petty officer in the Navy, and his family is from Iowa. Because he was to serve aboard ship, he moved her and the two boys to his family home in Iowa. Mr. Martinez did not want her to go because of the children, but she says that his drunkenness continued and was too much for her to bear. She left her new address at the bank so that her husband's checks for child support could be forwarded. She feared his acting out against them if he knew their exact location. Although she had been awarded them, she says that Mr. Martinez was enraged over her taking drapes, furnishing, and fixtures from her house (she had continued to live in a house on Mr. Martinez's property after the separation and divorce), and also her automobile. Shortly before she left, her ex-husband had traded her car for another one, and unbeknownst to her he had registered it in his name only. She took this car with her, but her husband later persuaded her to send it back to her former husband in order to prevent further trouble.

The family lived in Iowa from October, 1976 to May, 1977, when Mr. Little returned from shipboard duty and was transferred to Norfolk, Virginia. The move did not take place until school was out in Iowa. Because of the change of climate represented by Iowa, the boys developed numerous upper respiratory infections, and they each developed asthmatic bronchitis. They were worked up medically for asthma there and in Norfolk where they were treated actively. Among the large sheaf of materials brought by Mrs. Little is a letter from the treating pediatrician at the Naval Regional Medical Center at Portsmouth, Virginia, who described the conditions of the boys. Mrs. Little says that when the boys would be sent to visit their father, they would be sent with medication and instructions, but the father would not let them take it, saying that they had no problems here. Last year, with a stronger letter from their doctor, Mr. Martinez gave them their medication, and this year, because they developed more asthma here since their return from their trip to Costa Rica in July (after which they were to have been returned to Mrs. Little in Panama), Mr. Martinez is having them seen, treated and desensitized for allergens by Dr. Z in San

Diego. It must be pointed out here that this is in direct contradiction to the data provided Dr. _____ when she wrote her report, in which she refers to the notion that neither boy has had asthma here.

The current situation dates from this summer, when the boys were routinely sent here for their two-month summer visitation with Mr. Martinez. Mrs. Little describes her agitation when she learned of the crash of the DC-10 in Chicago, not knowing if this affected her boys. She says that when she was finally able to reach them by telephone at Mr. Martinez's house, she could hear him screaming at them from the background, ridiculing her for her worrying. The children were to return to the mother on July 25th, by which time she and her husband were to have moved into new housing provided for them in a Navy enclave in the Canal Zone to which Mr. Little had been transferred. When Mrs. Little called San Diego the week before the boys' scheduled departure for Panama, she spoke with Bobby and told him about the tickets which had been arranged, but she heard nothing further from the boys after that. She had hoped that her husband would have sent the boys back to her from Costa Rica because it would have been much cheaper, but instead, he took the boys back to San Diego. The boys had become ill there because of having eaten contaminated food. Whenever Mrs. Little would call near the scheduled time of return to Panama, Mr. Martinez would answer and tell her that the boys were not home. Also, he would not say whether they were going to come home on the day in question, and when Mr. and Mrs. Little went to the airport to meet them, they were not aboard the plane. The day after that, she called her attorney here, and he found out that Mr. Martinez was keeping the boys and suing for custody!

Mrs. Little described her current living situation in the Canal Zone as an excellent one, and a convenient one for the boys. Pictures of the new home and its environs are part of the package she brought, and prominently displayed are the nearby swimming pool and playground. She says that there is no danger in Panama, and that the atmosphere is peaceful. Her husband expects to remain there for three years, and they have enrolled the boys in St. Mary's School in Balboa. The boys have always attended parochial schools.

Mr. Little, 47, confirmed all of this when I saw him in a joint interview with his wife. He has obviously devoted himself to his wife's cause, and he describes the attempts he has made at intervention in Panama, pointing out the conferences he has held with the Director of Medical Services and the Child Advocacy Representative of the Navy there. The letter from him is also part of the portfolio they brought.

Mr. Little is the youngest of six living siblings, and in Iowa, to which he took his new family, he has an elderly mother and many aunts and cousins. He was first married in 1956, and that marriage lasted for 18 years. He describes his first wife as very domineering, controlling the children and trying to control him. He did not want a divorce because he feared losing his children, but this finally happened in 1974. The first wife is Hawaiian, but now she lives in California. The oldest child is married. Next is a girl, now living independently. The two younger children are in the twelfth and eighth grades, respectively. Mr. Little states that his wife had set up numerous restrictions regarding his visitation, and his protests led to too many fights. Eventually, he gave up and went his own way, although he still hears from the second and fourth children.

He says that he is very comfortable with his current wife, and that he and the boys hit it off right away. They had not learned to play ball; he taught them, and also taught them to play checkers and card games. He says that they are competitive, but they always were rather placid with their father who did nothing with them. With Mr. Little, the boys are not placid at all but, rather, they keep asking him to play with them. While home with them, he is with them all the time. He is the cook at home, and he enjoys this; Mrs. Little takes care of the rest of the domestic chores. He says that they all enjoy family life together, and that both he and Mrs. Little are the disciplinarians. Despite reports to the contrary, Mr. Little states emphatically that he has never hit either boy with a belt, a shoe or his hand. Instead, he talks with them and tries to teach them to be good out of a sense of love and expectation. Mrs. Little once used a belt on Bobby when he picked on the younger boy, Scotty.

Mr. Little says that he is well able to care for the boys and assume the duties of fatherhood, and although he welcomes the support payments made by Mr. Martinez, he makes enough, and receives enough perquisites, to support them all on his own. Mr. Little said that Mr. Martinez sent $200.00 per month before, and now, because of his age and injury, Social Security is sending $370.00 per month. Mr. Little says that Mr. Martinez wants them to send him the difference!

Mental status examination of Mr. Little reveals no signs or indications of any neurotic or psychotic process. He is not anxious, and he relates quite well and warmly, not only with me but with the boys as well. This was noted when they were all together in my waiting room. The boys eagerly gather about him to play a game, with Mrs. Little seated adjacent, beaming, and Mr. Martinez seated on a bench away from them. The relationship between the boys and Mr. Little is obviously a warm and loving one, and laughter comes easily to all of them. There appears to be no forcing or artificiality.

This observation in no way is intended to diminish or downgrade the feelings that Mr. Martinez has toward his children, although it is apparent that he is somewhat more distant from them than Mr. Little. When Mr. Martinez first came to see me, he brought some friends with him to act as interpreters. However, because of the necessity to try to obtain as much nuance as possible in order to gain as firm a measure of personality as possible, I decided to see him alone. Mr. Martinez speaks what might be charitably described as "Spanglish," with much more Spanish than English intermixed in his sentences. However, there is really no trouble understanding him, and he is always willing to stop and repeat so that he makes sure that I understand him. At the end of the initial interview with him, he and I agreed that he could leave his friends at home next time. He felt as secure as I did in regard to his being understood. It should be pointed out that Mrs. Little is also a native-born Spanish-speaking individual, but her command of English is far better. Likewise, she appears in far better emotional control and is able to stop and think so that she can express herself more carefully. A plethoric, red-faced and excitable obese man of 63 (Mrs. Little says that he is 67) with jet black hair, Mr. Martinez tended to focus mainly on two topics, money and the boys' health, which also was reflected in his discussions of money and of how much money the medical workups of the boys have cost him. Sometimes it is difficult to tell if he is complaining about spending so much money or whether he is taking pride in taking such expensive care of his sons. He is much more overtly angry than his ex-wife, and often he complains to me of her actions, again centering his complaints about financial matters. For example, he says that he bought the boys their bikes, not his wife. He angrily charges that she buys them nothing, and that everything they have comes from him! He also describes her as very punitive toward them, accusing her of physically abusing the boys. Parenthetically, it should be pointed out there that the same types of accusations were made during the earlier divorce battles and were found to be invalid by the investigating probation officer.

Mr. Martinez speaks at length of the boys' health, and he shows me several letters from Dr. Z, and from an opthalmologist who is treating them for an eye infection. Mr. Martinez states that he fears that his wife will not take as good care of the boys as he does, and he cites as an example the fact that the younger boy does not have braces. In contrast, Mrs. Little says that the dentist told her that Scotty is not yet ready for braces. The most flagrant example of parental neglect, according to Mr. Martinez occurred when his ex-wife took the boys to Iowa, a cold place to which they made no adaptation. It was there that asthma developed, but he speaks of the asthma from two contrasting views. First, he blames his wife for creating it, and then he says that when the boys were with him they were well and there was no asthma! After that, he reverses himself again and complains about the bills from Dr. Z! Dr. Z's report, by the way, details his knowledge of both boys' asthma over the past several years. He has seen them every summer and the alternate winter holidays when they would become ill while staying with their father. This contradicts the history provided Dr. _____, who reported no asthma while the children were with their father.

Mr. Martinez also states that he always found the younger boy to be a very nervous child who had sleep problems and many fears. The younger boy is also described as somewhat disturbed, and a boy who keeps to himself and does not play when he is with his mother. Mr. Martinez says that he plays at school with other children here, and this provides a cue for further complaints about money, this time related to the tuition for the parochial school in which he had enrolled the boys. Mr. Martinez describes the climate of Panama as bad, and says that the trip to Costa Rica provided an example of how the climate of the tropics affects the boys. When I reminded him that the boys became sick due to food poisoning and bad water (the latter a diagnosis he proffered), he counters by saying that the climate is bad, too, and that he is, further, worried about the possibility of Panamanian uprisings against the Americans there.

Mr. Martinez says that he has five children by his first wife, in contrast to Mrs. Little's statement that he had four. The youngest was five when he brought his wife and family to San Diego in 1961. He had kept them in Costa Rica until then because it was much cheaper to do so, even though he saw them much less often. His wife had developed a lung lesion diagnosed as tuberculosis, and she was hospitalized in San Diego. A pneumonectomy was performed but an embolus intervened and she died during the acute, post-surgical convalescence. She had converted to Mormonism, and many of her Mormon friends helped Mr. Martinez rear the children.

Mr. Martinez's second session with me was notable for his being 25 minutes late. He shrugged as he told me that traffic was bad and that he needed to make sure that the boys got off to school. The second session was mainly devoted to even more complaints about money, especially centering about the fact that his wife does not send him any of the Social Security money for the boys. He also showed me the address and telephone number he had been given when his ex-wife moved from Virginia to Panama. This consisted of a FPO address and telephone number, a standard procedure at times of overseas moves by service people. He did not respond when I pointed out that the boys had been given their mother's telephone number in Panama when she first called them from there, except to complain that it costs too much to call Panama!

Bobby and Scotty were seen in my office, each for about a half-hour, on October 20th, 1979. Each related quite well in the interview setting, demonstrating active awareness of all the concepts centering about their being the focus of a custody battle. Each also demonstrated remarkable verbal capacities and relative sophistication. Bobby, nearly 12, was generally quite sad during the session with me, and on one occasion he began to spill over just a bit with some tears. This occurred when we were discussing how unfair it was for him to be placed in the middle in this fight, and to have to give up either parent for the sake of the other. I would have wished to be able to spend more time with Bobby as well as with his brother, but the stringent dictates of time prevented this. By and large, my findings reflect many of those described by Dr. _____, especially those centering about Bobby's affect and his relative isolation. In further discussions with him regarding his future, it is apparent that he is at least far more ambivalent regarding his wishes than indicated when he spoke with Dr. _____. He spoke of his possible home in Panama in positive terms, and he also discussed his relationship with Mr. Little as a good and warm one. As is the case with his brother as well, Bobby especially appreciates Mr. Little's ability to work with him on problem homework, a situation in which his real father cannot participate. A specific aspect of the relationship with his father was noted by me. When Mr. Martinez brought the boys to see me (a rather passive-aggressive and manipulative act, by the way, because he had known that Mr. and Mrs. Little were to pick them up in the morning and bring them down to see me), we discussed the arrangements to follow, when the Littles would come to the office to meet them. As I began speaking with Mr. Martinez, Bobby began translating my message into Spanish, and then restated Mr. Martinez's response, already understood by me. In the privacy of my conference room, I spoke with Bobby about this and wondered about his need to look after his father. Bobby agreed that he did this because it "smoothed out things," and this appears to dovetail with the remark he made to Dr. _____, i.e., that his father loves him so much. These types of comments and interactions make me wonder about the real motivations of the child, and their stimulus by the father. Is the child being made to feel responsible for the guilt-provoking, sad father with whom the child is identifying? The psychologist, in his tests, came up with the finding that Bobby is struggling with some pressure for maturity which he feels unable as yet to meet. I can only contrast these ideas with what I saw when he was sitting with his stepfather, laughing as he was playing a game with him.

Scotty, in contrast, is much more outgoing. I can only agree with Dr. _____'s assessment of him as a "charmer." He smiled frequently and displayed a cheerful affect of some considerable depth. A voluble talker, he is less guarded than his overtly more fearful brother who obviously feels the pressure of the internecine surrounding warfare more than Scotty. In the main, Scotty reflected what Bobby said about his relations with his parents and his stepfather. He also expressed his anxiety about being placed in the middle of the custody battle; he expressed it nonverbally, with a change of expression from the otherwise nearly-constant smile to a frown and a negative shake of his head. Otherwise, he was hardly ever at a loss for words! Most notably, after we spoke of how hard that decision was going to be, he opined freely that he was hoping that he could go to live with his mother and come back every summer to visit his father, like he used to do.

This particular litigation is certainly an excellent example of one which is sufficiently ugly for anyone's purposes. The effect on both children is severe and, to my mind, unjustifiable. Bobby is overtly depressed. Although I am not able to discern this clinically via interview, psychological tests indicate that Scotty is possible covertly depressed. Both are feeling pressures which threaten to become intolerable and which can easily result in definite and overt psychopathology of even deeper dimensions than now seen.

In sum and substance, my recommendations in this case can not be summarized any better than by quoting the remark passed by the probation worker when she told that me she saw no need for any change in custody. She pointed out that the boys appeared to have been doing well while with the mother and stepfather, and that the allegations to the contrary were easily disproved by considerable evidence.

My point of departure in any child custody case is the standard of the best interests of the children. The initial question to be answered by anyone who considers himself a child advocate is why the custody should be changed, because changing custody is always a terrific wrench for the children, even if there is good cause. In this case three significant categories of inquiry must serve to illuminate that issue and those are the ongoing development of the children, the relationships with the custodial parents, and the motivations of the father in requesting changes in the custody.

First, the children appear to be doing relatively well in terms of baseline. I believe that the many positive features noted by me, as well as by Dr. _____ in her observations, represent plusses for their rearing by their mother, whose concern is obvious. That concern is measured in clinical interviews with me, as well as by all of the letters from friends and neighbors, doctors, etc., and the attitude of her remarkably supportive husband. The psychopathology noted in the psychological tests, as well as in the clinical interviews with Dr. _____ and with me, may well represent the children's responses to the struggle surrounding them rather than any ongoing, baseline problems. Had there been no custody battle, with all the stresses imposed upon the children, the clues to stress phenomena noted in the findings might well not be present. I think that Bobby might still be somewhat of a "loner" and a quite, reflective child; but the relationship with his stepfather is one which tends to cause him to become more outgoing and social. Likewise, living in the type of enclave provided by the family's housing in Panama will further tend to push interaction—and besides, he is only 12 years old, and adolescence is approaching with its trends toward socialization. Although Scotty may not be the best determiner of his own future at his age, his feelings expressed toward living with his mother and stepfather ought to be at least recognized as significant and meaningful.

Second, the relationship between the children and their mother and stepfather is a markedly positive one, not marked by the ambivalence I noted in regard to the relationship with the real father. The goals shared by Mr. and Mrs. Little for the children all appear realistically constructive, and many of the difficulties noted during the periods in Iowa and Virginia will not be present in Panama. First of all, Mrs. Little will not be working, as she needed to do in Virginia. Second, she will be in the midst of a culture with which she has definite familiarity, that of Latin America. She has considerable family in Costa Rica, only a comfortable drive away on the Inter-American Highway (she and her husband have driven it); and she will extend the children's family lives by visiting them often. She will also arrange for the children to visit with her ex-husband's family there, a distinct contrast to the attitude of the husband, who, according to Scotty, did not allow very much visiting with the mother's family in Costa Rica. Mr. Martinez, according to Scotty, spoke very badly about the mother's family as well as the mother to the children. Scotty told me that his father used bad words and he quoted, "Bitch," here.

Increased comfort and stability on the parts of Mr. and Mrs. Little will obviously reflect itself with the boys who will thereby benefit. As regards the father, I am very impressed by the remarks of all the other observers who report how much they are all moved by the obvious love shown by Mr. Martinez for his children. This was noted by Dr. _____, and the probation workers both commented to me about it. I have no doubt that such love is present, but I must confess that I looked at this man with a far more jaundiced eye, one that perhaps had too much of a filter to allow me to see that love as clearly. What I saw even more clearly was the father's preoccupation with finances, which over-rode nearly everything else, and which made me suspect the possibility that financial reasons may be more important than emotional ones to his achieving custody. These are only suspicions based upon my clinical interviews with this man, but aside from that aspect, I would wonder about how well the boys would do with their father on a permanent basis. Mr. Martinez is an obese man in his sixties whose temperament makes me wonder about his eventual physical stability. According to what I read, he is to get remarried to a younger woman who will come to this country and who will take care of these children. This arrangement represents a definite risk. The father's health must be considered a variable here, and any uncertainty here would only contribute further to the stresses felt by the children. The father's handling of his rage toward the ex-wife is also seen as a problem here. The expressions, the covert and passive-aggressive expressions of such feelings, will also create more problems for the boys, who will be placed even more in the middle by the guilt-provoking father, who will be seen increasingly as a pitiable object. Certainly, I do not see the father operating in such a manner as to bring Bobby out of his so-called shell.

I would hope that there would be no interruption of the annual trek to San Diego to visit with the father. I would also hope that the father would be able to take advantage of his opportunity to see them over alternate Christmas holidays. Scott told me that his father had not been able to afford to do this in the past.

Thank you very much for having referred this case to me. In view of the limited time available for this workup, I would have liked to have seen all the parties more, but my definite impression is that a valid picture has been obtained of the family, nonetheless. I hope that the findings and recommendations expressed in this report are helpful to all considering this case.

Very truly yours,
Melvin G. Goldzband, M.D., F.A.P.A.

In brief, the sage quoted at the beginning of this case study was wrong: both parties were not right. Although in many situations both parties demonstrate excellent qualities as parents, they generally cannot both be "right" as the judge must define that term. Perhaps if they can constructively share the upbringing of the children—if not specifically through joint-custody maneuvering and moving about, then by the more metaphysical arrangement in which the custodial parent encourages free and open access by the other concerned and active parent—they may both be said to be "right." In such a case, however, there is usually no need for a judge to raise the victor's hand.

Perhaps if the initial psychiatrist had had more forensic experience, she would have insisted on more background from independent sources. Of course, if, as she was told, the children were never sick while visiting with the father, then there would be no known allergist to contact. However, the father did mention to her that two pediatricians had recommended that the children discontinue their medications for asthma; at least those doctors ought to have been contacted. Even so, on the basis of what was presented to her, the first psychiatrist's conclusions were both pertinent and ethical. She reviewed the relationship between the father and the two boys, using her own observations and those of a psychologist as well as the history provided by the father. It should be noted that she commented on the lack of opportunity to evaluate the mother or her relationship with the boys.

The first psychiatrist was legitimately not embarrassed by the turn of events; the judge and all observers recognized that she had done her best within a very limited (and, as it turned out, dishonest) framework. The father and his attorney were eventually seen as the goats here, tripped up by their own attempts to "pull a fast one." Their strategy of entering the court with a psychiatric recommendation that custody be remanded to the father backfired. The end result was that the children were ordered returned to their mother. She promptly booked passage for all of them on the first available flight, and they still are doing well together in Panama. The court requested monitoring by the local probation department, which has good communication with the navy social-service workers at the base in Panama. The next extended visitation with the father in San Diego was carried out without problems and with only a single asthma attack on the part of one of the boys. That may indicate a decrease in tension in the father and his home following the battle. It also may indicate that at least a good portion of the anxiety symptoms noted in the boys by the psychologist may have resulted from the stresses of the contest itself, rather than from their lives with their mother and stepfather.

I was not the better psychiatrist here; I was the luckier one, provided with all the help and time I needed. Obviously, we should insist on that, once again in order to make sure that we function as true advocates for the children and not as dupes for either party.

12 No Miracles

Experts are often appropriately defined by cynics as people who come in from out of town carrying briefcases. In my own lucky career, this appellation has been applied to me over some years in a number of courts in a number of jurisdictions. Lately, however, it has been applied a little more frequently. This is a consequence of the publication of *Custody Cases and Expert Witnesses—A Manual for Attorneys,* in which I attempted to introduce unknowing and/or suspicious attorneys to the thoughts and practices of the mental-health professionals to whom they must turn in dealing with troublesome custody cases.

The publicity surrounding the writing and publication of that textbook for lawyers led to a number of invitations to address and confer with several law societies scattered across the country. These kind invitations, though providing ego boosts, also gave me an awareness of some of the worst aspects of handling custody disputes. I was surprised at how little information lawyers had about the very idea of approaching cases from the viewpoint of child advocacy. In many jurisdictions, even in large metropolitan centers, no concept seems to have been established of seeing the contestants and their children in conferences with the goal of resolving the cases without resort to trial. This, of course, also testifies to the scarcity in those same areas of behavioral scientists who promote child advocacy.

The biggest surprise was that beachheads in that direction had not been established even in cities with large, long-standing, active psychiatric and child-psychiatric training centers. In Chicago, where I received my medical and psychiatric training, I developed the impression that the rigid, fault-finding approach of the divorce laws disastrously affects the ways in which child-custody issues are determined. The statutes there seemed only to increase resentment and bitterness between the divorcing members. Perhaps over the seemingly interminable duration of divorce actions there, it may be unreasonable to expect that the approach to cases outlined and suggested in this book would be uniformly adaptable, let alone successful.

Following the announcement and publication of my textbook for lawyers, I was contacted by a family-law specialist in Chicago. He asked me if I would be willing to come there and to review some cases for him. Because I had already arranged to attend two medical meetings in Chicago, scheduled on two successive weekends, I readily agreed. My presence there at that time would pare the costs of those consultations somewhat; the lawyer and his responsible clients appreciated that. However, the arrangements made provided me with a remarkable surprise. I had expected to call him on my arrival and set up a series of conferences on as relaxed and leisurely a basis as my limited time would allow. Instead, when I called him, he told me that he had already arranged for me to see all four cases in a single day, and that he had arranged appointments with all the parties. After all, I was a well-known miracle worker with an approach representing reason and concern, as my book implied.

What a humbling lesson I learned! Authority, waving a book in the air, still cannot make miracles happen. Impressions can be gained and perhaps some recommendations made, but these need to be discussed fully and often repeatedly with both the parties and the lawyers. Also, considerable work must be done by the effectuating agents, whether lawyers or psychiatrists, over some time. Nonetheless, my contacts with the attorney who called me, as well as with the lawyers for the contending spouses and with the lawyers who served as guardians *ad litem* for the contested children, were very constructive. Perhaps even more so were my meetings with several judges who sit in the Cook County Circuit Court's Domestic Relations Department. In one case, following the initial evaluation, it was necessary to go down to the courthouse because the case was scheduled for trial. Instead of trial, a conference took place in a room adjacent to the courtroom especially provided for that purpose, and the contestants reached a tentative agreement regarding custody of their disputed children.

The judges were interested in that, and we had a few good talks. Judges, of course, are the real keys to custody procedures. All the attorneys and judges were receptive to some degree to the idea of settling these issues by conference, if possible—the judges most of all. When divorce actions are conducted on a fault-finding basis, lawyers and judges have plenty of work to do, and no threat to the attorneys' livelihoods is posed by making the custody aspects of the cases easier for all concerned. There is still plenty to fight about, more than in no-fault, community-property jurisdictions. However, as will be seen in the case presented in this chapter, that may well work against real acceptance of the ideas and conclusions reached during conference.

Of those four cases seen in Chicago during that crowded week, one was especially noteworthy for a number of reasons. The fault-finding concepts were highlighted so that observers could see how these adversely affect attempts to settle any and all issues and how the participation of an extended family complicates resolution attempts. All the participants in this case were seen in the offices of the referring lawyer, in a ranch-style, rambling office park in a Chicago suburb. The setup of the offices allowed for each contesting party to sit in a space of his or her own, without too much contact with the other parties, which likely would result in conflagration. The children were shuttled from one area to another, to one contestant and then to another, providing some interesting observations. So did the hurried nature of the lawyer's arrangements, which prevented ideal communication to all of the meaning, goals, and purposes of my intervention. I assume the responsibility for that in the end. The psychiatrist should always try to determine and set the pace for the evaluation procedure. After all, he or she knows how much subsequent sessions are influenced or even called for because of what happened in preceding interviews, whether with that party or a different party.

Following is the first of two reports I dictated to the referring lawyer, in which the background of the case as well as the findings are presented.

Dear Mr. _____:

Thank you very much for referring your client, Beverly Smith, to me for psychiatric evaluation.

Prior to seeing your client and other members of her family in your office on [date], I had the opportunity to review a lengthy sheaf of material you provided me. This included a letter from Mrs. Smith's former attorney, _____, Esq., who provided his own impressions of the principals in this case, as well as the abstracts of the transcripts of the depositions of each of the principals. These include Mr. and Mrs. John P. Smith, Jr., and Mr. and Mrs. John P. Smith, Sr. Mrs. John P. Smith, Jr. is your client, Beverly Smith. Over and above that material, I saw the evaluations by their schools of the three Smith children, Debbie, Christina and John as well as a letter from Dr. _____, an ear, nose and throat specialist who had operated on little John Smith for his bilateral otitis media. Little John Smith is in a special program in a suburban school district, and his teacher submitted a brief report to the County Department of Supportive Services. A fairly lengthy report from the Department of Supportive Services by one of their caseworkers was also provided me, and this gave a considerable amount of background material of all of the parties involved. Finally, a lengthy handwritten memorandum to you by Beverly Smith was provided me. She disputes a number of contentions made by her antagonists in this child custody matter, as well as some of the conclusions reached by the caseworker.

As can be expected, this is a highly charged, emotionally laden and internally conflictful matter which would be expected to provide considerable difficulty for anyone sufficiently unfortunate as to have to make specific recommendations, conclusions and dispositions regarding this complex case. I appreciate the confidence in me which you expressed by asking me to serve as a consultant to you here, and I hope that the materials contained in this report, the recommendations and the conclusions, will be helpful to all concerned in considereing this case.

Three hours and fifteen minutes were devoted to my interviews and observations with and of all of the parties in this case. Beverly and John Smith, Jr., came to your office, as well as John's parents, Mr. and Mrs. Smith, Sr. This day was one of the days in which Beverly had visitation with the three children, and she brought them to the office. When she was scheduled to come to see me, she left the children in the care of John and his parents, and I was able to observe the specific relationship between the children and their paternal grandparents.

The paternal grandmother appears to be the major influence over the three children, and the individual who appears to assume most of the responsibility for their care. She has to devote most of her attention to the little boy, who appears to me to be severely emotionally disturbed, as well as quite possibly organically mentally ill. He is best described as "hyperactive," although my use of the term here does not necessarily imply the organic brain disorder which is so often associated with that term. I know that the relationship between little John and his grandmother (by observation) is such that the remarkable anxiety she feels over his situation is transmitted to him. This must perforce create further anxiety within him which, in turn, leads to further hyper-activity which only leads to further anxiety on the part of his grandmother or whomever else takes care of him. A vicious cycle is thereby created, and regardless of how this case turns out, that cycle will have to be broken.

The two little girls seem to adopt a relatively patronizing attitude toward their brother, a mixture of a small part of compassion and a large part of resentment. With little girls this age, this is hardly unexpected, and when they came in to talk with me later, this became quite evident and transparent. They seem, however, to have a very warm and close relationship with their paternal grandfather, who, although extraordinarily authoritarian and seemingly gruff, really appears to be "a pigeon" when confronted with these two little girls. He softens considerably, but nonetheless maintains good control. I noticed that there was actually little attention paid to the little girls by the grandmother because of the obvious necessity to spend most of her time and efforts with the little boy.

John Smith, Jr., the children's father, appeared to assume a sideline role in the waiting room where the children were playing with their grandparents. He appeared to be under the aegis and influence of his parents just as much as did the children, and he was seemingly bewildered at the necessity to be in your office, and totally unsure as to whether or not they would all be talking with me. As it turned out, he apparently decided on his own that he would talk with me despite the fact that his own parents decided that they would not.

This decision was, as I observed it, basically made by Mrs. Smith, Sr. Mr. Smith, Sr. appeared ambivalent about seeing me, but Mrs. Smith was quite adamant in her refusal. She likewise insisted that her husband not talk with me. This was based upon her impression that Mr. Jones, the advocate for the children, would be here and would be in the office with them and me during the interview. When I told them that I would not interview them in the presence of anyone else, she became quite incensed and felt that she was in "enemy territory" because, after all, I had been hired as your consultant. I attempted to explain that my point of departure was, like Mr. Jones's, that of a child advocate, but it appears that the feelings in this case had risen so high that this would not be accepted. [This was the case despite my urgings that they consult with the guardian *ad litem* by telephone. His attempts to reassure them were unsuccessful.] Thus, I am left with the impression of the grandparents only by observation and not by interview. My impression, however, is that of a set of individuals who operate in such a manner that they become exceedingly controlling. They seem to control their son, for the most part, and as it turns out, he becomes a carbon copy of his own authoritarian father, relating to the other people by giving firm orders rather than most other ways.

The paternal grandmother is a very anxious lady, perhaps seemingly more anxious under these circumstances than she might otherwise be. However, given a stress situation, a person generally lets it be known how he or she operates under stress, and this lady does not appear to operate too well. She allows her feelings to carry her away, rather than her judgment, and by this I do not only refer to her refusal to see me. I am also referring to the manner in which she deals with the grandson and the two grand-daughters. She would complain long and loud in the grandson's presence about his behavior and the demands that his behavior places upon her. Likewise, she commented about such things as the fact that the child does not even know who his real mother is, an obviously defensive comment which followed his referring to her as "Mama." Of course, this gives rise to some suspicion that little might be done at home to discourage him from calling her "Mama" because of the possibility of underlying satisfaction on her part upon being addressed as such. I point out that I have no specific indication or evidence for this, but it appears to be consistent with the general approach I noted in their behavior. That is best described as "running the show." I believe, on the basis of my observations and my interview with John Smith, Jr., that were it not for the strength and insistence of his parents, this litigation would not be taking place, and that probably the children would be left with their mother.

I spent thirty-five minutes observing the children with their grand-parents. This was sometimes interrupted time because of the telephone communications with the child advocate and the attempts to keep Beverly away from the grandparents, thereby preventing the stimulation of another overt fight. Following that period, I spent fifty-five minutes interviewing Beverly. She was overtly hostile toward her divorcing husband and his parents, and she had no difficulty in expressing that hostility, verbally, succinctly and pointedly to me. "If they didn't want to come here, they shouldn't have set this up, and they're really handling it badly in front of the kids. They poisoned the kids' minds." This type of allegation continued almost throughout the session with me.

Beverly is a fairly attractive white lady of 30, who looks about her stated age. Oriented in all spheres, she relates with excellent verbal fluency and facility in the interview setting, demonstrating a vocabulary and a capacity for abstract conceptualization which tends to place her level of intelligence well within the normal, perhaps toward the high-normal range. This is in distinction to her lengthy, handwritten memorandum. That document is filled with all types of grammatical mistakes, as well as grotesque misspellings and misuse of words, hardly suitable for a woman with three years of college education at the University of Minnesota. As she describes in that memorandum, however, it was written very late at night over a period of several nights, and her tiredness at that time, might have taken its toll. One might have expected better, however, from a person with that type of education. Therefore, the thought must occur that one might expect better from her under stress and under tired situations than that which she perhaps has to offer given those circumstances. Those circumstances are the ones which would be the rule were she to have custody of her children.

Her affect is generally appropriate to the verbal content expressed, although a great deal of it is colored by the hostile feelings toward the opposing parties. There is a great deal of expression of warmth toward the children, and genuine tearful affect is produced during the time that she discusses the accusations made against her of hitting the children, especially her son. This leads to a great deal of obviously defensive discussion on her part about her treatment of the children and what can really be expected. She differentiates her approach to the children, generally live and let live, with what she considers to be the over-controlled and over-controlling approach of her divorcing husband and his parents. Thought processes, themselves, are not remarkable; she is neither hallucinatory nor overtly delusional, and the train of associations is logical, relevent, coherent and chronological. There are no indications of overt neurosis and none of psychosis. Memory appears intact. Judgment, however, is highly doubtful and appears to be under the aegis of a markedly immature, impulse-ridden personality which also demonstrates and manifests some definite signs of a masochistic trend. In her discussions of the relationship with her husband, characterized by her descriptions of repeated beatings of her by him, she fails to see how she ''gives her hand away.'' She obviously is capable of being extremely provocative and also appears to anticipate the kinds of beatings of which she complains. In fact, she even gives verbal clues and cues that were she to marry again, she might anticipate the same type of behavior from her future husband.

Aside from all of the anger, in the midst of this material there is indication of at least a former genuine love for her spouse. She describes having ''four good years'' with him, and she says that they did very well in Arizona. Insofar as her relationship with her in-laws, she even acknowledges the kindness of those people when she and her husband first came to Chicago and lived with them. The deteriorating of this relationship, however, is such that one cannot really expect any type of meaningful cooperation between these antagonists.

Further, considerable material was elaborated by Beverly regarding the ''poisoning of the kids' minds'' by their grandparents, and she gave some specific examples. However, it is noted that during all of this time with me, she would inadvertently let slip some material which indicates her own ''pumping'' (her term) of the children, especially her ''laying guilt trips on them'' in which she would complain to them about her in-laws and her divorcing husband placing the children in the middle, but she appears to be very well practiced in doing the same thing.

John Smith was also interviewed, this time for only forty-five minutes. He is a stocky, muscular 30-year-old, white male whose verbal capacity and fluency does not appear to match that of his divorcing wife. Oriented in all spheres, he relates fairly well, but with considerable tension and unease, giving me the impression that he felt considerable ambivalence about talking with me, probably based upon the fear of disapproval by his own parents who did not want him to do this. The fact that he decided on his own to do so indicates that there may be a kernel of potential independence within him, a kernel which has not yet sprouted into any type of seedling. Likewise, as with his divorcing wife, there are no indications of psychosis or frank neurosis within this man. However, the basic conclusion reached via observing him and interviewing him, is that this man unconsciously sees himself as grossly inadequate, and that he suffers from a self-image which is probably unrealistically low. He is a man who had over three years of college education in Minnesota, where he was a pre-veterinary student with a major in chemistry. This is not an easy curriculum, and he ''made it,'' although he left college because of his personal difficulties. He had to marry his first wife, and then married Beverly. It is unfortunate that he was not able to continue his education, but it is significant that he has chosen not to, even subsequent to the original crisis surrounding the necessity for the marriages. He had little to go in order to receive his college degree, but there appears to be no impetus in that direction. One must contrast his educational background with his contentment at doing what he is doing. He is a maintenance man and earns a relatively meager salary. He is a hard worker and he worked several part-time jobs in order to provide funds for the marital home he bought during the better years of marriage. However, he seems to have no ambition to better himself at this time, and says that his current job and lifestyle suit him just fine. By this, I think he not only refers to his employment, but to his status insofar as his own parents are concerned. He lives with them and is basically under their dominance. I have the impression, although this would need further investigation to validate thoroughly, that this is a state which is preferential for him.

His affect in describing the situation between him and his divorcing wife indicates some considerable guardedness on his part. He is very defensive. There is a generally fixed smile through which he discusses the horror stories of their marriage. This, of course, is an inappropriate affect and places the listener on considerable guard. Mr. Smith glosses over the beatings he administered to his wife and rather prefers to talk about his impression that she "intentionally" provoked him into this type of behavior. On the basis of what I obtained from her, he may be quite right. However, there does not appear to be any sense of regret on his part over the beatings and his mishandling of her.

A great deal of the time Mr. Smith spent with me was devoted to his descriptions of his wife's beatings of his children. He talked about the bruises he found on his son, and his feeling that his wife provides few clothes or care for him. He further complained about the sexual activity observed by the children in his wife's home, and was incensed at his wife's comment, ostensibly made to him, that she did not think that they would know the difference about what was going on. Basically, he is not really able to talk about the background of the marriage, or even of his own background and his observations of his parents' marriage. Instead, he appears to be obsessed with his wife's alleged pecadilloes.

He talked about his own relationship with the children, however, in a rather surprising vein. He, himself, was surprised at how close the children have become to him and says that they have become very attached to him. When asked what type of time he spends with them, he speaks mostly of helping them with their homework, and this appears to be characteristic of the type of behavior I noted in him when I observed him with the children. The best example of this can be given by describing the end of the interview with me, when he said that he wanted to say goodbye to the children because his wife would be taking them home with her for the rest of the weekend. He walked into the kitchen of your office (followed by me) and I expected him to wave to the children and wish them a goodbye, telling them that he would see them on the following night or whenever it was scheduled for them to return to his home. However, he did not do that at all. Instead, he barged into the kitchen and immediately ordered the children to sit in their chairs and behave themselves. This was done in a rather angry "top-sergeant" type of tone and voice. The children, then taken care of by their mother, were wandering all around the kitchen, opening drawers and playing with whatever they could find in a rather free style. Nothing actually was being harmed, but it was apparent that they were not really being structured by the mother who was sitting at the table with the young son on her lap. Like her mother-in-law, just about all of the attention needed to be given to him, and the girls were operating freely and untrammeledly. I noted that there was nothing in the way of tenderness expressed by the father toward the daughters when he said goodbye to them. All that really was communicated to them was that they had better sit in their chairs and behave themselves. No comment was made by their mother.

Insofar as the two parents are concerned, I see each of them as grossly deficient. My impression is that their marital relationship was almost clasically sadomasochistic, and that they seemed to fulfill each other's neurotic rather than realistic needs via getting together. The wife describes eight years of beatings, even though she says that the first four years were better. Why were there continued beatings and why did the relationship stay as it was for that length of time? The wife certainly had the wherewithal to leave earlier just as she found the wherewithal to leave later. Mr. and Mrs. Smith appear to operate at the opposite ends of the spectrum insofar as their relationship with the children is concerned. Mrs. Smith appears to favor an almost totally unstructured approach, whereas Mr. Smith, like his own parents, favors an almost militaristic, overstructured, rigid and authoritarian appraoch. Obviously, a place someplace toward the middle of that spectrum would be ideal, but I rather doubt that at this time either of these principals have the capacity to work their way toward that goal.

I spent twenty-five minutes with Debbie and Christina, and I found this interview a revelation. The two girls have an interesting relationship. Debbie appears to be identifying with her rather authoritarian, somewhat demeaning, grandmother, and this is her method of attempting to control her rival, her younger sister. Christina is a seemingly irrepressible, perfectly charming and giggly girl, whose anxiety is betrayed by her almost total inability to prevent herself from constant talking. During that time, she sometimes says very little, but on occasion, as will be noted, she says a great deal. By and large, the mental status of each of these two girls is unexceptional, and they seem to have sufficient fiber to withstand a great deal of the stress which goes on around them. However, there is considerable danger by virtue of their having been placed in the middle, especially with the kinds of pressures placed upon them to favor one or the other side. Beverly Smith is quite right when she describes the pressures placed upon them by their grandparents and by their father. However, she lacks the self-recognition to know how much pressure she applies to them as well. Nothing but harm can come to the girls by virtue of the attitudes of the contestants for them. No matter what happens in terms of actual custody disposition, this is a matter which will have to be remedied strongly and immediately. The manipulations applied to these girls by their grandparents and father became transparent to me in the interview. Toward the close of the interview, after I told the girls that I was through with them, Christina looked at me and asked me if I were not going to ask them with whom they wanted to live. When I responded that I certainly would not ask them that question and thought that it would put them into a terrible position in order to have to answer it, Debbie immediately began to talk with me about the adultery, committed by her mother, which violated God's Command-ments. She tumbled this material out in such a way that I had to help her with a couple of the simple words, such as "commit" and "command-ments." It is noted that she had no trouble at all with "adultery." When I commented to her that it seemed terribly important that she tell me about this, even though I said that we were through with the interview, she did not blink an eye and did not even stop or think about what she was doing. Instead, she proceeded in an uninterrupted manner to repeat the same material and to tell me more about it. It was obviously mandatory that she do so, and, to my mind, this gives away the pressures under which she must be placed by her grandparents who coach her. Debbie also talked about her mother's boyfriends and how this bothers her, but there did not appear to be any real affect underlying or accompanying these statements. These were obviously rote statements.

These girls are in grave danger of having a needed relationship with their mother destroyed by the obvious resentment toward that parent on the part of Mr. and Mrs. Smith, Sr. and their son, John, Jr. I speak of the concept of "grave danger" here because, with girls the ages of Christina and Debbie, a relationship with their mother is quite important. A relation-ship with their mother as she is now constituted emotionally might not be the most healthful thing for all concerned, but I think that the mother can be reconstituted to some extent via treatment, and I would hope that this would be instituted.

The report of the Department of Supportive Services obviously favors the father and his family. My observations are both similar and different from those of the caseworker. I note the father's and grandfather's rigid authoritarianism to almost militaristic extents, and I note the grandmother's marked nervousness, almost to the point of agitation, dur-ing the time that whe was supervising young John. I also note that this took place in an atmosphere of considerable anxiety provocation (i.e., the seem-ingly enforced meeting with me in a situation they did not really under-stand), but a great deal of that was self-induced via the grandmother's own suspicion and unwillingness to listen even to the advice of the child ad-vocate over the telephone. I note the mother's lack of insight into her own provocativeness and into her own relationship with her daughters. She is so angry with her husband that she uses remarkably poor judgment in her in-terviews with practically everybody who might help her in her fight against him, such as the caseworker and me. It is easy for any listener to develop an impression of her which is quite negative.

Conclusions and Recommendations

This difficult case is one of those in which one feels that nobody wins, especially the children, regardless of how the case turns out. Neither parent appears at this time to be sufficiently capable of providing "good parenting" for all three of the children, but I really doubt that any but an excep-tional parent might be able to do that because of the severe illness manifested by the little boy.

I spoke for some time with Mr. Jones, the child advocate, who arrived at your office late that afternoon. He gave me some of his impressions regarding the situation. He told me of a report made on the little boy which was disparaging of his relationship with the mother. However, very appropriately, he pointed out that the person who made that report did not have any input from the mother, and was probably influenced by the resentment of the father and the father's family. I believe, on the basis of the fact that I have no real input regarding any complete workup of this child, that this child's situation demands such a workup. I do not know what is wrong with him. He certainly manifests many indications of severe emotional disturbance, but I have no idea how much of this is predicated upon an underlying organic brain disturbance, an underlying perceptual disturbance (such as his longstanding early difficulty with hearing) or predicated upon the pressures applied to him currently via the cyclone which is going on all around him. The situation which surrounded him during his first several years, that of the constant battles between his parents who were living together, also did him no good. This child needs to be seen for a complete and thorough workup at an institution which can provide such for him. Not being a Chicagoan at this time, I am not really able to recommend such a place, although I am well aware of the excellent reputations of the Institute for Juvenile Research and of the Isaac Ray Center of the Rush Medical College. Either of these two places should be able to have facilities (at reasonable rates) for the type of workup which is mandatory here. I would not doubt that following such a workup, further consultation insofar as the best disposition for this child would be necessary. I would not doubt that it might be recommended that a residential treatment setting for him be obtained, because no one in his family is really able to take care of him to the extent required. If they were able to do so, no one would be able to take care of his two sisters who would thereby suffer.

It appears, on the basis of the report by the Department of Supportive Services, that the two girls are doing well where they are, with their father and grandparents. I believe that if the brother is placed in an appropriate residential treatment setting, the degree of tension currently characteristic of that household might lessen, and that the girls might benefit thereby. However, if the girls remain in that household it will be essential that their father become involved in some type of psychotherapy which will have as its goal an investigation of his underlying self-concept problem, and a hoped-for change in that very self-concept. If their father would feel better about himself, it is quite likely that he would not have to respond to these girls in the same way that he does, that is, as militaristically rigid and authoritarian as he has learned to be from his own father. This would benefit them greatly, and would also lead to the likelihood that the father would move out of his own parents' house and lead an independent life with his daughters. I believe that under such circumstances, the relationship between father and mother might improve to the extent that the constant pressure applied to these two girls would diminish, thereby allowing the girls a little more freedom and less anxiety insofar as their own desire to relate to their own mother is concerned. Mrs. Smith is not a bad mother. She has a considerable wellspring of good feeling toward her daughters, and has the intellectual capacity to rear them well. I do not believe, however, that she represents a good role model for them by virtue of her marked masochistic tendencies, as well as the frankly manipulative pressures she places upon the two girls. If she were able to recognize what she does as well as she sees what her opponents in this case do to these two girls, she perhaps might be able to control this. However, I thnk that she, too, is in need of help. Were she not to receive this, I believe that it is a safe bet that her subsequent marriages would turn out to be as unsuccessful as her first one, and that she would provoke considerable resentment toward her (perhaps violent) just as she did with John Smith.

Thus, in summary, I hope that the disposition of this case is handled as follows:

1. The little boy must be evaluated at a full-scale evaluation center, which might be able to make recommendations for adequate intensive and meaningful treatment for him. Although everyone seems to be in favor of the current program in which he is involved in his school system, to my mind, this does not represent adequate or sufficient treatment for him. He may very well need a residential treatment unit.

2. Both parents need psychotherapy. They have severe and stringent personality problems and are fixated at grossly immature stages in life. They have the capacity for growth, but they have not exercised this. With treatment, I think that they can both benefit to the extent that their affected children will positively benefit.

3. On the basis of the indications provided by the Department of Supportive Services, the girls seem to be doing well in their grandparents' home, and if they are doing well they should not be moved. They should, however, be able to maintain a free and open relationship with their mother, and such a relationship might well turn out to be even freer and more open following the commencement of therapy on the part of their father, as well as on the part of their mother. The girls will need a relationship with their mother, not for the sake of their mother, but for their own sakes. They must not be allowed to see themselves as rejected by their mother. The grandparents must not be permitted to speak of their mother in the disparaging manner in which they have done so, because this will cause the girls to wonder about themselves and about their likely identification (quite appropriate) with this demeaned mother. I believe that if the boy is away from the home, the tensions and demands which are provoked by his presence will be lessened, and this may allow the grandmother and grandfather to "listen to reason" and obtain some fair counseling which will allow them to rear the girls in this non-demeaning, non-punitive atmosphere, for the sake of the girls' own welfare.

Thank you once again for having referred this very complex and difficult case to me. I am sorry that, unlike Solomon, I can provide no easy and simple or magical answers. The type of case this represents must be dealt with step-wise, and I hope that some arrangements can be made to follow through with the recommendations I have made.

Very truly yours,
Melvin G. Goldzband, M.D., F.A.P.A.

Upon study by the lawyer and subsequent telephone communication between us, we agreed that it would be worthwhile to attempt to set up another session with the adults in this case, including the grandparents, who are so crucial to any resolution. As would be expected, the demands of the psychiatric meeting that originally brought me to Chicago created considerable scheduling difficulties, but the lawyer was finally able to arrange for all of us to meet on the afternoon before I was scheduled to fly back to San Diego. The following report, written after I returned to San Diego, describes the second conference session, in which all of the adults, including the lawyers, met together. Unfortunately, the grandparents were still unaware of my role and of the real purpose of this meeting. As it turned out, so was the Smiths' counsel. This only emphasizes the importance of effective communications between the mental-health expert and both attorneys, as described in previous chapters.

Dear Mr. _____:

This is an addendum to my previous report regarding your client, Beverly Smith. I was very pleased to have had the opportunity to have spoken with her, her children and her ex-husband, although I was very sorry that her former in-laws were unwilling to speak with me during the time allotted for my evaluation of the situation. Unfortunately, that time was truncated because of many restrictions, and I think that probably as we go along doing our missionary work (you and I, and I hope, other Chicago attorneys as well), the task of evaluating contesting parents, their families and their children with an eye to keeping the cases out of trial will become more easily done. That will allow for far less suspicion and more understanding on everybody's part of the role of the expert witness, that is, that of child advocate.

I was very pleased that you were able to have arranged a follow-up meeting with the principals in your office on [date]. I met with Beverly Smith and her ex-husband, and also her ex-husband's parents at that time. We were together for somewhat over three hours. Before meeting with any of the principals, I met with Mr. Smith's attorney, Mr. Ames. It is unfortunate that he had not seen my report before. When he saw me, he spoke of his impression that I was there to interview the in-laws because I had not interviewed them before. I told Mr. Ames that I was there for the purpose of holding a family conference, for the purpose of allowing all of them to know of my conclusions and recommendations in this case, and for the purpose of attempting to reach a series of decisions which the principals themselves could implement without having to have the court impose externally implemented decisions upon them. Mr. Ames, to his vast credit, saw the value of this approach, read the lengthy original report, and discussed it with me in considerable detail before I saw any of the principals. I had, by the way, told the in-laws that I would not talk with them nor would I do anything further prior to Mr. Ames's having seen the report and discussing the situation with me. I would not do anything if he did not want me to do it. Fortunately, Mr. Ames wanted me to proceed, and we had an excellent family session.

Mr. _____ of your office was present, representing your client. My only regret was that the child advocate, the guardian *ad litem,* Mr. Jones, was not present. Once again, I think that in the future the communications regarding these meetings, their purposes and the necessary attendees will be much smoother as the concept of avoiding litigation and encouraging conferences gains popularity in your community.

In sum and substance, group therapy was the order of the day, and all of the participants had opportunities to vent considerable feelings. Mr. Ames was very helpful as a "co-therapist" with me, as he was also able to point out to the senior Smiths their insistence upon maintaining the wellspring of rage toward their former daughter-in-law. I was able to demonstrate situations in which this was brought out on the part of all of them. Suspicions were raised, vented and clarified, and I was pleased to note that at the end everyone seemed relatively satisfied with the likelihood that arrangements could be made between all of them without court-imposed orders.

Mr. Smith, Sr. (the grandfather) especially vented considerable, tearful, rageful affect. He feels very close to his grandson to whom he specifically referred as his namesake. His wife, the grandmother, is as we had previously discussed. She is a very angry and vindictive woman who hides these feelings under a torrent of cliches and good intentions. However, she did respond to confrontations with some of her underlying feelings, and there is a possibility that she might, with some anxiety relief, cease to put such heavy pressure on her grandchildren.

Beverly accepted the need for psychiatric treatment. This was expected, but I am somewhat dubious regarding her motivation. This will have to be monitored by your office if not by the court, and frequent communications with her regarding her relationship with her psychotherapist will have to be maintained.

My major concern is the husband in question. He is extraordinarily defensive, and I fear, even more fragile than I thought before. He was hardly able to participate. I wonder what his parents said to him following his independent decision to talk with me during our first session. He spoke to some extent but was unable to bring out a great deal of feelings other than resentment toward his wife. When I confronted him with his poor self-image, he was extraordinarily defensive and commented that I had derived that information from Beverly. He was seriously taken aback when I pointed out to him in no uncertain terms that he provided me with this information himself, and I cited chapter and verse to him to back up that statement. From that time on, he was quite reserved and his eyes frequently brimmed with tears. He needs a great deal of help and, even more significant, I believe that he knows that he needs a great deal of help and this frightens him. Mr. Ames, with whom I spoke at some length later, will need to provide enormous emotional support for him.

I recommended to all that the little boy be seen at the Institute for Juvenile Research or at the Rush Medical College, or at some comparable facility. Everybody seemed to be in agreement, especially the grandmother (somewhat surprisingly). Now, all I can do is leave it in your hands, and in those of Mr. Ames and of Mr. Jones. Again, I really regret not having him present, although I feel quite certain that he would have backed up my approach and my goal. Obviously, copies of this addendum must go to each of these gentlemen.

We left shaking hands all around, and I think that a great deal of tension was dissipated. At least now there is some fertile ground which can be worked, although how much actual underlying motivation can be positive enough to offset the wellspring of resentment, I cannot say. However, we are all far better off than before insofar as this case is concerned.

One final comment must be made, not about that meeting, but about the fact that something had been left out inadvertently of the earlier report. Comments were made by the children during their interview with me regarding the behavior of their little brother. It appears that it is characteristic, according to their description, for him to deal with his frustration (and he has a very low frustration tolerance) by simply running almost blindly into walls or other projections. The specific instance in which he came back to his grandparents' home from the visitation with Beverly, the instance during which the grandparents felt that Beverly had beaten the child, was described by the little girls. It became apparent that his facial injuries were due to the little boy's frustration-relieving behavior rather than to any assault by his mother. This is obviously a very important issue, and I regret not having put it in the original report. I hope that in future cases, a little more time can be granted so that people can be evaluated a little more leisurely and reports can be dictated and edited to a much finer degree.

Once again, I thank you for the confidence you have expressed in me via asking me to confer and consult with you regarding this extraordinarily difficult, complex and frustrating case. I am pleased that I left Chicago with the feeling that I was able to do something to keep this case out of court, and to allow the principals to sit down among themselves and make some plans regarding the disposition of these seriously disturbed children. As I say, the rest I must leave up to you, Mr. Ames and Mr. Jones.

Very truly yours,
Melvin G. Goldzband, M.D., F.A.P.A.

Euphoria is not the appropriate term to describe my feelings about what we all thought we had accomplished during our two sessions in Chicago. However, my hopes and perhaps my naivete allowed me to think that more was accomplished than subsequent examination of the facts revealed.

Follow-up five months after the meetings revealed that considerable battling was still going on between the parties and that the grandparents had succeeded in inducing their son to add adultery as another ground for the divorce action. This had predictable effect on Beverly, whose passive-aggressive tendency created further avenues for provocative acting out on her own. A good example is provided by the not unexpected—and not really unreasonable—insistence by the grandparents that Beverly have no men visiting her during the visitation times. However, the grandparents, obviously more aggressive than their son, went a controversial step further when they insisted that Beverly not bring in a baby-sitter for the children. That, of course, would effectively prevent Beverly from going out after the children were already in bed. As a formally accused adulteress, Beverly was being forced to wear her scarlet letter.

The referring lawyer commented that the fault-finding aspects of the divorce statutes in Illinois, with their encouragement of name-calling, probably create an environment within which any recommendations could well be undercut by the sanctioned antagonisms of the contestants. The experience in no-fault states, however, has been that even when the divorce procedures create a situation in which the hostility of the former partners is funneled into a fight over the children, that hostility can often be dealt with effectively through intervention of the type described throughout this book.

Index

Index

About the Author

Melvin G. Goldzband, M.D., has practiced psychiatry in San Diego for more than twenty years. Although most of his professional time is devoted to treating patients, he has also developed a considerable national reputation as a teacher and lecturer. He is an associate clinical professor in the Department of Psychiatry of the University of California at San Diego, has served as visiting professor in many medical and law schools throughout the United States and Canada, and is often asked to lecture on various aspects of psychiatry and the law.

A diplomate in psychiatry of the American Board of Psychiatry and Neurology, Dr. Goldzband is an associate editor of the *Bulletin of the American Academy of Psychiatry and the Law* and a member of the Academy's Ethics Committee. He is a Fellow of the American Academy of Forensic Sciences and has shared his experiences as a consultant to many courts and attorneys with numerous colleagues. Dr. Goldzband has published many articles on both clinical and forensic psychiatry as well as the book, *Custody Cases and Expert Witnesses,* a practice manual for attorneys.